Do-It-Yourself

GUNSMITHING

AN OUTDOOR LIFE BOOK

Do-It-Yourself
GUNSMITHING

by Jim Carmichel

With Photos by the Author

OUTDOOR LIFE

HARPER & ROW

New York, Evanston, San Francisco, London

To
FRED HUNTINGTON

*My good friend and worldwide hunting pal,
with whom I've shared freezing tents,
steaming jungle huts, and terrible food,
but always had a good time.*

Contents

PART III

Stock Decoration: The Stylish Extras

PART IV

Metalsmithing: The Professional Look

Contents

Introduction

How often have you looked at an eye-catching piece of custom gunsmithing and said to yourself: I could do that if only I had the tools?

Actually, expensive tools aren't necessary for good gunsmithing. In fact you don't need many tools at all. What's more important by far is that you have the *right* tools and know how to use them. I once knew a very fine gunsmith who turned out some of the most beautiful Kentucky style rifles and pistols ever built. Yet, his entire collection of tools could easily be stored in a shoe box!

Full time professional gunsmiths need high priced equipment such as lathes, milling machines and bandsaws for highly specialized work such as barrel fitting and chambering, action rebuilding and high production stock work. This is the kind of work an amateur need not attempt.

But this in no way means that the amateur is prevented from accomplishing scores of projects which make his guns more accurate, more functional, more beautiful and more valuable. In fact, the features gun lovers treasure most: clean stockwork, beautiful checkering, accuracy refinements and custom touches, are all accomplsihed with the simplest of tools—rasps, files, chisels, checkering tools, sandpaper and screwdrivers. This book *shows* you how to use these tools.

When I was in college I kept body and soul alive by making reproductions of muzzle loading guns, plus some stockwork on modern guns. None of my collection of tools cost more than three dollars until I splurged on a five dollar electric drill in a second-hand shop. Since I didn't have fancy tools I learned to make do with the few tools I had. Often I surprised myself, and others, with how many seemingly complicated projects I could complete with only a file, a drill, and a hacksaw.

Introduction

The purpose of this book is to show how much you can accomplish with these same simple tools. If the best instruction is an actual demonstration then the next best thing must be the step-by-step photos used throughout this book. You will see how simple tools are used on a variety of fascinating and worthwhile projects with both wood and metal.

By following these simple instructions you will surprise yourself and draw admiring glances from all who see your results. I know you can accomplish these projects because, you see, I'm an amateur also. Many of the projects and conversions pictured here were *first time* attempts on my part! I just thought to take pictures as I went along. So if my efforts came out so well on the first try it's a snap that yours will too.

As you move from one project to another you'll discover that you've gained greater confidence, and respect, for your natural skills. Each project is a stepping stone to more difficult and complicated jobs and soon you'll find yourself accomplishing with ease projects which you previously thought far beyond your abilities.

As your skill and confidence increase you will also begin to get ideas for projects which will be distinctly your own. You will be a *creative* gunsmith.

No tool can accomplish very much without some determined and skillful application. This is the real key to successful gunsmithing, be it in the home workshop of professional shop. The best tool of all is a desire and willingness on your part to spend the necessary time and physical application to see a project through to completion.

JIM CARMICHEL
Prescott, Arizona

I

Basic Gunsmithing Tools and Skills

1 / The Right Screwdrivers

I doubt if there are many homes which do not have a screwdriver or two lying around somewhere. It is the number-one basic tool of a world that seems to be held together by screws. Firearms are no exception, and most guns can be completely taken apart, adjusted, and repaired with only a screwdriver. *But not with just any screwdriver!*

Ordinary household screwdrivers and gunsmithing screwdrivers are as different as buggies and racecars, and there is *absolutely no* gun application I can think of where a plain screwdriver is suitable. If you've ever tried to mount a scope or disassemble a gun with a plain screwdriver you've probably already proved this to yourself. Most likely the screw slots were marred and twisted out of shape, leaving the gun not nearly so pristine as before.

The screws used in guns almost always have slots deeper and narrower than wood and machine screws. This is simply because narrow slots have a neater appearance. Ordinary screwdrivers have a wide, tapered bit and are usually made of relatively soft steel. If the screwdriver has been used much the bit is also apt to be battered and rounded. So if the household screwdriver fits the gun screw at all, the chances are that it will not fit very deeply into the slot because of the taper. Then, when you apply pressure to the screw all of the force is directed to a very small area of the screw's slot. This has the immediate effect of bending it out of shape and ruining its appearance. The screwdriver's taper will also make it want to ride up out of the slot. When this happens, and it usually does, the screw is severely scratched and mangled. Sometimes the screwdriver itself bends or twists and then proceeds to ruin the screw.

Other sins of household screwdrivers are that they are usually too wide or too narrow. When they are too wide the metal surrounding the screw is scarred, and when they are too narrow the screw slot is twisted open.

The first and foremost law of gunsmithing screwdrivers is that no one screwdriver will do everything. You will need a screwdriver for just about *every screw size!* I have a special screwdriver rack in my basement workshop which holds fifteen different screwdrivers. This may sound like a lot of trouble and expense, but I promise you that good screwdrivers, and a lot of 'em, are a very wise investment. A perfectly fitted locking screw for a fine sidelock shotgun may cost twenty dollars to replace if the slot gets butchered up with an ill-fitting screwdriver.

To give you an idea of how screwdrivers should be used, consider that the heads on many scope-ring screws are about the same diameter. Supposedly, therefore, the same screwdriver can be used for all. But no, the slots come in varying widths, so you need screwdrivers with different blade thicknesses. In order to keep from marring a screw head the screwdriver must fill the slot completely.

If a screwdriver is to fit a gun screw properly, the bit, or blade, must be hollow-ground so that the sides of the bit are parallel. This way the screwdriver puts as much force on the bottom of the slot as on the top.

One other necessity of screwdrivers used in gun work is that the metal in the blade be *hard.* If it is soft it will bend under pressure and ride up out of the slot. When this happens the screw is mangled for sure. Therefore, I like blades so hard that they will break before they bend. As a matter of fact, my

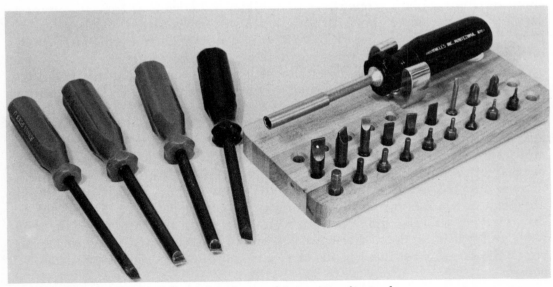

At left, an assortment of hollow-ground screwdrivers manufactured by Bonanza. At right, Brownell's gunsmithing screwdriver set, which utilizes replaceable bits fitting into a single handle. The bits are held in the universal handle magnetically.

At left, a correctly shapened gunsmithing screwdriver. At right, an ordinary household utility screwdriver. The latter will not fit gun screws properly and is liable to disfigure them and thus give them an unprofessional look.

screwdrivers occasionally do break, but the screw head is invariably left unmarred. It is no problem to grind or file the screwdriver back into shape.

A basic set of gunsmithing screwdrivers is an eight-piece outfit manufactured by Grace and obtainable through Brownell's. This is only a *basic* set. As you progress you'll find that you'll need additional shapes. But the Grace set will get you in the habit of using proper tools to turn screws. One of the best screwdriver sets for gunsmiths is made by Bonanza, the reloading-tool manufacturers. They offer fifteen specialized screwdrivers which will cover just about any gunsmithing job.

Another good outfit is the Brownell Magno-Tip set, which includes twenty-four bits which fit into one universal handle. The set, which comes in a wooden holder, includes a dozen hollow-ground bits of assorted widths and thicknesses, three sizes of Phillips-head bits, and ten hex (Allen-type) bits. This set, which will handle almost all gunsmithing jobs, sells for less than twenty bucks in the current (1977) Brownell catalog. The bits are tough and well shaped, and the only disadvantage is the time lost changing bits.

An alternate route is to collect a batch of cheap, ordinary screwdrivers and reshape the bits for gunsmithing purposes. Sometimes the metal in cheap screwdrivers is good and sometimes not. But in any event the steel will be too soft and will require hardening. Test this by buying only one screwdriver to begin with. With a brazing torch heat the tip until it is red-hot, then plunge it into oil or water (try both). If this hardens the steel so that it is difficult to cut with a file, you have what you're looking for.

Even the best screwdrivers become battered and dulled with use, so give them a periodic check and true up any rounded or chipped edges. Good gunsmithing is largely a matter of good work habits, and proper screwdriver use and care is a very good habit. So much so that you can look at a gunsmith's screwdrivers and get a pretty accurate idea of the quality of his gun work.

2 / Files and Rasps

The fine art of filing steel is one of the all-time best examples of skill rather than tools being the secret to success. One of gunsmithing's most essential tools, files are not expensive and, with care, will last a long time; the work that can be accomplished with a file is astounding. Whole rifle, pistol, and shotgun actions have been filed from solid steel with an ordinary file—plus lots of work, of course. When I was a youngster I lived not far from the famed Hacker Martin, who at that time was about the country's only maker of muzzleloading guns. Hacker was a true gunsmith, making virtually every part of his rifles, lock, stock, and barrel. The barrels for his slender Kentucky-style rifles, which were sometimes as long as 50 inches, were round to begin with, then filed by hand to their finished octagon shape. Much of this hard filing was done by his daughter. As soon as she got home from school each day, she changed clothes, picked up a 14-inch mill file, and filed barrels until dinner. None of the boys at our school dared arm-wrestle with her.

Nowadays, with readymade parts for just about everything, knowing how to use a file is not as important as it once was. But just the same, there are enough projects requiring work with a file that even the amateur needs a few files and the skill to use them.

I think the amateur can get by very nicely with only three files—one 6-inch triangular, one 8-inch round, and one 6-inch flat. To help speed up bigger jobs a 8-inch or 10-inch flat mill file is handy. Also needed are handles, a file card, and, for delicate work, a set of fine-cut "needle" files. These little files come in all shapes, usually ten or twelve to the set, and have a terrific range of uses from making delicate metal parts to stock detailing. A file card, or cleaner, is a must, as will be explained later.

Back when I was a farm lad we made handles for files simply by jamming a length of corn cob on the file shank. Today cobs are about as hard to find as

An assortment of files for the amateur gunsmith. At left, a 12-inch file for speedy, rough finishing of metal and also for finishing cuts on stock work. Next, a couple of smaller files with finer teeth for finish filing. Next, straight-side pillar file, which cuts on either side top and bottom, but not on the sides; a round chain-saw sharpening file; and a triangular file. Also shown is a set of fine-bit needle files and a file card, used for cleaning accumulations of metal from the file.

elephant burgers so you'll need to buy or make some wooden handles.

When you check your local hardware store you'll probably find several grades and prices of files. Be sure and buy the best, such as Nicholson or Black Diamond, because some of the economy-priced files are really terrible. In gunsmith's tool catalogs you'll find some exotic files for special jobs. These aren't necessary for any of the do-it-yourself projects discussed in this book, but who knows what other projects you may tackle in the future.

A European-trained gunsmith once told me that one of the periodic tests he took as an apprentice was to file a piece of steel into a simple cube. This sounds like an easy task until you give it a try. Filing a flat surface just ain't all that easy. Most of us apply to much pressure, for one thing; and for another, we do not make uniformly level strokes. This results in a flat surface that isn't quite flat, but somewhat curved, especially at the edges.

This can be overcome only with practice, but it helps to place your work

Proper filing means holding and positioning the file correctly and putting the work in a comfortable, convenient position. The file is controlled better when held in both hands.

(the piece being filed, etc.) at a comfortable level so that your arms can move smoothly. Working at an awkward angle is perhaps the most common cause of poor file work. Grip your file by the handle in one hand and at the tip with the thumb and forefinger of the other hand. This will give you best control and a better "feel" of what you're doing. Do not drag the file back and forth across the work but lift it on the return stroke. This gives you a chance to see the cut after every stroke and increases the life of your files.

By all means do not apply too much pressure. A file can only cut so much at a stroke, and additional pressure just increases friction. Excessive pressure also is a leading cause of poor control and uneven cuts. I also think too much pressure causes a file to "load up" or clog.

When a file clogs, metal particles collect in the file's cutting surfaces and form a noticeable bump. This bump or bumps will, if allowed to remain, keep getting bigger as you continue filing. Pretty soon it will even begin cutting an ugly groove across the work surface. This is awful.

Some metals and alloys, especially softer metals, seem to have a natural tendency to clog files, and one must inspect the cutting face of the file after every few strokes.

The file is cleaned with a few passes of a file card, a stiff wire brush of sorts

It is essential that a file be cleaned thoroughly and often with the card. Once metal particles begin to build up in the teeth they become increasingly difficult to remove.

which gets into the teeth and removes the collection of metal particles. Do this often, because metal particles can pock into the cutting surface mighty hard. Once an accumulation gets started it can be damn hard to remove.

A sure death of a good file is trying to cut steel that is too hard. If a file screeches across the work, hardly makes a cut, or makes no cut at all, stop right there. If you continue, all you will do is knock the sharp edge off your file and ruin it. Hard surfaces must be cut with a grinding wheel, or their temper (hardness) must be removed with a torch. I keep an old file handy to try on metals which I suspect of being glass-hard. Sometimes gun parts have only a hard surface, or shell, only a few thousandths of an inch thick. This is common for "case-hardened" parts. Once the shell is broken through, the underlying metal may be comparatively soft. When I suspect this condition, I break through the shell with an old file. Sometimes it works and sometimes it doesn't.

Happily, the projects outlined in the following chapters involve rather mild, easy-to-file steels.

A rasp is a type of file with bigger, coarser teeth designed for removing comparatively large amounts of material. Rasps of different shapes are the principal tool for shaping gunstocks because they remove wood with comparative ease and are adaptable to nearly all shapes of cuts on wood.

I keep some six or eight rasps on hand, but this is because I do more stockwork than other kinds of gunsmithing. A "general practitioner" can get by with half as many. Stockmakers of a few decades ago had to do much of their rough shaping with heavy, rough-cutting rasps of the type used by blacksmiths to trim horses' hooves. These rasps made a terrible mess of the wood, requiring considerable dressing and smoothing with smoother-cutting, but slower, cabinet rasps, planes, and spokeshaves. This era ended, and the stockmakers'

The half-round cabinet rasp is excellent for stock work. The flat side (top) is used for straight or convex surfaces, while the rounded side (bottom) is ideal for inside curves like the underside of a cheekpiece.

labors lightened, with the introduction of the Stanley "Surform" rasp. This tool looks and handles like a rasp, but the replaceable flat and rounded blades are actually a series of small knives that smoothly slice the wood. The cutting action is so smooth that you can actually slice a stock in half in about a minute. The Surform tool is not flexible enough for finishing or close-quarter work, but for hogging away large quantities of wood no hand tool is better.

After rough shaping with the Surform tool the stock is smoothed and worked to final shape with a half-round cabinet rasp or file. These come in several lengths; the 10-inch length is a good all-round choice. The flat side of the rasp is used for all straight and convex surfaces, and the half-rounded side is ideal for inside curves such as the inside of the pistol grip and the underside of the cheekpiece. If you want to spend the few extra dollars you can get cabinet rasps in progressively finer cuts which smooth wood down until it is ready for final sanding. An alternate way of doing this is to wrap 80-grit or 120-grit sandpaper around the rasp for the initial smoothing-up operation. When metal-cutting files get too dull for steel they can still be used for final shaping and smoothing of wood.

In order to get the longest and best use from your files and rasps do not store them loose in a drawer or tool kit where they get banged about and chip at each other. Keep them dry and clean, and, if possible, hang them on a wall fixture where they'll be out of harms way.

3

Chisels and Other Stockmaking Tools

Over two decades ago, when I began my hobby of amateur gunsmithing, I bought a set of six small Millers Falls carving tools. The price then, as I recall, was $5.95. At today's inflated prices a similar set probably costs three times what I paid, but it's still a hell of a useful bunch of tools. The cutting edge of the widest chisel and gouge is only about ⅜ inch wide, so one makes haste very slowly. This is not such a bad thing, because it helps guarantee that your mistakes will be small ones. I inletted dozens of stocks with this simple, inexpensive set of tools before I owned a single larger chisel.

It is nice to own a collection of finely made carving tools in a wide variety of shapes and sizes. But chances are you'll use only a few basic shapes for just about every job. Some years ago I invested in a fancy eighteen-piece set of tools only to discover that I used four or five favorite shapes for nearly all the work. The point is that you'll save money by buying an inexpensive four- or six-piece basic set, then adding individual tools as you need them. The gunsmith-supply catalogs have a terrific assortment to choose from.

Don't let the terminology of carving tools throw you: A *chisel* has a flat blade and makes flat or straight-edged cuts. A *gouge* is curved and makes rounded cuts, such as for a barrel channel. These come in a wide variety of radiuses and widths. The other common shape used by stockmakers is known as a parting tool, veining tool, or simply a V-tool because of the V-shaped cutting edge. These are used to sharpen up corners in inletting, but their principal use is in cutting the border around checkering panels and other forms of decorative carving. The chapter on carving pistol grips shows extensive use of this handy little tool.

Most carving tools are meant to be powered by hand *only*. If you try to drive

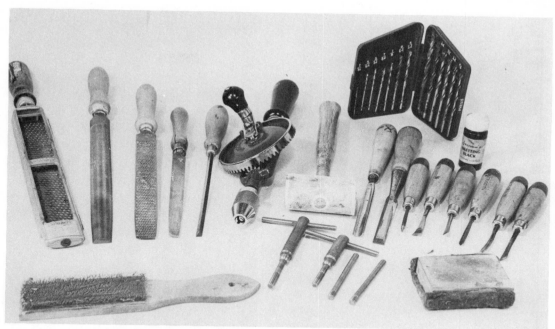

This simple assortment of tools is all that's needed to do really first-class stockwork. More elaborate tools may make faster work but not better. At bottom, a file card to keep the rasps and files clean, a stock of T handled guard screws and inletting pins, and a simple homemade sanding block fashioned from a bit of felt tacked to a bit of wood. At top, a Stanley Surform shaper, , three different rasps, a small triangular file for delicate shaping operations, a simple hand-cranked drill, a rawhide mallet, a half-round and a straight chisel, and an inexpensive set of six carving tools. At the back, a small bottle of inletting black used for spotting-in operations and a set of drill bits.

them with a mallet or hammer the handles will split and all sorts of other bad things may happen. So if you must bang at a carving tool, get chisels and gouges which were made to take such abuse. Such a tool will have a metal or leather reinforcement at the top of the handle or perhaps have a handle made entirely of shock-resistant material. By and large, you'll find that chisel hammering is seldom if ever needed for stockwork. If the tool is as sharp as it should be, it will glide through wood with moderate pressure. Fine carving tools are delightful to own and use—so much so that I suspect many professionals and home hobbyists eventually wind up with more than they really need. Pride in ownership of fine tools is not a sin, unless you abuse them.

Beginning stockmakers are invariably surprised to learn that the precision fitting of firearms mechanisms into wood is accomplished by *scraping*. That super-close metal-to-wood fit when a barreled action is inletted into a stock is

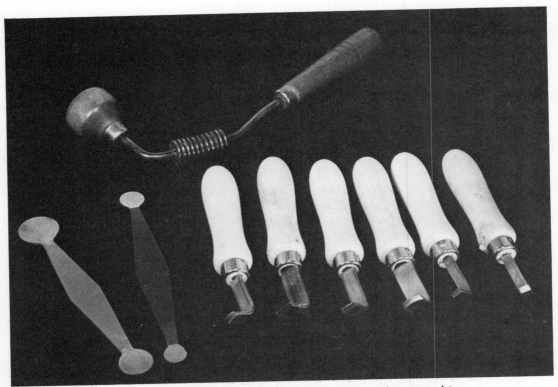

Scrapers such as these are a tremendous asset to the stockmaker who wants his inletting to be precise and so close that it looks as though the metal grew into wood. At left, a couple of scrapers made by ace stockmaker Jerry Fisher. At right, a set of six scrapers of different shapes sold by Brownell's. In the background, a Gun Line barrel-channel scraper which removes a lot of wood in a hurry.

achieved by delicately scraping away thin wisps of wood until the fit is perfect. Therefore the stockmaker needs a scraper or two. The best of these for scraping rounded surfaces is a two-piece set made by ace stockmaker Jerry Fisher. The four radiuses (two per tool) will do for just about every surface you'll encounter in inletting. Another set of scrapers is a six-piece outfit by Brownell's with three curved edges and three flat, of varying widths. Grace makes a two-piece set, sold by Brownell's, one straight and one curved. The Brownell's catalog lists other types of barrel-inletting scrapers shaped more or less like a plane for two-handed work.

The trick to using a scraper successfully is to keep the edge sharp, working with the grain and not trying to cut too much at a time. The correct inletting procedure is to inlet the action to *nearly* all the way into the stock with carving tools. Then use the scrapers for fitting the last small fraction. The scraping action smooths the wood so that it looks as though it were actually molded to the metal. Fortunately for the beginner, scraping is easy to learn and relatively foolproof. It's mainly a matter of patience.

There are, of course, quite a few other widely used stocking tools, but none that the home hobbyist really needs. The drawknife, for example, is a big two-handled tool traditionally used by stockmakers to slice off big chunks of wood from oversize stock blanks. But with today's really excellent choice of semi-finished stocks there is no need for the amateur to consider making a stock from a block of wood.

Spokeshaves and an assortment of planes were also once widely used for shaping and smoothing stocks. But these have been made all but obsolete for stockmaking the availability of semi-finished stocks and a plentiful assortment of wood rasps and wood files. Nowadays it is possible to do an entirely creditable job of stockmaking with three carving tools, a couple of scrapers, a Surform shaper, and a cabinet rasp.

4/

Drills and Drilling

I think most professional gunsmiths would agree that the single most indispensable power tool in their shops is the drill press. They would further agree that the drill press ranks only behind the screwdriver and drift punch in frequency of use. But sadly, drill presses are too expensive for most amateur shops, so we must do our hole boring with less elaborate tools.

Here of late, due to the wizardry of solid-state electronics and high-impact plastics, some junior-size drill presses have been marketed which sell for a fraction of the cost of full-size models. These tools, which are sold by Sears, Montgomery Ward, and others, offer sufficient power for most drilling operations, variable speed, compact size, and easy portability. These last two features may make the little drill presses even more desirable than the big presses in home shops where space is at a premium. Prices for these little presses run between fifty and seventy-five dollars. They are a great Christmas or birthday gift to hint for. This is how I got mine.

But all this talk about drill presses is not to say you can't do a first-rate gunsmithing job without one. There are times, to be sure, when a drill of some sort is necessary, but nearly all jobs can be managed very nicely with a simple, inexpensive hand-cranked model. Or for a few more dollars you can own an electric hand drill.

Drill bits can be bought in sets of ten or twelve ranging from $1/16$ to $1/4$ inch. One of these sets in a protective holder will handle 99 percent of your drilling needs, so there's no need to spend a lot of money on a sackful of odd-sized bits. I get by very nicely with one of these sets plus one $5/16$ inch drill which is handy for drilling guard-screw holes in rifle stocks.

If you want to spend some extra money for extra bits, you'll be smart to buy a set of the flat, funny-looking spade or "paddle" type wood-boring bits. These can be bought separately or in sets of six or so. Sizes range from $1/4$ inch up to an inch or more, but all have ¼-inch shanks so they will fit in small-chuck electric hand drills. They are especially handy for such chores as boring bolt holes in bench tops when you mount a vise or reloading tools, and I've used them for boring clean, deep holes when making my own cartridge-holding blocks.

The rule for buying drill bits is simple: Buy the very best you can afford. Money spent for cheap bits is wasted. Gun steels are tough and require top-quality bits. If the better brands are unknown to you, a good rule of thumb is that bits that *look* sharp and well finished are the good ones. Avoid most imports unless you know they are of top quality.

Three drilling options available to the amateur workman. The old-fashioned hand-cranked drill is hard to beat and is a handy accessory in any shop. The electron hand drill saves time and energy, when drilling metal. The junior-size drill press is relatively inexpensive and does not require much space. However, it offers the advantages precision drilling at a variety of drill speeds. These are available from several manufacturers. A simple set of cased drill bits is all that the amateur requires. However, the bits should be carefully stored and cared for in order to assure a long life. Drill bits are easy to lose unless they are kept in a container in this type.

5 / Soldering and Brazing Torches

Soldering, welding, and brazing are essential skills in the gunsmithing trade with dozens of applications. For example, front and rear sights are often soldered or brazed to rifle barrels, and on occasion scope mounts are brazed to actions. Double-barreled shotguns have the barrels joined by soldering, and many are soldered into a monoblock breeching system. Broken parts are sometimes welded back together. All sorts of deluxe refinements are added to custom guns by welding and soldering. And, of course, welding torches are a source of high heat for the tempering of steel.

Among the more spectacular welding projects done by gunsmiths is action shortening. This involves cutting a bolt-action rifle mechanism—receiver, bolt, firing pin, magazine, follower, and floorplate—in half, removing about an inch, then welding everything back together. This makes a handy little action for cartridges in the .250 Savage, .22/250, and .308 Winchester class. If the gunsmith is a true expert welder, it is all but impossible to detect where the parts were welded together.

Jim Clark, the well-known pistolsmith, makes a super-accurate adaption of the Colt automatic pistol by welding an extra inch of length to the slide. The weld is so perfect that the unit appears to have been machined from a single piece of steel.

Many gunsmiths even reline worn-out rifle barrels by soldering a new rifled liner in the old barrel. Obviously, these projects are beyond the capabilities of nearly all amateur craftsmen and, for that matter, many professional gunsmiths. The purpose in mentioning them is to give you an idea of what *can* be done.

Since electric-arc and acetylene welding require special equipment and training, they are beyond the scope of this book. But many types of soldering can be done with simple equipment and a minimum of skill. In the chapter on

A simple-to-use and inexpensive propane torch is capable of performing a wide variety of gunsmithing services. It can be used for surface-hardening or tempering small parts as well as soldering. The solder is force 44, which does not break down in hot caustic-type bluing solutions as does ordinary cold solders. This solder is available from Brownell's and other gunsmithing supply houses.

making a hinged floorplate, for example, a simple silver-soldering project is managed with only an inexpensive propane torch.

Soldering falls into two general categories: "soft" soldering with an alloy of lead and tin, and "silver" soldering with a harder alloy of mainly silver and copper. This latter is also sometimes called silver brazing. The advantage of soft soldering is lower cost of material and equipment. Soft solder melts at less than 500° F. Thus it can be melted with inexpensive, low-temperature torches. The most common use of soft solder in gunmaking has been joining the two barrels on double-barreled shotguns and rifles.

The disadvantages of soft solder are that it is not as strong as silver solder and suffers the particular misfortune of being attacked by caustic bluing salts.

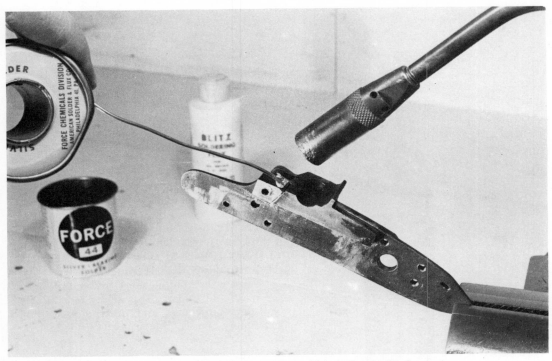

A propane torch being used to solder the pan assembly to the lock plate of a flintlock mechanism. The torch can also be used to surface-harden the frizzen of this lock to ensure a good sparking action and to heat the barrel and other steel parts as necessary for the browning operation.

Back when guns were blued by the old-fashioned rust process, this was no problem. Many a gunsmith has made the mistake of trying to reblue an old set of double barrels in his hot-blue process only to have them come apart before his eyes. Bob Brownell sells a solder called Force-44, an alloy of mostly tin with a bit of silver, which flows at 475° F. and is said to resist hot blueing.

The advantages of silver solder are its strength and resistance to caustic blueing solutions. The disadvantage is that most silver solders melt and flow in the 1000-1200° F. range. This means that more elaborate heating is required for many jobs. Relatively small parts such as the hinged-floorplate project can be silver-soldered with an ordinary propane torch because the heat is not rapidly lost. But when heat is rapidly dissipated in larger masses of metal, such as a rifle barrel, torches of this type are not adequate.

Until fairly recently this meant that oxyaceylene welding torches had to be used for silver soldering. Recently, however, several brands of small, light-weight, and comparatively inexpensive brazing torches have been marketed which add rich oxygen to propane MAPP gas. This increases the flame heat tremendously and permits one to do firearms-related silver soldering with ease. The source of oxygen is oxygen pellets which are converted to gas. Though the price range of these new soldering/blazing kits varies, some cost less than thirty dollars.

Silver soldering is not at all difficult. The only real secrets are to use ample flux and plenty of heat. Perhaps the most convenient way to use silver solder is in a prepared paste form. These soldering pastes, which I understand were developed for and by the aircraft industry, have finely ground solder particles mixed with soldering flux. The paste is simply spread on the two surfaces to be joined, the parts are clamped together, and heat is applied until the solder melts and flows. This is a super-convenient way to attach sights, etc.

Another serious disadvantage of silver solder, and sometimes even soft solder, is the potential damage to gun metal when excessive heat is applied. When steel gets red-hot it oxidizes rapidly and forms a rough, ugly coating of shale. If a rifle barrel is heated red-hot, say to attach a front sight base ramp, the mirrorlike surface of the bore will become disfigured and there will likely be some loss of accuracy. This can usually be avoided by coating delicate surfaces with a protective nonscaling compound. These protective agents are available from welding shops and gunsmith-supply houses. Brownell's also supplies a heat-control paste which prevents heat from spreading to areas where it is not wanted.

Another helpful use of soldering torches is the heat treating of special-use steels. A good example of this is the hardening of frizzens and flintlocks. It takes a *hard* frizzen to make the necessary sparks to fire a flintlock rifle, and I've made wonderful frizzens by heating them red-hot with an ordinary propane torch, then dumping them into a can of Kosenit or a similar surface-hardening compound.

Soldering torches can also be used to good advantage by do-it-yourself muzzleloading fans for heating parts to be browned with Birchwood-Casey's Plum Brown metal browner. I've gotten long Kentucky-rifle barrels hot enough to brown beautifully simply by playing a propane torch over the barrel's surface. The trick is to support the barrel in such a way that the accumulated heat is not lost. I do this by bending simple barrel-holding rods from a couple of clotheshangers. Wire doesn't have enough mass to steal much heat.

6/

Other Basic Tools for the Amateur

One basic tool no amateur gunsmith can be without for very long is a bench vise. It can be elaborate, with all sorts of fancy extras, or it can be the ordinary garden variety. But you can't do much without a vise. As you thumb through these pages you'll note that I'm working with a plain bench-mounted 4-inch vise. Vises similar to this can be found in most hardware stores and cost in the neighborhood of twenty bucks. When the vise was new it had rather sharp teeth in the jaws. I filed these off so they couldn't mar stocks. I also fitted the jaws with soft plastic protectors so I could clamp metal parts tightly without damaging the finish.

For years I got by with a little three-dollar vise which clamped to the bench by means of a thumbscrew. The home craftsman who has only limited space can use one of these attached to the kitchen table. In fact this is exactly what I did for a while, even for such major projects as stockworking. But the best advice when it comes to vises is get the best you can afford. After all, it's a lifetime investment.

Another essential tool is the common hacksaw. The one I own and use is a very cheap model but I make up for it by using the best blades obtainable. Gun steels tend to be especially tough, requiring top-quality blades with small teeth. If best-quality blades seem to cost a lot just keep in mind that good blades make sawing much easier. Besides, some of the cheaper blades I've tried simply shed their teeth on the first pass across gun steel. So cheap blades aren't very economical after all.

Since nearly all guns make use of pins to hold some parts together you won't get by without some drift punches. Some home hobbyists get by with just a few nails of different sizes with the points filed off. Whichever way you

My work bench. Rasps and files are hung in brackets, screwdrivers are in a special rack to the right, and a small-parts cabinet is out of the way in a corner. Oil and other often-used materials are in easy reach and a small but adequate vise is mounted on the bench. The flexible-armed light is a valuable aid.

decide be sure to use a punch that is only slightly smaller than the pin. I use readymade punches which come as a set in a nice wooden holder. The sizes range from about $1/32$ inch up to $3/8$ inch and fit every gun pin I've encountered yet.

In my bench drawer is a $1/4$-inch diameter brass rod about 4 inches long. It's been around so long I can't remember where I got it but it has been absolutely essential for driving front and rear sights in and out of dovetail slots. The purpose of using a *soft* rod of brass, copper, or nylon is to keep from battering the sights themselves and making them look ugly and abused. Brownell's sells all sorts of soft punches of this sort if you can't find a piece of scrap brass rod.

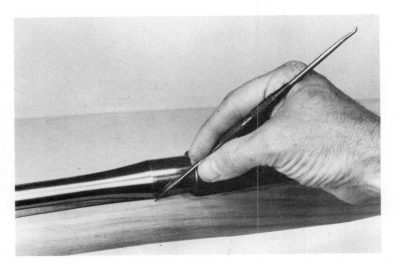

A rawhide mallet or nonmarring hammer with plastic head is good to have for driving punches and other uses.

This brings up the matter of a choice in hammers for driving these punches. You *will* need a rawhide mallet or a nonmarring hammer of some sort with a plastic head. Also I use a little 4-ounce ball-peen hammer for light tapping on punches, etc. The only other hammer I've ever needed was a carpenter's hammer to build my workbench. So don't burden yourself with unnecessarily large hammers.

If you've done much woodwork you're probably accustomed to doing your marking with a pencil. Pencils are handy for some gun work too, but not nearly as handy — or as accurate — as a sharp-pointed scribe. A scribe will make a narrow, precise mark on wood or metal which will not smudge or easily wipe away. A gunsmith must learn to work in tolerances of only a few thou-

A sharply pointed scribe is best for marking on wood, rather than pencil point which can dull quickly and doesn't mark as precisely.

sandths of an inch. The only way you can measure and mark this fine is with a scribe. A pencil is too coarse. If you do much marking on metal you'll appreciate some layout blue. This is a fast-drying paint which forms a thin coat on metal that clearly shows scribed marks. Its use is illustrated in the chapter on making and fitting skeleton gripcaps.

To help you make straight, precisely measured lines with the scribe you'll need a 6-inch steel machinists' rule. These usually come with a pocket clip so you'll always have it handy in your shirt pocket. They are calibrated in 64ths of an inch, which is plenty close enough for most stock work. But they're probably handiest of all as a reliable straightedge. I keep about three on hand in case one gets lost in the mess on my workbench.

The next time you're in a paint or hardware store be sure to ask for one of their free yardsticks. That is, if you don't already have one. Nothing is handier for measuring barrel lengths and length of pull on rifles and shotguns, and for preliminary stock layout. If you want to spend some dough on a fancy piece of measuring equipment you might consider a dial or vernier caliper calibrated in $1/1000$ths. If you reload rifle or pistol ammo you should have one of these anyway. Nearly all gun measurements are given in decimal fractions, so a caliper is essential for precision work. A 4-inch or 6-inch caliper is handier and far more versatile than a micrometer.

Pliers are handy for many jobs, but they can also get you in trouble, so I recommend their use with definite reservations. Do not use pliers on gun screws, pins, sights, knobs, or bolts. This is because pliers usually mar anything they grip. So restrict their use to springs and other such items which occasionally require manhandling. Pliers are at their handiest for holding and maneuvering parts being heat treated, soldered, etc. A pair of needlenose pliers and a set of the ordinary household kind will do you just fine. Small C-clamps are also mighty handy for soldering and brazing jobs, especially for holding sight ramps in place while you apply the heat.

A little wire bristle brush about the size of a toothbrush is one of those items you think you can do without until you've used one for a while and gotten the habit. They are especially handy for scrubbing hard pocked accumulations of powder fouling, grease, and dirt from hard-to-get-at places. A softer bristle brush will be needed for cleaning out checkering and other such delicate tasks.

One piece of equipment no gunsmith is a stranger to is the sanding block. You can buy it or you can make it, but you gotta have it. When the world was young I tacked a thin piece of felt to a little scrap of lumber and it has been my official sanding block ever since. I simply wrap a piece of sandpaper around the block and have at the stock I'm finishing. The idea of using a sanding block rather than simply holding the sandpaper in your fingers is that the

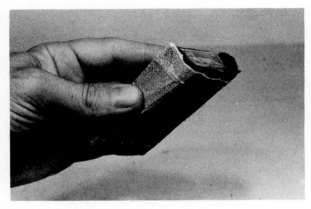

The author's official sanding block is a block of wood with a piece of felt tacked to it. Sandpaper is wrapped around the block.

block ensures a flat, ripple-free surface. If you hold the paper in your fingers it tends to make hollow spots, which will make your work look more amateurish. Store-bought sanding blocks are usually about 4 inches long by 2 inches wide. This is fine for sanding forends and other large, flat surfaces, but a smaller block is better for all-round stock sanding.

Another honest-to-goodness necessity for good gun work is a good light. I used to work in a basement which had a single overhead bulb. My work looked pretty good as long as I kept it in the basement, but when I took it out in the daylight it looked pretty bad. In my current workshop there are full-width windows along two walls, large lights overhead, and two flexible-arm lamps over my workbench. It makes a tremendous difference in not only the quality of your work but, just as important, your *attitude* toward your work. A well-lighted work area will make your hobby more enjoyable, and you'll find that you can work on tedious jobs longer without fatigue. In addition to large overhead lights which provide ample light for the entire work area I think it is also essential to have a flexible-arm lamp which can be directed to the work area. This is especially important for carving and checkering.

If you intend to do much stockwork involving the inletting of bolt-action rifles you'll do well to get a set of inletting pins. You'll need a different set of pins for every action make because of the difference in guard-screw threads. But they cost only about a buck a set so you won't go broke.

Inletting pins, or guide screws, fit into the guard-screw holes and serve as a guide when you drop the barreled action into the stock being inletted. Since you have to fit the assembly into the stock quite a few times during the inletting process, the pins help ensure that the action is positioned in the wood the same time after time. I'm not saying that inletting pins are an absolute must for good inletting, but they sure make it easier to do good work.

Another helpful tool for speeding the inletting job is a set of T-handle action

Another handy gunsmithing accessory is a hand grinder such as the Dremel Moto-Tool. This tool performs a variety of jobs on both wood and metal. More recent models of the Dremel Moto-Tool feature a variable-speed control, which is especially handy for gunsmithing jobs.

screws. When the barreled action is almost completely inletted it becomes necessary to tighten the action screws with every fitting. Constantly screwing the action screws in and out with a screwdriver gets to be a chore, and you run the risk of disfiguring the screw heads.

The easy way around this is to use specially made screws with handles which make action tightening both faster and easier. They cost about three dollars per set. Like inletting pins, they are available from all gunsmith-supply houses and are also listed in semi-finished stock catalogs. So every time you order a semi-finished stock for a different type of action it's a good idea to order pins and hand screws. They last forever.

Sooner or later every amateur stockmaker will want to try his hand at checkering. Checkering tools, however, are so specialized that it is all but impossible to describe the tools without explaining how they work. Therefore, both tools and their use are described in the chapter on beginning checkering. A checkering accessory worth thinking about is a "cradle" or fixture to hold the stock while it is being checkered.

Just to keep the record straight, entirely satisfactory checkering can be done

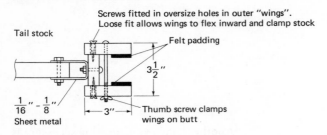

Screws fitted in oversize holes in outer "wings".
Loose fit allows wings to flex inward and clamp stock

Tail stock

Felt padding

$3\frac{1}{2}$"

$\frac{1}{16}$" - $\frac{1}{8}$"
Sheet metal

3"

Thumb screw clamps
wings on butt

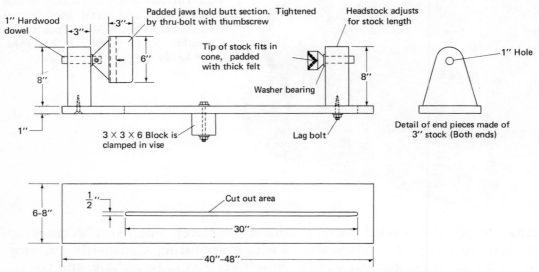

1" Hardwood
dowel

3"

3"

Padded jaws hold butt section. Tightened
by thru-bolt with thumbscrew

Headstock adjusts
for stock length

6"

Tip of stock fits in
cone, padded
with thick felt

8"

8"

Washer bearing

1" Hole

1"

3 X 3 X 6 Block is
clamped in vise

Lag bolt

Detail of end pieces made of
3" stock (Both ends)

6–8"

$\frac{1}{2}$"

Cut out area

30"

40"–48"

The author's stock cradle consists of a base of heavy lumber with felt-lined grips
at either end to hold the butt and forend tip to the stock. The cradle itself is held
in a bench vise.

by holding the stock in a vise, on a padded workbench or table. You can even
hold the stock in your lap and checker to a fair-thee-well.

For years I used a cradle made from a piece of heavy lumber with arms at either end which held the stock at the butt and at the tip of the forend. The
cradle itself was held in the bench vise. Beginners don't need to worry about
owning a cradle, but if you plan to checker one or two stocks a year, owning
one is worthwhile. The commercially made cradles I've seen aren't so hot, so
you can make one yourself when the need arises.

When you begin to collect tools and equipment you should also give some thought to storing and caring for them. If allowed to just lie around they get lost, battered, and rusted. If they are well stored they not only give longer service but are easy to find when you need them.

I hang files and rasps on hanger clips above my workbench. This way they are both out of the way and within easy reach. There are all sorts of tool-hanging gadgets available, so get the kind you like best. I keep smaller tools in a cabinet which has several plastic drawers. These storage cabinets are also available at most hardware stores. It seems to me that they cost more than they should, but I must admit that regardless of what they cost, they are mighty handy. I keep drills and other often-used tools in a small storage chest right on my workbench. Less-often-used tools are in another cabinet under the bench.

One more tool that will make your life easier is a wide bench brush for sweeping chips and sanding dust from your workbench. If you take the time to keep a clean work area it will pay happy dividends. Think neat—it will show up in your work.

The final *and most important* equipment you can own is personal-protection gear: a breathing filter and safety glasses. Anytime you grind, drill, polish, hammer, solder, weld, or even drive a pin you should wear eye protection. Likewise, get in the habit of wearing a nose shield if you do your stock sanding in a confined area. All that dust can't be good for your respiratory system. A nose guard or respirator is also a smart idea when you polish or buff metal on a buffing wheel. The fine particles thrown into the air are bound to be harmful if you inhale enough of them.

Good gun work is *smart* work, and there's nothing smart about taking chances with your eyes and lungs.

7 / Sharpening Knives and Shop Tools

It was more than a few years ago, back when I was in the seventh or eighth grade in school, but the memory is as fresh as though it were only yesterday. One of my classmates pulled a knife from his pocket, opened the blade, and casually began shaving the hair from his arm. I was fascinated.

"How did you get that knife so sharp?" I asked.

"Can't tell you."

"Why not?"

"My granddaddy showed me how to get this knife as sharp as a razor, but I can't tell anybody because it's a family secret."

I was dejected almost to tears. I would have given almost anything to have been able to sharpen a knife like that, but now it looked as though I'd never learn because it was a closely guarded family secret. Nonetheless I resolved to learn to sharpen a knife to razor keenness. Within a few weeks of asking questions of all the old-timers in the community, plus a bit of experimenting on my own, I learned not one but several ways of honing a blade to hairsplitting sharpness. Each of the old-timers who shared his "secret" formula with me was of the opinion that he alone possessed the ultimate technique of knife sharpening. Thus their demonstrations were accomplished with considerable ritual, and the prescribed honing fluids ranged from stagnant water from a hollowed-out gum stump to common spit laced with a variety of chewing tobaccos and snuffs. One old fellow whom I'll never forget went into considerable detail with his demonstration of knife sharpening, then promptly dulled the edge on a rusty bolt, "because," he admonished, "it's a sin to have a knife that sharp."

One thing I did learn for sure, though, is that there are any number of ways to sharpen a cutting tool.

Be that as it may, the fact remains that putting a fine edge on a piece of steel is as mysterious to some people as it was to me as a schoolboy. As a result many otherwise fine knives, chisels, and carving tools are giving only half service, and their owners are producing not nearly so fine a quality of work as they might otherwise. In truth, getting a razor-fine edge on a cutting tool isn't at all difficult, nor does it take much time. All you need is a proper technique and the right sharpening stone for the job. Here's how to go about it.

Selecting a sharpening stone

First, the sharpening stone. For general gunsmithing work such as stock-making and related woodcarving one needs to be concerned with only two or possibly three grades of stone. These include the Washita or Soft Arkansas, the Hard Arkansas, and the India stone, the only artificial stone of the three. Actually there is no exact grading system for Arkansas stones. Being a natural mineral (novaculite), it is found in different densities or hardnesses, from the soft, open-grained Washita to the hard, fine-grained, blue-black Arkansas.

The synthetic India stone generally has inferior sharpening qualities to a good Arkansas stone but is still useful to the home craftsman because it is available in a useful shape for sharpening curved chisels. Also it is less expensive than a natural Arkansas stone.

Generally speaking, the softer, coarser-grained stones are faster-cutting than the harder stones. At the same time, however, the coarser stones impart a characteristic roughness to the edge of the blade which limits the final degree of sharpness possible with that particular stone. In other words, a soft stone will get an edge just so sharp and no more regardless of how much care and effort you put forth.

It is like sanding a piece of wood with coarse but fast-cutting 80-grit sandpaper—no matter how hard you try it will leave scratches on the wood. If you use a powerful magnifying glass to observe the edge of a blade which has been sharpened with a soft stone you will observe that the edge appears somewhat rough and jagged, with the roughness matching the grain size of the stone. Thus if a greater degree of sharpness is required a harder, finer-grained stone must be used.

It would seem, in light of the above, that the smart thing to do is to use only a fine-cut hard Arkansas stone for all your sharpening. Unfortunately, the hard stones cut so slowly that it would take a mighty long time to bring a dull edge to a fine edge. Therefore one must think in terms of two stones for a single sharpening job, or better yet, a compromise medium-soft stone called a

Washita/Soft Arkansas such as marketed by A. G. Russell's Arkansas Oil-stones of Fayetteville, Arkansas. These relatively fast-cutting stones are selected for the proper hardness which will combine fast cutting action with relatively fine edge sharpening. Such a stone will get shop tools such as stocking chisels sharp enough for most jobs with the possible exception of carving tools used for extra-fine relief carving.

For most sharpening jobs an oilstone 2 inches wide by 4 inches long will do, but a 6-inch stone is more convenient.

Using the stone

To sharpen a knife, hold it with the blade at about a 20° angle to the stone and draw it *edge first* across the face of the stone. In the same motion draw the knife toward you so that all the edge will contact stone somewhere during the cycle. Now reverse the blade and take an identical pass in the opposite direction. Continue this back-and-forth action until the blade is evenly sharpened from rear to point. It is important that you maintain the same angle (or patch) with each pass or the stone will be cutting at different places and causing a rounded edge.

Also it is important that the stone be lubricated with some type of oil or even water during the sharpening operation. The fluid will hold the metal particles in suspension and keep them from clogging the pores in the stone. A clogged stones cut poorly, and the metal particles will build up in tiny clumps that will cause nicks in the blade's edge. The type of lubrication fluid is not really so important as long as something is used. Light oil such as gun oil is fine. Even with the best of care a stone will sometimes "load up" and require a cleaning out to get it back in best condition. Just give it a good scrubbing with water and a stiff brush. If it is really bad, a dash of kitchen scouring powder will help things along.

Straight-edged chisels can be sharpened up in jig time with a simple back-and-forth motion on the oilstone. However, be sure to sharpen from the beveled side only and at the same, or near the same, angle as the bevel. Also keep an even straight-down pressure, as an uneven pressure will cause the side receiving the most pressure to become somewhat rounded and you'll wind up with a curved edge. If you don't like the back-and-forth technique a circular motion will do just as well. Just watch the angle, keep the pressure even, and keep the stone well oiled.

This sharpening from one side only will cause a fine bead or "wire edge" to build up on the edge and curl toward the side which is not being honed. This wire edge can be removed by a light pass or two with the flat side of the chisel toward the stone. It can also be removed by alternately drawing each side

The first step in sharpening a knife or chisel on a stone is applying a liberal coat of oil to the stone. The liquid keeps the metal particles in suspension so they will not become imbedded in the surface of the stone. A dry stone quickly becomes coated with metal particles and does not sharpen as well as an oiled stone.

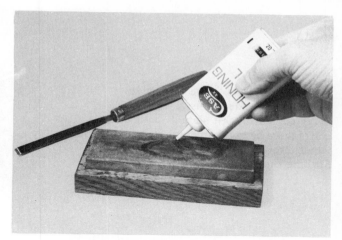

The secret to efficient sharpening is holding the knife or chisel at a correct angle. Be sure to position the stone so that it allows your hand to move freely and maintain a constant angle. Cut forward against the stone as if you were trying to cut the stone.

A chisel is being final-honed on a strip of leather tacked to a piece of wood. If you draw the knife backward over the leather, alternating sides, any "wire edge" that may have accumulated during the honing will be honed away.

A contoured India stone is used to sharpen the inside radius of a gouge. Every gunsmith's kit should include one of these handy sharpening stones, which are available from all gunsmithing supply houses.

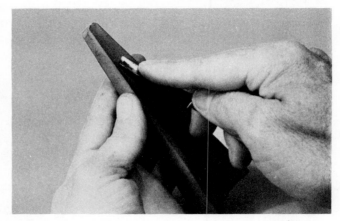

The other side of the contoured India stone has a concave face for honing the outside radius of carving gouges.

across a strip of clean, smooth leather. You can test for a wire edge by drawing the edge of the blade backward across the thumbnail. A wire edge will scrape up a fine curl of whatever it is thumbnails are made of. Keep honing on the leather until the blade slides freely across the nail.

For curved gouges, Norton Abrasives Company manufactures an India stone with a curved surface which can be used for sharpening both the inside and outside edges. As most gouges are beveled on the outside it is possible to sharpen them with a side-to-side motion on the concave side of the curved India stone or even on a flat Arkansas stone. The wire edge which builds up on the inside of the curve can be cleared away with a bit of leather wrapped around a dowel or, better yet, a round Arkansas stone such as is available from Russell's. Sharpening curved gouges and carving tools is a tedious task and it is best to give the tool a frequent touching up with the stone rather than let it get too dull. But this is the best advice for *any* cutting tool.

Veining chisels can be sharpened just as you'd sharpen a flat chisel provided the bevel is on the outside. For getting at an inside bevel you'll need a knife-edge slipstone to get down in the tight corner. These are also available from Russell's.

For extra-sharp edges for fine carving a bevel of less than 20° will take a sharper edge. However, the slighter the angle the more delicate the edge. Since these delicate edges do not hold an edge too well they must be sharpened more frequently, and too, a hard Arkansas will be needed to keep the kind of edge required.

All in all the trick of knife sharpening is just getting the blade on a sharpening stone and moving it around. If there is any "secret" it is holding the blade at a constant angle and using the right stone for the job.

Finally, there is the cost of sharpening stones. At upwards of six dollars for a $6 \times 2 \times 3/4$-inch soft Arkansas and twice that for a hard Arkansas, good stones cost a lot more than the common hardware-store synthetic stones. With proper care, however, a good stone will last a lifetime and become a family heirloom.

Sharpening with a hand grinder

Sharpening may be a chore to you, but you must do it. When it comes to cutting wood, especially the delicate cutting of wood associated with precise stock inletting and related stock carving, nothing is more important than a razor-sharp carving instrument. Yet the importance of keeping one's tools honed to a fine edge is ofttimes lost on most amateurs and more than a few professional gunsmiths and stockmakers.

Actually I think most folks realize the importance of sharp tools and appreciate using them. Their hangup, however, is going to the trouble of sharpening and resharpening a knife or chisel when there are more interesting things to do. Then on top of this it always seems that one never has just the right size or shape of stone to fit a particular gouge. Thus we are inclined to give it a lick and a promise with a mismatched stone and try to make do.

In truth, I've long suspected, and have been told by professionals, that many if not most amateur or part-time-professional stockmakers could upgrade the quality of their work by half again if they'd only keep a sharp tool. This holds especially true during the inletting process. Unsightly gaps between wood and metal, for example, are frequently caused by a chisel that was only sharp enough to cut itself into the wood but not sharp enough to cut its way back out again without causing the grain to part and split because of the excessive pressure needed to drive the tool. Thus the wood splinters off at a "tender" spot and an unforgivable gap appears in the inletting.

I know for a fact that there are more than a few stockmakers who have never had the pleasure of working with really sharp tools. How do I know? I can tell by looking at their work.

Going to the other extreme, there are those few who go overboard on sharpening. By this I mean that they lose too much valuable production time just stoning and honing their tools.

I once knew an old German woodcarver who must have spent at least half, or so it seemed, of his workday sharpening tools. He had a good assortment of chisels, knives, and gouges, and I think he had a stone for just about every tool.

"In der old country," he would say, "ve learn to sharpen knife, den ve learn to cut der wood." An admirable viewpoint, I agree, but I also think that if he could have spent less time sharpening "der knife" he could have made a lot more money at his trade.

Too bad the old boy didn't have an electric hand grinder and an assortment of felt polishing tips and wheels. He could have gotten his tools sharp in a fraction of the time.

Actually there's nothing new about using a polishing wheel for sharpening. It's not at all unusual to see a stockmaker or gunsmith step up to his felt or muslin wheel and "tough up" the edge of a chisel. It's fast and easy, and if done properly puts a super edge on fine steel.

The difficulty with using the typical shop wheel, however, is that it is too big for some tools and doesn't fit the narrow radius of the smaller gouges.

The answer to all of these problems, even lazy craftsmen who have an aversion to the sharpening chore, is a hand-grinder setup complete with tool stand and speed control. A typical product of this kind is the Dremel Moto-Tool, but there are also other grinders available from Chicago Wheel & Manufacturing Co. (Handee), Weller (Mini Shop), Sears, Roebuck & Co. (Li'l Crafty) and Foredom Electric Co. (flexible shaft tools). Addresses of these companies are listed at the end of this book. The beauty of this compact little tool arrangement is that you can keep it right there on the bench only a few inches from where you're working. Thus when the fine edge of your tool starts to fade all you have to do is flip a switch and bring back a fine edge in only a few seconds. Simple? You bet!

When I first tried using the Dremel tool for sharpening I encountered a few problems. I'll explain these right now so you'll be saved the trouble:

The first problem was charging the small felt and muslin wheels with buffing compound. At 30,000 rpm the centrifugal force was just too great. Before the compound could "set" it was slung off the wheel. Thus for a while I charged the wheel by working compound into the felt with the motor turned off.

Using the Hand Grinder to Sharpen Tools

A complete set-up for sharpening carving chisels with the Drmel Moto-Tool. The Moto-Tool is mounted in the Dremel stand. The Dremel motor speed control is especially handy for sharpening, because different speeds tend to produce better results' on different types of metal. (Dremel also offers a Moto-Tool with a built-in speed control.) The Dremel tool fixture, which can be mounted in a lathe or held fast in a vise, is a particularly handy accessory for sharpening and buffing. The chisels shown can all be sharpened with the tool. In the center, a couple of buffing wheels and a container of buffing compound.

Here's a detail of the Dremel solid state motor control. By experimenting with different speeds the most efficient speed can be found for different sizes of buffing wheels.

An assortment os small buffing wheels and various shapes which can be used for sharpening different sizes and shapes of carving tools and chisels. Clockwise from top, a muslin buffing wheel, a spindle which fits each of these buffing wheels, a cone-shaped felt button which fits the inside radius of different darving chisels very nicely, a small-diameter felt wheel, and a medium-size felt buffing wheel. The blackened area on the larger felt wheel was caused by buffing compound.

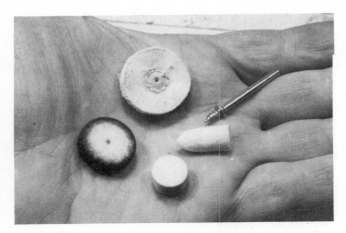

The buffing wheel being charged with polishing compound. This is best done with a motor speed control set at relatively low rpm. At higher speeds centrifugal force tends to throw the polishing compound off the wheel before it has a chance to set.

A small gouge chisel being sharpened with the felt wheel. Notice that the chisel is held at such an angle that the edge itself does not seem to be in contact with the wheel. This is the correct angle for bringing the edge to razor sharpness.

The cone-shaped felt polishing button fits very nicely inside this small curved gouge.

The same gouge shown in the previous photo is sharpened on the inside edge with the cone-shaped polishing button. The ability to sharpen odd-shaped chisels such as this is one of the principal advantages of the Dremel buffing system.

The small buffing wheel powered by the grinder is used to sharpen the outside radius of a large gouge.

Another problem was that while some tools could be buffed to a razor edge, others could not. My guess was that different wheel speeds tend to work better for different shapes of tools. Subsequent experiments and experience have proved this true.

When using the wheel at high speed with a thin bevel edge, for example, the edge would seem to get just so sharp and then no more. Finally I realized that small fibers on the edge of the wheel, traveling so fast as to be invisible, were backlashing around the edge of the tool and, in effect, whipping the edge away. I was able to solve this problem to some degree by angling the edge farther away from the surface of the wheel. In fact it looked as though the wheel wasn't even touching the edge, but it was getting mighty sharp anyway. Those little invisible fibers were doing the job, I guess.

Things got a lot simpler when I ordered a Dremel speed control, a universal holding stand, and a lathe mounting bracket for the Moto-Tool. The speed control lets you slow the rpm down enough to charge the wheel without slinging polishing compound everywhere. Also, with the speed-control unit it is possible to adjust to the speed that is most efficient for any given tool. This takes a bit of experimenting, but the difference it can make is astounding. If a certain speed doesn't give you a satisfactory edge, try adjusting the rpm up or down. One way or the other the blade will begin to get sharper, so from this point on it's easy to pinpoint the ideal speed. Next time you sharpen that tool you can go right to the required speed merely by setting the indexed speed-control knob.

Perhaps the greatest convenience of all is sharpening small, tightly curved gouges that no stone ever seems to fit. For this you use the bullet-shaped No. 422 felt tip. This ³⁄₈-inch tip tapers to a point which fits all sorts of tiny curved carving tools.

For larger gouges or flat-blade chisels and knives there is a 1-inch diameter muslin wheel and felt wheels of even smaller size. Each of these wheels and tips is mounted by means of a universal mandrel.

If you want to change the bevel angle of a certain tool all you have to is use one of the small grinding wheels. These handy little mounted stones are small enough to get inside the curve of very small gouges and reshape them to your liking.

With a little practice at this remarkable new way of sharpening your tools you'll find that you're keeping your tools a lot sharper and spending less time doing it. You'll no doubt notice an improvement in the quality of your wood cutting, too. Who knows? For the very first time you may discover what a joy carving and inletting a stock can actually be. All it takes is a *sharp* tool.

8/
Making Your Own Low-Cost Electric Wire Brush and Polishing Fixture

One of the handiest power tools in any gun shop is a motor-driven circular wire brush. Though the uses are too many to list here, one of the most common is removing rust from guns and tools. A quick touch of the wire wheel knocks even heavy rust loose in a jiffy and leaves the metal bright and clean. Wire wheels are also great for cleaning hard-caked grease, grime, grit, paint, and varnish from gun parts or just about anything else. The rapid scrubbing action not only cleans tiny grooves and other difficult-shaped parts but also has a burnishing effect which leaves the part looking like new.

Gunsmiths and machinists also make frequent use of the wire wheel to blunt sharp edges left on metal by grinding, milling, and even filing operations. In short, once you have used a wire wheel and learned to appreciate its multiple uses, you'll never be able to live without one again.

Another motor-driven tool which is a standard fixture in just about every gun shop is a buffing wheel. These are layers of cotton muslin stitched into wheels about 1/4 to 1/2 inch thick. Usually two, three, or even four wheels are stacked together into a wheel an inch or more wide.

Before a polishing wheel is used it is "charged"—that is, a mild abrasive agent is applied to it. Thus when metal is placed against the wheel it imparts a bright shine. Different grits of polishing agents are available which, when used in progressively finer order, will reduce a roughly turned or filed surface to mirror brightness. Buffing of this type is the standard metal-preparation procedure for gun blueing.

Another super-handy use for a buffing wheel is putting a final razor edge on knives and carving chisels. A quick touch against the wheel is handier, quicker, and better than a stone when a final honing is needed. Buffing wheels are especially handy for putting keen edges on curved gouges and veining tools, which are often difficult to sharpen with stones.

Despite the obvious handiness of electric-motor-driven wire wheels and buffing rigs, many amateur shops have to get along without them because of the high cost of such equipment. This means that jobs which could be done in minutes or even seconds must be done by time-consuming hand labor.

Actually, at a cost of ten dollars or less you can build yourself a very serviceable combination wire wheel and polishing setup. The most expensive component of ready-made power tools is the electric motor. But usable ¼-, ⅓-, or ½-horsepower salvage motors can be had for only a few dollars. Sometimes they are free for the asking, or you may even have an old washing-machine or electric-dryer motor just waiting to be used. Check with shops that do appliance or furnace repair. Most motors have a listed speed of 1725 rpm, and this is just right for your purposes. Most motors have only one driveshaft, but if you can find one that has the shaft extending from both sides this is even better. But either kind will do. Of course you want to make sure the motor runs on standard 110-volt household current. Some motors are wired for 220 volts. The motor should have an identification plate which shows the proper voltage and rpm. Most salvage motors will not have an electric cord with plug, but one can be easily attached by splicing to the existing lead-out wires or, better yet, attaching a new cord directly to the terminals. Before buying a salvage motor make sure it runs.

Since nearly all electric motors have a smooth, unthreaded driveshaft, the problem is how to attach the wire wheel and buffing discs. This is managed very easily by attaching a threaded adaptor. Adaptors come in several size combinations so you can get different threaded shanks for different driveshaft diameters. Most appliance-size electric motors have a ½-inch or ⅝-inch shaft. Adaptors are easily available for both these, and other sizes, but be sure the adaptor has a ½-inch threaded shank. This is the correct size for nearly all wire wheels and buffing wheels. The adaptor, which locks on the motor shaft by means of one or two set screws, comes with a lock nut and a couple of large collars to hold the wheels in place.

If you are lucky enough to find a double-driveshaft motor you can fit the wire wheel on one side and the buffing wheel on the other. Otherwise you have to change wheels as you go from one job to another.

The next chore is mounting the motor. It can be bolted to the workbench, the wall, or even some portable stand such as a sawhorse. It is important to fashion some sort of shield around the wheels if for no other reason than to keep debris and buffing compound from scattering all over your work area.

Making the Electric Wire Brush and Polisher

This homemade wire brush and polishing rig was made at a cost of less than ten dollars. The motor is an old ¼-horsepower motor salvaged from a discarded furnace fan. The shield around the wire brush was made from plywood and bent tin. It required only a couple of hours to assemble the unit, and it has saved me many hours of otherwise difficult handwork.

My rig with the shield removed to show how I wired the electric motor into an on-off switch. Looks crude, maybe, but it works fine.

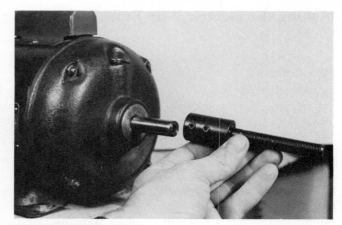

A detail of an adaptor unit, showing how it fits over the driveshaft of an electric motor. It is held fast by two Allen screws. These adaptors come in a variety of sizes for all motor shafts.

A wire wheel is one of the most effective rust-removing tools you can have around. Here it cleans paint and rust from a hammer. A wire wheel also does a beautiful job of cleaning gunk and hardened oil and grease from gun parts. Note how the tool is conveniently mounted at the end of the work bench with the on-off switch immediately underneath.

The wire wheel is easily and quickly removed from the unit and replaced with a cloth buffing wheel as shown here. With a buffing wheel you can put a mirror-bright finish on metal parts such as the rifle bolt shown here. Proper buffing and polishing is also a vital part of the bluing process.

This can be easily made from a piece of tin and a few scraps of wood nailed together.

Most salvage motors will not have an on-off switch, but you can handle this easily enough by running the wiring through a simple wall switch. From there the wiring runs to a plug-in outlet. The complete brushing-and-buffing setup shown on these pages cost some seven dollars and was assembled in about two hours.

It will occur to you that this unit would also make a fine grinding tool simply by fitting it with a grinding wheel. If you should decide to do this it is important that you fit safety devices such as a clear-plastic or shatterproof-glass shield to keep sparks and particles from being thrown in your eyes and face. Also you will need a tool rest to help you support the object being ground or sharpened. Take a look at a ready-made grinding tool to see what is needed.

II

Stock Making — The Custom Look

9 / Inletting the Semi-Finished Stock

Whenever gunsmiths, be they amateur or professional, get together they talk about guns. And when they talk about guns it is more than likely that quite a few opinions will be expressed on how a barreled action should be fitted to a stock.

Despite all this discussion—or possibly because of it—proper inletting continues to be a mystery to more than a few shooters. By and large, "good" inletting is generally meant to be close inletting. But this may not always be the case. Really good inletting not only is a close wood-to-metal fit but also holds the metal firmly in the stock so that it does not shift about with each shot, the action does not bind, twist, cramp, or bend when the action screws are pulled tight, and the wood itself is not sprung or forced.

I once owned a beautifully stocked rifle with inletting so close that one would think it to be about perfect; there wasn't the slightest gap between wood and metal. But as it turned out, the fit was actually too tight. The side pressure on the barrel and action forced the receiver into a bind so that it couldn't seat or "bottom" in the stock very well. As a result, accuracy was never very good. During one particularly damp spell the stock absorbed a lot of moisture, began to swell, and since it already was too tight, it cracked all the way up the forend.

The problem in this case was that the stockmaker had made the inletting close by pounding and squeezing the action and barrel into the wood and compressing the grain. When that compressed grain began to swell, something had to give.

Taking the other extreme, it is possible to inlet a stock with wide, unsightly gaps between wood and metal but have the action bottomed well with good contact on the recoil lug and have a finely accurate rifle. In fact, some amateurs (and even some so-called professionals) defend their ragged-looking inletting with a fierce but inane "What difference does it make how it looks as long as it shoots good?" In general, however, a stockmaker that can't do a close inletting probably doesn't know enough about the craft to bed a rifle for accuracy either.

Frankly, I think good inletting is overrated! Overrated, that is, in terms of how difficult it is to achieve a really good job. There's certainly no mystery or black magic involved, and contrary to what you may have heard it doesn't take all that long either. More than one topnotch professional stockmaker has admitted to me that in one working day he can completely inlet *and shape* a stock from a solid, unformed block of wood! Granted, of course, these are highly experienced craftsmen who know when, where, and how much to cut and how to make every move count.

It takes the inexperienced stockmaker somewhat longer because he occasionally has to step back and figure out what to do next. Even so, a few evenings' work should result in a nicely fitted job even if you've had little or no experience. I'll qualify this prediction and state that you should end up with an inletting job you can be proud to show *provided* that you *want* to do a good job and *pay attention to what you're doing!*

I've already discussed the importance of the scraper in stockmaking. If you don't have one, you can make one of anything from a power hacksaw blade to a beercan opener. Trim it to a uniform width of about ½ inch and make it short enough to be easy to handle; 3 or 4 inches is about right. Curve one end with a radius of about ¼ inch and put a ½-inch radius on the other end. Now file a bevel on the ends so that the scraping edges are pretty sharp. This is not a cutting tool but rather a scraping tool and is the "secret weapon" for close inletting. It keeps the inletted surfaces peeled smooth and slick and will take out a shaving as thin as a gnat's wing when you're down to that last few thousandths. The small-radius end is for working in the barrel channel and the big end is for the action area. Of course the degree of curve can be altered to suit your particular action or barrel size. To keep it sharp, just touch up the edges with a file once in a while.

The first big step is selecting a piece of wood for your stock. By all means use a semi-inletted, semi-shaped stock for your first effort. The variety of stock styles available from Fajen, Bishop, Pachmayer, Biesen, and others is so complete that you're bound to find just about anything you're looking for, and they speed up the job considerably. The cost, by the way, is only slightly more than a plain block of wood.

If your action has a one-piece magazine-box and trigger-guard assembly such as Mausers and Springfields, the guard assembly should be inletted first. This way the guard-screw holes will act as a positive guide for the inletting pins when you inlet the action later. Rifles such as the Winchester Model 70 which do not have a one-piece guard assembly should be inletted action first and trigger guard last. But for our purposes here we'll be discussing a Mauser-type arrangement.

Since semi-inletted stocks already have the magazine-box mortise cut, it is a simple matter to establish the proper position for the assembly. Simply drop the box as far into the magazine cut as it will go (don't force it) and check the alignment of the holes in the guard and the stock holes. If they are properly aligned you may proceed to inlet the assembly straight down. It is possible that the guard assembly will have to be shifted to the front or rear for proper alignment. This is no problem, as the stock manufacturers usually leave extra wood to allow for any adjustments that might be necessary.

The magazine box, you'll notice, is tapered inward and tends to wedge tight in the stock. The sides of the mortise cut can be opened easily and smoothly with a rasp or file, but don't attempt to drive the assembly in. Too much pressure and the stock will split. Just keep shaving the sides of the cut and let the box "fall" by itself. Be sure to check from time to time to see if the holes are still properly aligned. When the underside of the trigger-guard extension and the front extension come to rest on the wood, use a sharply pointed scribe to mark the complete outline. Occasionally the inletting is so nearly complete that the whole assembly will go all the way in. Usually, however, the cuts need to be widened and lengthened slightly. Actually, very little, if any, "spotting" is required for inletting the guard assembly. After scribing the outlines of the front and rear extensions, simply cut straight down to the bottom of the precut recesses.

Every semi-inletted stock I've ever worked with was made so that the guard assembly went in deeper than flush with the stock's outside surface before "bottoming" in the recess. This allows for variations among different makes of guards. Mauser trigger guards vary considerably. So if your guard seems to go in too deep, don't worry about it. Later we'll simply cut the wood down flush with the guard.

Beware of inletting the guard assembly *too* close! Guards that are too tight are liable to jerk out splinters around the inletting when they are removed. Thus make the inletting free enough to allow the assembly to slip in and out rather easily.

With the guard assembly in place it's time to turn the stock right side up and get on with the main order of business.

The first step is to screw the inletting pins into the guard-screw holes. If you don't have any inletting pins, hold everything until you get or make some. They don't cost much and are available from nearly all suppliers of gunsmithing tools, semi-inletted-stock manufacturers, and well-equipped gun shops. The purpose of the pins is to hold the barreled action in strict alignment with the stock and guard assembly. During the inletting process you'll be moving the action in and out of the stock a lot, and the pins help make sure that you always put it back in the same position.

Now we're almost, but not quite, face to face with the much-discussed "spotting-in" process. Before beginning the rather slow-paced spotting-in you can save yourself a lot of time by roughing out a lot of the wood which obviously has to come out. I recall a fellow who was so determined to do a perfect job of inletting that he began spotting in his barreled action when the barrel channel was only ½ inch wide. Patiently he spotted and scraped on his stock every evening for weeks. Finally, when the job was pretty close to completion, his patience wore out and in a fit of temper he hogged out the final — but crucial — last ¹⁄₁₆ inch of wood and all his previous time and effort went to nought. So do all your hogging out to begin with and save your patience for when it counts. My technique for the preliminary roughing out begins by inserting the barreled action into the precut inletting as far as it will go and tracing the outline on the top edge of the stock. By keeping within this working boundary, and dropping the action in occasionally to see if everything is going right, it is possible to get the inletting pretty well finished in a relatively short time. The only thing you need to be especially careful about here is to get the recoil-lug cut started right.

Your stock will come with a precut mortise for the recoil lug, but it's purposely cut undersize so that you can get an exact fit for your rifle. Thus during the inletting you will find it necessary to make way for the lug before the inletting can progress further. At this point the bottom of the lug will have come to rest on the bottom flat of the pre-inletting. Now, making sure that the action is perfectly aligned, give the front receiver ring a solid whack with a mallet or padded hammer. This will cause the bottom of the recoil lug to make a clear impression on the wood. Using the rear edge of this impression as a guide, it is possible to enlarge the mortise so that the rear of the lug will be in perfect, solid contact with the wood. Simply use a straight-edged chisel and cut straight down.

When you feel you've roughed out everything except the last few thousandths it's time to start the spotting-in. This is nothing more than coating the metal with some sort of marking agent that leaves a distinct mark on the wood whenever the two come together. Traditionally this is Prussian blue, an artist's oil-type paint that comes in a tube. The Prussian blue is of about the same consistency as heavy grease, takes fairly long to dry, and makes a clear mark on wood. During my early stockmaking days I was pretty messy, I guess, for I always seemed to get the blue in my ears, hair, shirt, pants, tools, and

Steps for Inletting a Semi-Finished Stock

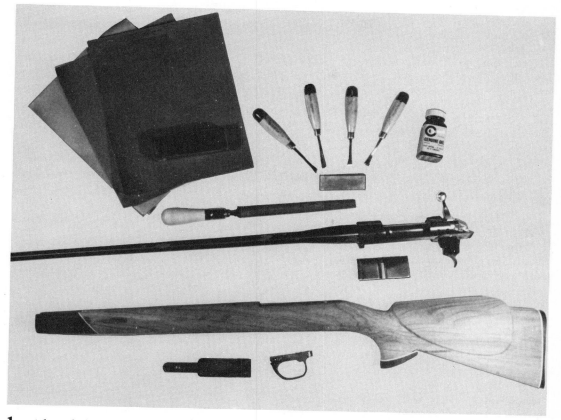

1 A barreled action, a Herter's semi-finished stock, and the few, simple tools needed to do a thoroughly satisfactory job: a few chisels and sharpening stone, rasp, sandpaper, and sanding block.

2
This is what a semi-inletted stock looks like. Notice that the bulk of the wood has already been removed and the action holes are precisely located and drilled.

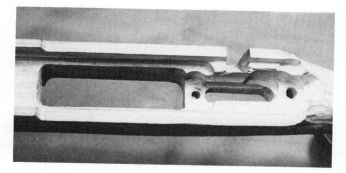

3

A homemade kerosene lamp is used to give the metal parts a light coating of soot. Commercial "spotting-in" preparations are available which are probably more convenient. Other spotting-in agents that work well are artist's Prussian blue and even lipstick. Be sure to recoat the metal parts with spotting agent frequently.

4

After coating the metal parts with soot or another spotting agent, the barreled action assembly is precisely located in the inletting and pressed into position. Inletting pins are a great aid in precisely aligning the action with the stock. Here a pointer indicates a soot smudge left where the metal pressed against the wood. This and other such smudges are carefully cut or scraped away and the metal parts refitted again and again. With each fitting and cutting the barreled action sinks deeper into the stock until it reaches the proper depth.

5

Here a small curved chisel is used to inlet the barrel channel. Notice that only very tiny cuts are made.

6

The blackened areas in this inletting show that the fit is uneven. This will cause the action to twist somewhat when the screws are tightened and accuracy will not be as good as it might be. Strive to achieve an even contact over all of the bottom surfaces.

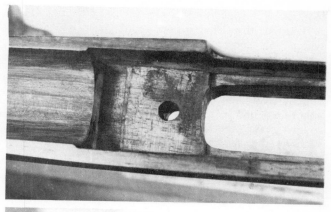

7

Notice that the blackened area is uniform all over the bottom surfaces. This means that the stock is fitting full and flush.

8

The action has been fully inletted into the stock and outside finishing can begin.

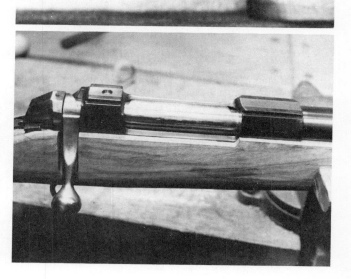

9

A detail of the fitted trigger guard, which was spotted in exactly the same manner as the receiver. Some rifles such as Mausers, Springfields, and Model 1914 and 1917 Enfields which have large one-piece trigger-guard assemblies should have the trigger guard inletted first. Others such as the Winchester Model 70 with multiple-piece trigger-guard units should have the barreled action inletted first, and then the trigger guard.

10

After inletting it is always necessary to protect the interior surfaces with a coat of water-resistant varnish or stock finish. This keeps the interior surfaces from absorbing oil and moisture, which could cause the wood to weaken and warp.

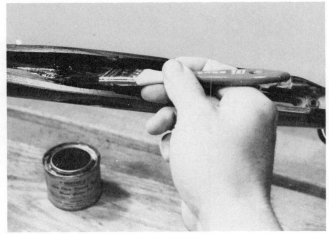

just about everything else I touched as well as the stock. So long ago I gave up on Prussian blue and never used it again. For several years I used a kerosene lamp made from a small bottle with a hole in the lid and a rag wick in the hole. Holding the metal over the smoky kerosene flame left a deposit of carbon black which was very nice for spotting in and didn't make such a mess as the blue. More recently, I've used Jarrow's Inletting Black (available from Brownell's). It seems to be a carbon black in an oil suspension (I'm just guessing), but whatever it is it's easy to use and does a good job. Just smear a thin coat on the metal from time to time and it leaves a clear black mark on the wood.

One just scrapes or shaves the black marks away, sets the action into the wood again, taps the action and barrel with a mallet, removes the metal, and scrapes away more black spots. This process is repeated until the bottom of the action comes to rest on the bottom of the action cut. When the bottom of the action cut is evenly coated with black where the bottom of the action has touched, your job is through. At this point, supposedly, the barrel will be inletted to exactly half depth. Manufacturers of semi-inletted stocks are quite careful to get this particular measurement right, and in my experience of inletting upwards of a hundred or more I can recall only a couple that didn't come out right in this respect.

Here is a trick worth mentioning that involves getting a visibly close contact between wood and metal. When the barreled action has almost reached final depth, *stop* scraping the black marks from the wood near the top 1/8 inch or so of the channel. If you keep scraping wood away here the metal will keep making another black mark until they no longer contact. *And when they no longer contact you have yourself an ugly gap!* So at least be very cautious about removing wood at the upper edge of the barrel channel and action cavity.

Some professional stockmakers prefer to inlet the action only first, then attach the barrel and inlet the channel. If this appeals to you, then by all means do it this way. To be sure, it allows you to concentrate on only one part at a time. I've never found it to be any advantage.

10 / Restocking Pump and Autoloading Shotguns

When the fine old pump-action shotgun had been purchased back in 1931 it was the best money could buy and the first of its kind ever to come to our town. Special features included a barrel with a ventilated rib, a rarity in those days, and a French-walnut stock with large areas of fine hand-cut checkering. It was a Remington Model 29-T, one of the finest trap guns available in an era famous for its high-quality shotguns. Whenever the shotgun was taken to the trap field or the duck blind there always seemed to be someone waiting to look at Dad's new shotgun. In fact, the shotgun somehow came to be called the "new" gun and for those who never tired of admiring the sleek, polished surface and the rows of sharply cut checkering the shotgun must have seemed new indeed, even years after it came from the store.

Then suddenly the "new" Remington wasn't new any more—it was old and tired-looking. Just when it stopped being new is hard to say, but perhaps it was on one of those drizzly mornings in the duck blind, on one of those frosty trips across endless rows of corn stubble, at a weekend trap tournament, or perhaps just while waiting in the closet where it had been stored without proper cleaning. The blue had turned to a dusty rust brown, there were numerous pits and scratches, and the buttstock, now blackened with sweat and oil, was cracked and chipped where the wood fit against the metal. In short, the gun had become old—old and ugly—by the time it came into my possession. Old and ugly like thousands of other shotguns deported to the backs of thousands of dark closets. Too ugly to be carried afield, but too dear an old friend to be disposed of.

A careful piece-by-piece examination indicated that while the old Remington was mighty rough on the outside the bore and the mechanism were still in excellent condition. All that was really needed was TLC (tender loving care), a new buttstock, and an overall slicking up. Nothing that couldn't be handled at home with a little care and a few simple tools. Here's how I went about fixing up the old Remington and made a silk purse from a sow's ear.

Chances are your old pump or autoloader is in need of a new buttstock or forend. Age isn't the big enemy of gunstocks, but gun oil is! Over the years the oil tends to soak into the wood and considerably weaken the junctures where the metal fits into the stock. This is especially true of a gun that has been stood butt down in closet corners and equally thoughtless places. Eventually a crack forms, and sometimes a whole piece of the stock breaks away. This is what had happened to the old Remington. A new buttstock was called for. The forend piece, on the other hand, had been kept relatively free from oil, so it was still sound.

New stocks for many vintage shotguns like the Remington Model 29 are no longer available from the manufacturer. This, however, is no cause for concern, for there are high-quality stocks available from firms specializing in producing semi-finished gunstocks. A semi-finished stock is one that has been pre-inletted and shaped to a nearly finished form but requires some final shaping, then sanding and finishing. These semi-finished stocks require a minimum of skill and tools, but finish into attractive, serviceable stocks which are often more handsome than the originals. The slight shaping required allows the do-it-yourself craftsman to add special features which give the gun a custom touch.

Three firms — E.C. Bishop, Reinhart Fajen, and Herter's — offer semi-finished stocks for a wide variety of firearms, obsolete and modern. The prices for these stocks vary, of course, with the grade of wood ordered, but the plainer grades are pretty inexpensive. Semi-finished rifle and shotgun stocks are available in a wide assortment of shapes and styles. Buttstocks, for example, can be ordered with a cheekpiece, Monte Carlo comb, and streamlined pistol grips as well as the traditional "field style." Or one may order the comfortable, hand-filling "beavertail" forend to replace the slender forends usually found on shotguns made a few decades ago. Of course, for those who prefer them, the light, slender forends are also available. It is wise to write to the manufacturers requesting brochures describing the various styles of stocks and accessories available. This way you'll be sure of what you're ordering. If stock finish and blueing materials are not available from your local sporting-goods shop they can be ordered with the stock.

While you're waiting for the stock to be delivered is a good time to get on with the metalwork — that is, if metalwork is required. My shotgun, in addition to having very little blue to speak of, was a pretty miserable mass of pits, dents, and burrs from the tang to the muzzle, so more than a little work was called for. Here is how I went about it:

After removing the butt and forend wood, I gave the exterior surface of the metal a heavy, soaking coat of oil. This oil, which may be cheap motor oil, should remain on the metal for several hours in order to penetrate and loosen the surface rust. When the oil is wiped off you'll be surprised how much rust comes with it. Then apply a second coat of oil and give the metal a good scrubbing with rather coarse steel wool. This pretty well removes the remainder of the surface rust and does a good job of cleaning out the pits and dents, thus allowing you to evaluate the actual condition of your gun. Now you can determine just what course of action is needed. If the cleaned surface of the metal shows no pitting, all that will be needed is a polishing with finishing paper and fine steel wool. On the other hand, if there are still pits and dents it will be necessary to remove them by cutting down the surface of the metal somewhat. Reducing the surface sounds like a lot of hard, tedious work, but actually, if you use the right tools and proper technique, it can be managed with little effort.

Good old-fashioned sandpaper will cut metal surprisingly well, and by wrapping it around a flat, stiff backer such as a file, you can shave a lot of metal away rather quickly. The pits are generally a lot wider than they are deep, so you actually need to cut the metal down only a very few thousandths of an inch. However, if your sow's ear is to come looking like a silk purse, considerable attention must be given to preserving the sharp shoulders and square edges of the original shape. Most receivers, for example, have flat sides with a rounded top and bottom. These rounded surfaces, you'll notice, do not flow into the flat sides but, rather, commence at a sharp, well-defined line running the length of the receiver. While you're dressing and smoothing the metal it would be very easy to round off these sharp lines. Actually nothing would be lost so far as function goes, but the finished product just wouldn't have that "as new" look you want.

This is why it is a good idea to use a sanding block or to wrap the sandpaper around a file. The flat surface of the file remains flush against the flat surfaces of the metal and all edges remain sharp. Also, there is less tendency to create waves or uneven spots. For dressing up the receiver on my Remington I wrapped 220-grit finishing paper around an 8-inch file for fast cutting, then switched to 400-grit for fine finishing. For rounded surfaces on the top and bottom of the receiver I used a sanding block with a 1/8-inch-thick rubber pad between the block and the paper. This allowed the sandpaper to conform to the various curves. All sanding strokes were kept lengthways with the receiver.

I used the same technique for the barrel and magazine tube, with each stroke running the full length in order to avoid any ripples. I dealt individually with smaller parts such as trigger guard, tip of magazine tube, screws, etc. Concave or inside curves such as the inside of the trigger guard are easily handled by wrapping sandpaper around wood dowels of the proper size to suit the curve. The ventilated rib of my Remington presented no special problem; I simply wrapped sandpaper around the sharp 90° shoulder of the sanding block and used the sharp edge to work up close where the rib joined the barrel and receiver. This polished the side of the rib as well as the barrel. The top of the rib was a textured surface for best sighting, so I used steel wool to scrub and clean this area.

After I had cleaned and polished all metal surfaces as much as possible with the 400-grit finishing paper, I gave the whole works a thorough scrubbing with super-fine steel wool. A hard polishing with fine steel wool tends to remove the light scratches made by sandpaper and brings the metal to a mirror-bright polish. Of course the steel-wool particles tend to pack into screw holes and other cracks and crannies, but don't worry about that now—just keep laying on the elbow grease. You might save yourself a bit of time by not bothering to put the final polish around where the stock will fit against the metal. During the stock-fitting operation you will find that you occasionally sand metal and wood together. Therefore, it's a good idea to wait until the stock is finished before putting the final polish on the steel.

If by now the stock you ordered still hasn't arrived, you can make use of the slack time by giving everything a careful inspection every evening or so. You'll always manage to find a spot or two which needs a little additional polishing. While you're on this final polishing, by the way, keep your fingers as dry as possible. Wear gloves if necessary, and by all means *don't get any oil on the metal!* Any trace of oil will play hell with your blueing job, and it's mighty hard to get completely off once it gets on.

When I finally was satisfied that all the surfaces of my shotgun were as slick and shiny as I could get them, I turned my attention to the forend. Despite the abuse which apparently had been rained on the old Remington, the forend wood had survived in remarkably good condition. The finish was pretty well gone and the checkering was filled to capacity with grime, but all that was really needed was a few coats of stock finish. Of course, before the new finish could go on the old finish, or what was left of it, had to come off. Frankly, after all the elbow grease I'd recently invested in polishing the metal, the prospect of sanding off stock finish was less than appealing. Also, there was the danger of the sandpaper hitting and dulling the checkering. Sanding around checkering without making a mistake is mighty tedious indeed.

Finish remover was the answer. Sold under several trade names, these paint

Restocking a Remington 29T Pump

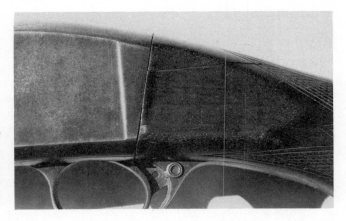

1

To start with, the old Remington 29T looked like this. The stock was almost totally black from wear and there were scratches, dents, splits, and cracks. The detail shows bad split at top of stock.

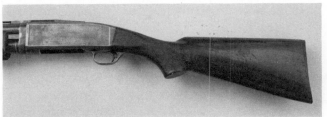

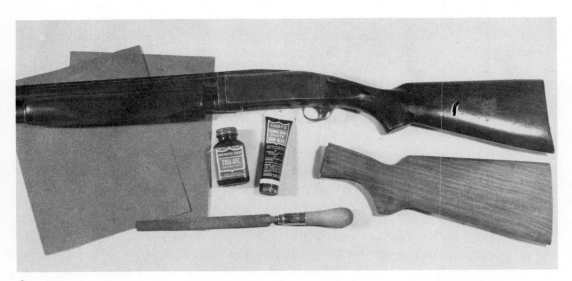

2   What it took to get the old Remington back in shape: a Bishop semi-finished butt-stock, a rasp, some sandpaper, cold blue, and stock finish.

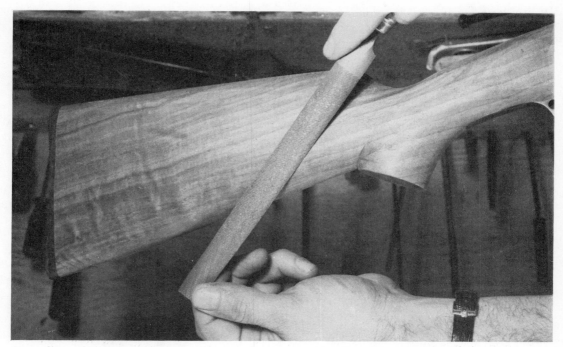

3 I use the flat side of a half-round cabinet rasp to shape and smooth the broad flat areas of the stock.

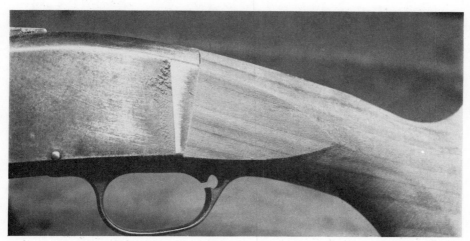

4 A closeup detail of the new stock being fitted to the receiver. Note the close wood-to-metal fit. Also notice that both wood and metal are being sanded together. When the metal parts are in need of refinishing and rebluing this is no problem, and by sanding both wood and metal together you get that "grown together" look. Otherwise care must be taken not to let the sandpaper or cutting tools contact the metal.

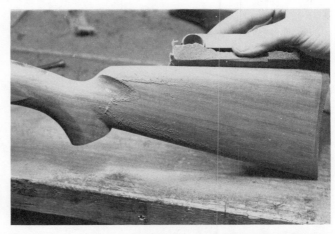

5

Sanding, sanding, sanding—professional stockmakers consider sanding a creative art. The final appearance of your stock will depend on how well you apply the sandpapeer. Always be sure to use a sanding block when sanding gunstocks. This way the lines and surfaces are kept smooth and ripple-free.

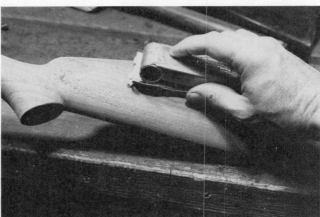

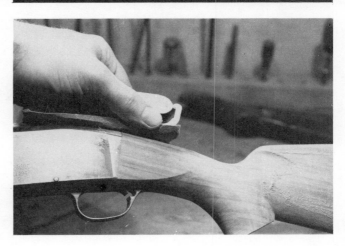

6

Note the very close woood-to-metal fit achieved by sanding wood and metal together.

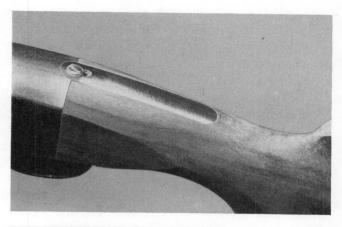

7

Stock finish being rubbed onto the new stock with the fingertips.

and varnish removers, which come in liquid or paste form, dissolve the old finish so it can be wiped away with a rag. The wood is left clean and dry. Though methods of application vary with the brand, it is usually simply brushed or wiped on. In about ten minutes the old finish blisters away from the wood and is easily wiped off. It's a lot easier and quicker than scrapers or sandpaper, and what's more it does a better job, and the checkering is un-damaged.

I found that the remover also tended to loosen the grime and junk which had accumulated in the checkering. A brisk scrubbing with a stiff-bristle brush practically restored the grime-clogged checkering to as-new condition. After this all I had to do was brush a coat of stock finish into the checkering, rub three coats of finish on the balance of the wood, and the forend was done. The whole thing was so quick and easy that it amounted to nothing more than a minor detail—thanks to the finish remover.

When the buttstock arrived I found that absolutely no wood-to-metal fitting was required. The receiver slipped smoothly but snugly into the inletted recesses of the stock, the bolt was drawn up tight, and there it was—a perfect fit! All that remained to be done was a bit of shaping up with the rasp.

Semi-finished stocks as they come from the factory are very nearly finish-shaped. However, a surplus of wood is left around the grip and at the comb so the individual can shape these areas to his own special liking. Thus a full-faced man can thin the comb enough for a perfect feel and fit, or a thin-faced fellow can leave the comb full. The grip can be thinned or left as full as maximum comfort dictates. The best tool for this finish shaping is a half-round wood rasp. Such a rasp has a curved surface on one side for cutting inside curves, such as the grip, and a flat surface for shaping and smoothing the broad, flatter areas of the stock.

First of all, trim down the surplus wood around the wood-to-metal joints so that everything is flush. Leave just enough wood elevated around the metal to be sanded to a flush surface to surface-fit later. About $1/32$ inch is enough to leave. When this is done, continue to blend the stock lines back through the grip. Shaping the stock of my old Remington was complicated by a raised panel which ran from the receiver to the grip. I dealt with this problem by simply copying the lines of the old stock, then shaping and blending the edges of the panel with the rounded side of the rasp. I also used the rounded side of the rasp to cut the flutes or grooves on either side of the comb. These flutes are not necessary but they tend to allow more room—and more comfort—for the hand. Also, they add an attractive detail to the stock and will give your efforts that added professional touch. After the grip is shaped—if necessary—to your liking, all that is left for the rasp is an overall smoothing-up job and you're ready for the sandpaper.

However careful your efforts up to now have been, the final appearance of your stock will depend on how well you apply the sandpaper. Professional stockmakers whose reputations depend on their beautifully detailed stockwork consider sanding a creative effort. This may seem a little much for the amateur, but the fact remains that if it's worth doing it's worth doing right! Starting off with 80-grit finishing paper, wrap a strip of paper around a sanding block and smooth out the rasp marks. The block is a must, because it keeps the surface flat and free of dips and wavy lines. I'm sure there's no need for me to mention that you want to sand *with* the grain at all times. Use strips of sandpaper folded into small pads to sand around curves and in areas you can't handle with the sanding block.

(Text continued on page 72)

Restocking a Winchester Model 12

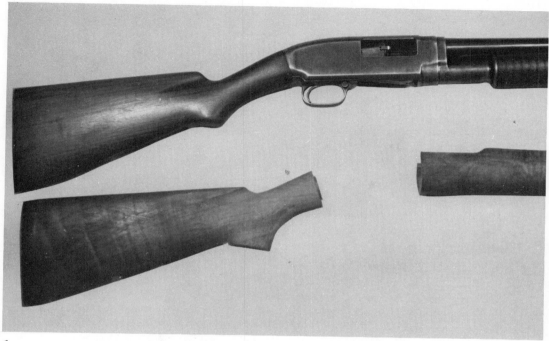

1 The most popular compact shotgun of all time is the legendary Model 12 Winchester. This one was the victim of many years of hard use and was in serious need of refinishing and restocking. The semi-finished stocks shown were manufactured by Reinhart Fajen.

2
The semi-finished stock fit flush with the receiver after only a small amount of trimming. However, note that the stock is still oversize around the receiver and will need to be trimmed.

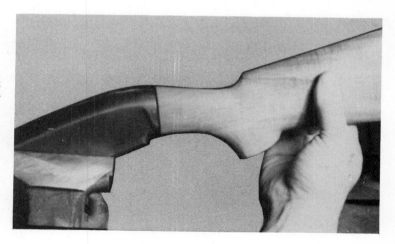

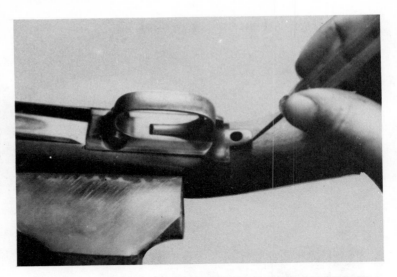

3

The Model 12 trigger guard is fitted into the stock by first tracing the rear extension with a scribe. The excess wood at this point will be cut out and removed with a small curved chisel.

4

Here a small curved chisel is used to cut the notch on the other side of the wood where the trigger guard extension is to be fitted.

5

The trigger guard has been completely fitted and now is tightened with a screwdriver.

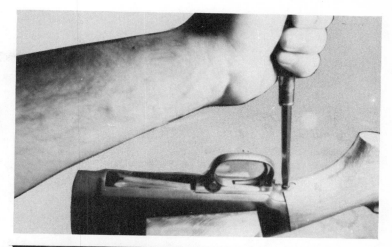

6

The detail of the stock after wood had been trimmed down to the shape of the receiver. Note the very close wood-to-metal fit.

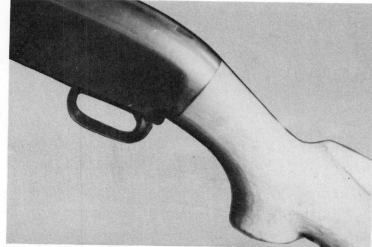

7

A gripcap being fitted to the new Model 12 stock. This adds a custom touch.

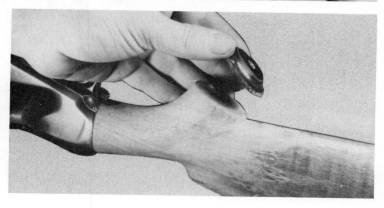

8

Here stock finish is being rubbed onto the Model 12 stock. The wood is a semi-fancy grade of black walnut which considerably upgrades the value of the shotgun.

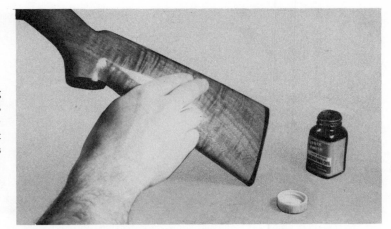

9

When the finish dries, it is briskly rubbed down with extra-fine steel wool. This process is repeated between each coat until the finish is smooth and deep with no grain pits showing.

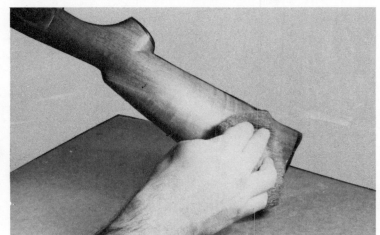

10

At top, the old original Model 12 forend; at bottom, a larger, more hand-filling semifinished stock. It is changes such as this which make restocking especially worthwhile, because they can actually improve the handling qualities of the gun.

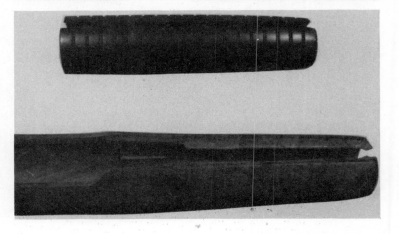

11

The Model 12 action slide being fitted into the semi-finished forend. The inletting for the slide sleeve was completely finished as it came from Fajen and required no further work. Otherwise, fitting the action slide is a difficult job demanding special equipment.

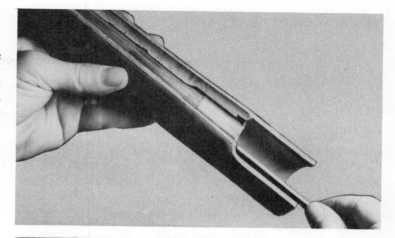

12

After finishing the stock, the finish is polished with a fine-grit rubbing compound. This gives it a rich, deep look.

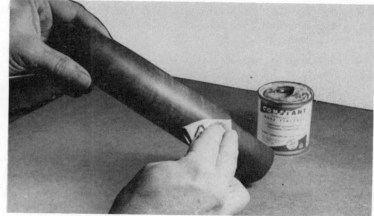

13

Do not neglect the inside surfaces of the stock. Here stock finish is shown being brushed into the inside surfaces so they will be more moisture-resistant. Otherwise this would be a good place for moisture to creep into the stock and cause it to swell and possibly crack.

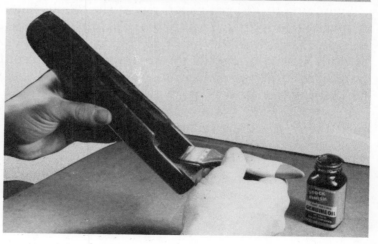

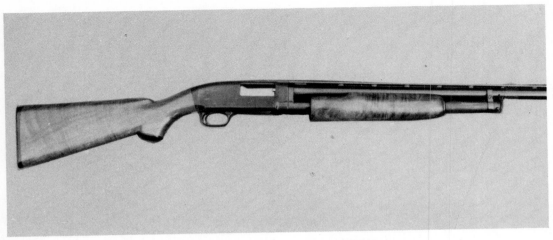

14 The Model 12 after being restocked. The gun was also reblued and fitted with a Simmons ventilated rib. The shotgun now is not only much more attractive but much more functional.

Remember back when I cautioned against putting the final polish on the metal around where the wood fits close? Here's the reason: For a perfectly flush wood-to-metal surface, sand the wood right down to the metal until you're sanding metal too! This is how the pros get that grown-together look.

Switching to 120-grit paper, repeat the whole sanding operation. Then do it all over again with 220-grit paper. This final sanding should remove the last traces of sanding marks made by the coarser paper and leave the wood dead smooth. It won't be ready for the finish, however, until you give it a good rubbing with extra-fine steel wool. The wool "polishes" the wood and snags off all the tiny wood fibers or "whispers"—hence no need for further grain raising.

Remove the stock from the receiver and soak a lot of stock finish into the inletting recesses and under the buttplate. This helps seal the wood against moisture and will help keep oil from the action from seeping into the stock. This is what ruined the old stock—remember? Though there is a wide variety of wood finishes on the market, the commercial oil-based stock finishes such as Birchwood-Casey's Tru-Oil are tops for the job. They are easy to apply and quick-drying, and they form a tough, long-wearing coating which is highly attractive. The technique I favor is using no wood filler at all but just rubbing on several coats of finish until the grain is filled with the finish itself. This takes a few extra coats, but the results are worth it. Between coats, rub down the finish with fine steel wool. This way the finish builds up without runs and ripples.

With the stock finishing underway you can return your attention to getting a sleek, lustrous blue to the metal parts. As you roughed up the metal a little with the stock sanding, you'll need to touch up these areas with 400-grit finishing paper and steel wool. While you're at it you may as well give the whole works one more good scrubbing. Keep your fingers off the metal from here on out; use clean cloths to touch the metal. Fingerprints are oily, and oily metal won't blue! Also at this point remove all exterior screws and lay them aside for further treatment.

There are several cold-blueing solutions, both liquid and paste, on the market and as far as I know all will do an excellent job *provided* the metal is properly prepared. Dissatisfaction with the so-called "cold" blues always seems to stem from poorly prepared metal. Those who voice dissatisfaction with cold blues may be interested to learn that the fine blueing on expensive European arms as well as some of the finest custom guns built in this country are in fact "cold" blues.

I blued my old Remington with a new blueing preparation marketed by Birchwood-Casey which comes in a paste form. As it is packaged in a tube, one simply squeezes a dab on the metal, spreads it with a cloth, and in a minute the steel is blue. A second and third application deepens the color to a rich blue-black color. If the metal was properly prepared prior to blueing it will seem to give off a glow of its own. A final rubdown with gun oil will set you to fairly jumping with joy. Now give each of the screw heads a final scrubbing with steel wool, clean out the slots, and apply the blue. Before reassembling everything, don't forget to give the firing mechanism a good cleaning and oiling.

With everything back together you'll no doubt be amazed and delighted at the miracle you've accomplished. The old blunderbuss probably looks as good as the day it came from the factory, and considering the extra custom touches you put on the stock it may even look—and feel—better. So now you can display the old sow's ear in a choice spot on the gun rack and no doubt you're eager to show it off to your shooting pals. A word of caution, however, here is advisable: Either they aren't going to believe you, or they're going to want you to work the same magic on their sow's ears.

Restocking the Winchester 50 Autoloader in Similar Manner

1 Another shotgun that one might restock in basically the same fashion is the Winchester Model 50 autoloader. The new semi-finished stock and forend are by Reinhart Fajen.

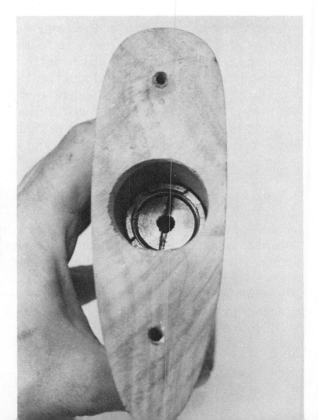

2
The stocks of some autoloading shotguns are attached to the receiver by a threaded sleeve, such as on this Model 50 Winchester. A special tool is necessary to remove the retaining sleeve. However, these can usually be easily made by a gunsmith.

3 A detail of the machined inletting on a semi-finished stock supplied by Fajen. With these basic inletting cuts already made there is very little left to be done. The time saved can be spent finishing the outside.

4

The Fajen stock fitted to the Model 50 Winchester receiver. Note that the wood is somewhat oversize in order to allow the stockmaker to work it down to a perfectly flush fit.

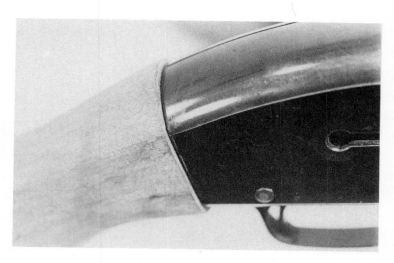

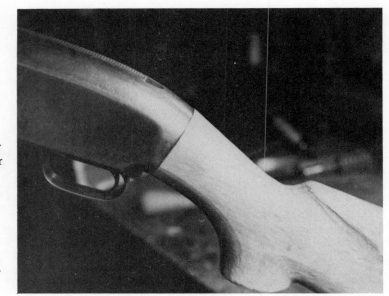

5
The Model 12 stock after being fitted to the receiver and rubbed and sanded.

11/

Restocking the Classic Double

A few years ago I owned an L. C. Smith side-by-side shotgun which I was right fond of. It was a 12-gauge, with 30-inch barrels, chambered for 3-inch magnum shells, and was just the right medicine for high-flying geese.

I'd bought the gun secondhand, and while the mechanism and other metal parts were in good order the stocks were terrible. The forend was one of those little splinter jobs which I could never hold on to, and the butt section looked as if it had been plowed every spring. Besides that, the previous owner had sawed the butt off so that it was too short for me to do my best shooting.

For a while the pitiful stockwork didn't bother me, but as my affection and appreciation for the Smith increased I began to grieve about the poor condition of the wood.

Finally, able to stand it no longer, I ordered a new semi-finished butt and beavertail forend from Reinhart Fajen in Missouri and put together an outfit that was mighty pleasing both to shoot and to look at. I added a classic touch by sawing off the pistol grip and making the grip in the traditional English style.

Though the work described in this chapter covers restocking the L. C. Smith, it is easily applicable to most other doubles, boxlock as well as sidelock designs. In fact, the L. C. Smith is one of the more difficult shotguns to restock.

Semi-finished stocks for most doubles can be ordered from Fajen, Bishop, Herter's, Pachmayr, and others in a wide variety of woods and grades of woods.

These semi-finished stocks really open things up for the home gunsmith. Broken stocks can be replaced in short order at a very nominal cost; old, drab, oil-soaked stocks can be replaced with fancy grades of wood, thus considerably upgrading the gun in both value and appearance; the old-fashioned slender forend can be replaced with the appealing and hand-filling beavertail type; and the new stock can be fitted to the individual shooter, thus allowing a better fit and better shooting.

The stocks come very nearly cut to shape, fully contoured with the comb fluted and the grip and forend already pleasingly sculptured. The field-style stock is turned to standard proportions but enough wood is left on to allow special features such as a fuller comb or grip. Additional features such as a cheekpiece, Monte Carlo comb, or extra length are available on special order.

Total de-assembly of most actions is not required or advisable. Removal of the parts required to free the old stock, namely the locks, trigger guard, and trigger plate (complete with triggers), will allow refitting the new buttstock. Actually the metal is fitted to the wood, as it is more convenient to mount the stock blank in a padded vise, at a good comfortable working height, and proceed to fit the smaller, more easily handled action parts. This method allows a rigid support for the wood which facilitates the small, precise cut required for perfect fitting.

The fitting of the action and tang is the first and perhaps the most critical part of the whole operation. The tang must fit snugly but not too tightly in its channel. If it is forced into place, splitting may occur at once or even worse, after the stock is completed. The recoil baffle areas must fit solidly and evenly, as should all areas where metal contacts wood. The total recoil area of the Smith action is less than ample, thus intensifying the need for flush, even fitting. Any areas which bear with excessive firmness will give under the pressure of recoil. Therefore all wood-to-metal surfaces must bear evenly; this cannot be overemphasized.

The inletting of the Fajen semi-finished stock was so nearly complete that only a few minor cuts and scrapes were required to complete the job. A final check for perfect fit can be made by coating the metal with soot, seating the action into wood tightly, and then inspecting the black impressions for irregularities. (A kerosene soot lamp can be quickly made by punching a hole in the lid of a small jar and inserting a rag wick.)

Once the action is in place, it serves as a very positive guide for the locks and trigger plate. If the action is properly seated these parts will fall into place perfectly. However, if it is incorrectly aligned, the lock, in particular, will not match up with the pre-inletted lock recess, thus causing all sorts of misery. It is wise, therefore, to make haste very slowly at the beginning.

The lock recesses are cut undersize so as to allow for the variations in locks. With the action fitted tightly into the wood, fit the forward tip of the lock into its slot in the action. This allows positive alignment, and the outline of the lock plate can be accurately traced onto the wood. Next cut away excess wood, leaving only a narrow margin for final fitting. A final no-gap fit can be achieved by "spotting in" the lock plate with the soot lamp. Simply cut away the blackened areas until the lock fits tight and flush. After repeating the operation on the other side it is a simple matter to line up and drill the hole for the through-bolt.

The trigger plate is fitted in much the same way, but care must be taken to see that the triggers work freely and engage the sear arms securely. At this point check to see that the safety works freely and that the safety yoke aligns properly with the trigger safety spurs.

After all parts are fully inletted, draw all the action's screws and bolts up tight, assemble the gun, and check everything out thoroughly. The hammers, safety, and self-cocking mechanism should work freely and crisply. With the safety in the off position only, the triggers should break cleanly and the hammers fall without drag or hesitation. Any sluggishness in this area probably means that the hammers or mainspring are rubbing against the wood. If such a failure occurs, take the lock off and remove the offending wood. It will probably be easy to find the spot because of the rubbed marks of the working part.

If the lock refuses to recock, the sear arm is either binding against the wood or is being held up by the trigger. In the latter case it may be necessary to file away a part of the internal trigger mechanism until proper contact is made. This situation is not too uncommon, especially when a slender-profile or straight-grip stock is fitted, causing the trigger plate to be rebent.

Fitting the trigger guard is a simple inletting detail, but in some instances special attention may be required. For example, if the old stock was of the straight-grip style, the trigger-guard strap will need to be cut off and curved to fit a pistol grip. On the other hand, a short, curved guard strap must be straightened if you plan on a straight or "English-style" grip. I chose this style for my gun. Though the new stock came with a pistol grip, I simply sawed it off flush with the bottom line of the stock. I reshaped the rounded tip of the guard strap for some extra "flair," straightened it, and then inletted it. The effect could be termed nothing less than classic.

The stocks, as they come, are so nearly shaped that very little outside work remains. Some wood may extend above the surface of the metal and should be worked flush. If the metal is to be refinished, use a fine-cut file to bring the wood down to the metal, removing a little of both on the final, smoothing cuts. Using a half-round cabinet file, stroke the stock gently all over, removing tool marks and other blemishes. At this point incorporate any special features such as reduced or lowered comb, shortened pull, slimmed grip, etc. It is a good idea to assemble the gun and try it for fit. Snap it to your shoulder several times to make sure your eye aligns naturally and correctly. If correction is needed, cut away only a small amount of wood and try again until a perfect fit is made. Fitting the forend iron of the field-grade Smith doesn't take more

(Text continues on page 84)

Steps for Restocking the Double

1

The buttstock of my old L. C. Smith before restocking. The wood was oil-soaked and the checkering worn, and there was a crack behind the lock plates. There was no sign of finish left and the recoil pad was worn out. Also, the shotgun had a splinter-type forend which I wanted to replace.

2

The semi-finished stocks made by Fajen came with the inletting very nearly completed and the outside ready for final shaping and sanding. The only disagreeable part was the white plastic spacer under the buttplate, which I immediately removed. The hand-filling contour of the semi-finished beavertail forend was quite a considerable improvement over the earlier splinter type.

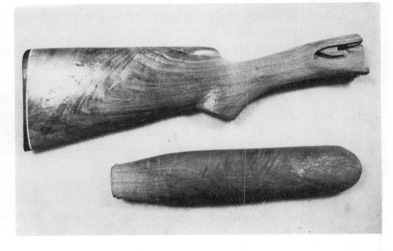

3

Wood must contact metal squarely and evenly. Otherwise recoil will cause splitting. And, of course, close wood-to-metal fit is always a sign of careful craftsmanship. Note here how the wood closely fits not only the outside surfaces but inside the frame as well.

4

A detail of the receiver with lock plate in place after final fitting. The wood still extends slightly beyond the surface of the lock plate and must be sanded flush.

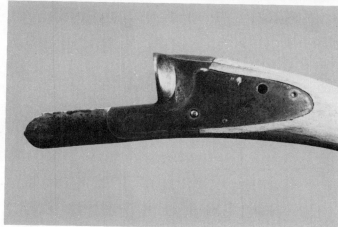

5

The trigger guard on this Smith was straightened and reshaped to fit the straight English-style grip. A final flush fit was achieved by filing and sanding both wood and metal together. This effect is classic. Though the semi-finished stock came with a pistolgrip, one has the option of removing it and building the stock in the classic English tradition.

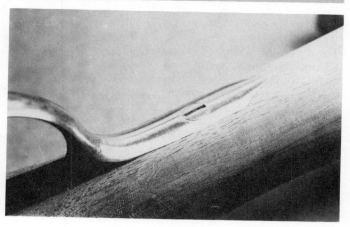

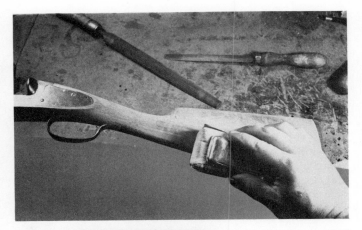

6

A sanding block is necessary to keep the edges straight and surfaces flat. Special effort must be taken to keep the edges around the lock plate sharp. This gives a very neat framing effect and is the sign of good workmanship. Rounded edges are a sign of sloppy work.

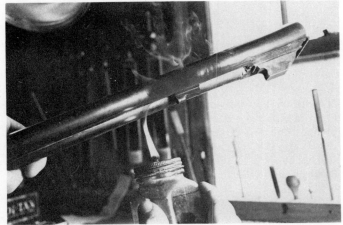

7

The barrels are blackened with a layer of soot from the flame of a homemade kerosene lamp. The lamp is made by making a hole in the lid of a bottle and inserting a rag wick. The coating of soot marks high places in the wood, indicating where to cut away wood.

8

A barrel-inletting scraper is used to whisk wood away. If you don't have an inletting scraper such as this, a simple scraping edge will do just as well but will be slower. Simply scrape away the soot-blackened spots until the forend fits snug against the barrels.

9
Final shaping of the forend is done with a half-round cabinet rasp. Note the close wood-to-metal fit.

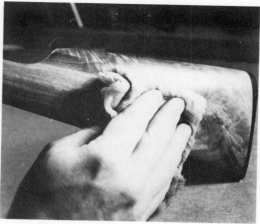

10
A painter's tack rag is used to clean the final sanded wood of particles of sanding dust. A tack rag is simply cheesecloth impregnated with nondrying varnish. They can usually be bought at any paint store. A final once-over with a tack rag gets the wood in final condition for finishing.

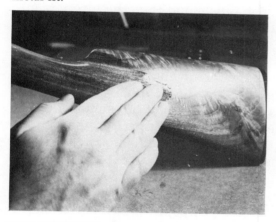

11
An oil type finish is applied simply by rubbing it into the wood with the fingertips. Apply several coats of finish, rubbing down each coat after it dries.

12   The restocked and finished L. C. Smith. The ventilated rib was mounted by Simmons Gun Specialties.

than a few minutes' work. Just make sure the fit is secure and the "knuckling tongue" rotates freely. The latch-type forends of the higher-grade guns require more time but present no problems unless you make some serious error in alignment. In the case of the automatic-ejector models, make sure the ejector springs have ample clearance.

Fitting the wrap-around beavertail forend calls for more cutting and scraping via the soot-lamp technique. Of course a barrel-channel scraper is speedier for this job, but almost any scraper with a sharp round tip will be satisfactory.

Best alignment can be assured by locking the barrels in place, fitting the forend to the forward action radius in the normal manner, and rotating the forend up against the barrels as if to snap it in place. The soot-coated barrels will, of course, spot the point of contact and can be cut away. This fit, spot, and cut procedure must be repeated until the forend is finally fully and firmly in place. Here again, as with the buttstock, use a cabinet rasp to remove excess outside wood and smooth to shape. At this point the butt and forend are fully inletted, shaped, and ready for sanding.

Sanding, regarded as a menial task by some, is, in fact, one of the most critical operations of the stockmaker's craft. The finish, and thus the ultimate appearance, of a gunstock is regulated by the workman's attention to certain basic, almost holy, principles.

Whenever possible (and this is most of the time), sand with the grain. When sanding rather large, straight areas, such as the forend and through the butt section, use a sanding block. This will remove any dips or high spots and avoid making any new ones. Sharp edges and corners must be sanded with special care. The only sharp edges on the L. C. Smith stock are on the lock-plate bosses. This narrow margin of wood surrounding the lock plates is one of the distinctive classic features of the sidelock double and its execution tells quite a story about the stockmaker. Therefore sand it with care and keep the edges *sharp!*

Preliminary sanding should be done with 180-grit paper, switching to 220-grit paper for additional smoothing up. Finally, polish the wood with super-fine steel wool. The steel wool pulls out a lot of loose grain fibers and shortens the "whiskering" process.

Remove the grain ends or whiskers by slightly wetting the wood with a damp cloth and immediately drying it over a heat source such as a stove eye. This operation swells and raises the grain so that the whiskers may be cut off with steel wool or 280-grit, or finer, sandpaper. Repeat this process until the wood remains smooth and glasslike. If the whiskers aren't properly removed at this point they will rise when the finish is applied, thus probably causing a violent vocal outburst not to mention a sloppy finish.

To use or not to use a wood filler is largely a matter of personal preference. I personally recommend filling the wood pores with oil-based stock finish. About five coats of this finish rubbed on with the fingers usually fills the grain and gives a smooth, flat surface. Be sure to apply the first couple of coats to the inletted surfaces and under the buttplate. This keeps moisture out and helps prevent oil from the mechanism from seeping in. As mentioned earlier, oil-soaked wood is one of the chief causes of L. C. Smith stock failure. After the finish has set hard, additional gloss can be had by hand rubbing with rottenstone and oil or one of the commercial furniture rubbing compounds.

The final frosting on any restocking is a nice, neat checkering job. Notice I say *neat*, for poor checkering is a far greater sin than no checkering at all. Properly laid-out and executed checkering, on the other hand, is a highly functional and attractive addition. If you are not accomplished at the art of checkering, I suggest you not attempt such work on your dazzling new L. C. Smith stock, at least until you have progressed to the chapters on checkering.

For guns of this type I prefer the traditional "point" patterns. Such patterns are relatively easy to lay out and checker and seem to add that final, quiet touch to your already elegant sidelock double.

My gun was done in the more modernistic basketweave technique, mainly to soften the rather stark lines of the straight grip and oversize forend. The choice, of course, is yours; you made the stock so you can darn well checker it to suit yourself. And too, you've proved that restocking the L. C. Smith or any other double is not at all a job for professionals only.

12/

Restocking Lever-Action Rifles

How many lever-action rifles there are in common use today is anybody's guess. But there's no doubt that the numbers run in the millions, many of which have been in continuous use for up to half a century and even more. Traditionally, a lever gun is for close, fast shooting where rough terrain, uncertain footing, and heavy brush are the rule. Thus the lever guns seem to get more than their fair share of abuse.

I know at least one hunter who has used his Model 94 Winchester .30/30 for so many years that the stock is battered to a mere stub of its former self. He occasionally claims that he's going to refinish the stock "one of these days," but the truth of the matter is that there isn't enough stock left to bother with refinishing.

Another guy I know, a sort of do-it-yourself home gunsmith, has refinished his stock so many times he has almost sanded it away. All the edges where the wood stock meets metal are so rounded that the stock bears only a casual resemblance to its former self.

These, and the thousand other tragedies which wood and metal suffer, have brought about thousands of lever-action rifles with stocks gone too far down that rocky road ever to be revived by a mere refinishing job. And this isn't even counting all those stocks that have been run over by cars, dropped off a cliff, or busted when the owner battered a crazed bear over the head.

Of course, in such cases the simplest expedient is to get a new stock from the factory. But then again, this may not be too practical in some cases. Not when a new stock will cost forty dollars and you figure the whole rifle isn't worth that.

The next choice is to make your own replacement. If you want it to be really easy all you need do is get one of the semi-finished stocks such as made by Reinhart Fajen or E. C. Bishop & Co. In fact, semi-finished isn't really the right word. *Nearly* finished is more accurate. These stocks are available for all makes and about all models of lever-action rifles going all the way back to the Winchester Model of 1873. According to how much you want to spend, you can also get some mighty fancy grades and types of wood—much fancier than that which came on your rifle when it was new.

If you yearn for more distinction there are models available with cheek-pieces, Monte Carlo combs, and swept-line pistolgrips, enough to satisfy the most jaded taste. Personally I am content to pass up the extra contraptions and spend my money for nice wood. The stock shown on these pages is Fajen's "Fancy" American black walnut. This grade costs more, no doubt, than many folks will want to pay. But it gives you an idea of the quality available.

For a plain grade of good walnut, about like what came on your rifle, you can get by for as little as twelve dollars for the buttstock and ten dollars for the forend. Other woods include maple (curly or plain), cherry, laminated (walnut and maple), two or three types of walnut, sycamore, myrtlewood, and mesquite. About 98 percent of those sold, however, are probably good old American black walnut.

As for the tools for a do-it-yourself restocking project such as this, all you need is a straight-edged chisel or a sharp pocket knife, screwdriver, a drill, a fine-cut wood rasp (even a file will do), two or three pieces of sandpaper, and some wood finish of some sort. Timewise, it depends mostly on you. But at any rate it shouldn't take more than a weekend, or a week of evenings.

The first fitting procedure, after removing the old stock, is to take a good long look at the inletting in the new stock and compare it with that of the old one.

In the old stock's inletting you'll note shiny places where it was in hard contact with the metal. Note also the clearance areas for the springs, and pay particular attention to where the wood absorbed the recoil, usually around the forward edge.

Next try fitting the action into the new stock. It probably won't fit all the way, but at least you'll get an idea of what needs to be done. By all means don't force the action into the stock or you'll split it.

Gunsmiths who do a lot of wood-to-metal fitting use various "spotting-in" agents such as cobalt blue, Prussian blue, soot in oil, and such. With a coat of this spotting agent on the metal a distinct mark is left wherever metal touches wood. This is where the next slice or scrape will be made. For no more spotting-in than you'll need to do you can just give the metal parts a thin coat of your wife's lipstick. This makes a nice easy-to-see mark. The idea is to fit the metal into the wood and cut or scrape away the red smudges.

Thus, bit by bit, the action can be fitted all the way into the new stock. Here's where you use the pocket knife or chisel. Either one will do fine as long as they're *sharp*.

When the stock is fully in place and all the recoil surfaces are firmly contacting, drill the holes for the screws or through-bolts and the inletting is finished.

If you are also fitting a forend it can be done in a jiffy. There are fewer manufacturing variations at the front of the rifle, and as a result the forearm will probably be a perfect fit as it comes—or at least pretty close. For rifles such as Winchester and Marlin with the tube magazines, the hole has already been bored in the forend, so there's no sweat. The only likely fitting of the forend is at the action, where the forend fits into a groove in the front of the receiver. So get out the ol' lipstick and spot it in.

With the new stocks firmly in place you can begin the trimming-down and smoothing-up operation. Probably around the tang areas the wood will extend above the level of the metal somewhat. Naturally this must be trimmed and sanded to a flush fit. The caution here is to avoid marring the metal with a woodworking tool such as a rasp. But on the other hand, if the metal looks pretty bad anyway and you are planning on a reblue, go ahead and sand metal and wood together. This makes a perfectly level fit.

I prefer to use a rasp for these trimming operations, followed by a brisk sanding. Also the rasp is great for getting rid of the turning-machine marks left on the surface of the wood. If you don't have a rasp, use a file or a bit of coarse sandpaper wrapped around a file.

As soon as you have the surface of the stock worked down smooth and flat, and have all the wood-to-metal unions flush, switch to 220-grit garnet sandpaper and start taking out all the little scratches left by the rasp, file, or coarser sandpaper. Use a padded sanding block and work *with* the grain. Next switch to 280-grit or 320-grit paper for a really smooth-as-glass finish. Now, for a really super finish give the wood a real polish with 400-grit paper or extra-fine steel wool.

The basis of a good finish is a good sanding job. If it doesn't look perfect, keep on till it does.

The choice of finish is up to you. The commercial finishes such as Birchwood-Casey's Tru-Oil or Linspeed are great. They make a tough, good-looking finish and are fast drying and easy to apply. About six coats of either of these smoothed on with the fingers, and rubbed down with steel wool between coats, forms a finish that will draw a lot of admiring glances.

How to Restock a Lever-Action Rifle

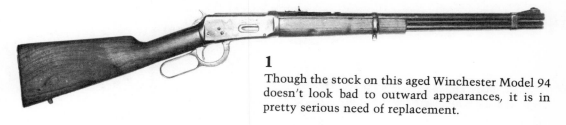

1

Though the stock on this aged Winchester Model 94 doesn't look bad to outward appearances, it is in pretty serious need of replacement.

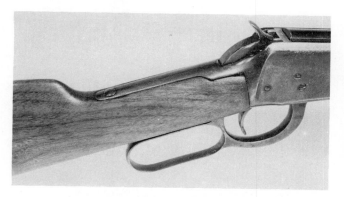

2

The closeup shows the deterioration of the stock around the metal areas, which in turn causes unwanted looseness between the stock and the receiver. When this condition prevails it is only a short time until the stock splits completely, usually at the worst possible moment.

3

The rifle with the new replacement stocks such as manufactured by Rinehart Fajen. Note that the semi-finished stocks are cut almost to final dimension so that very little shaping is required.

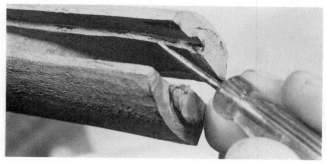

4

The spotting-in technique. The dark areas indicated by the pointer are where the metal has contacted the inletting in the stock. These dark areas are carefully scraped away until the fit is perfect.

5

A small, sharp chisel is used to shave away the dark area left by the spotting-in agent.

6

Note how the dark area is spread widely over the inletting surfaces. This means that the metal has come into full contact with the stock and that the inletting is finished.

7

A fine-cut wood rasp is used to trim the wood down very close to the surface of the metal.

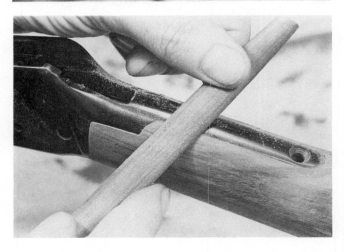

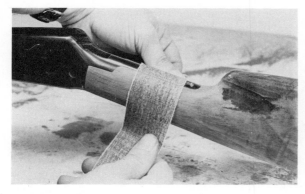

8

Cloth-backed sandpaper is used to sand the wood around the tang area. A quick shoe-shine motion gets the wood away fast.

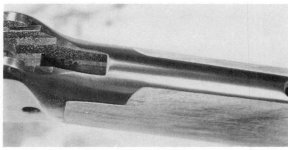

9

A detail of a properly inletted stock. Note that there are no gaps between wood and metal. All this work was done with a single narrow-bladed chisel.

10

The wood rasp is used to rasp away the machine marks on the outside surface of the stock.

11

The semi-finished forend for the Winchester Model 94 as it comes from Rinehart Fajen. Note that the barrel channel is cut and that the hole for the tubular magazine has also been bored. This can be fitted in place in a very few minutes.

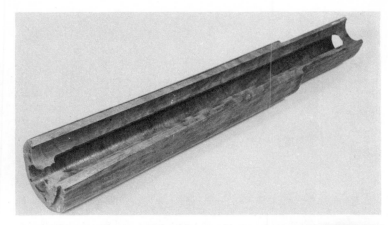

12

A detail of the tongue-and-groove fitting that holds the forend rigidly in the receiver.

13

The forend fitted flush with the receiver.

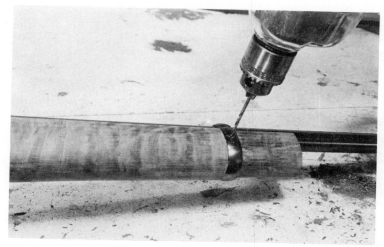

14

One of the few drilling operations is boring the hole for the forend band screw.

15

Note the very close wood-to-metal fit where the forend joins the barrel. This shows good workmanship, but in fact the forend was so nearly finished that very little fitting was required at all.

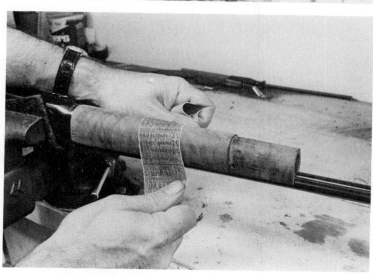

16

Here again the cloth-backed sandpaper and a shoeshine motion does a quick job of sanding the curved surfaces, such as this forend.

17
Final sanding is done with the grain with 120-grit sandpaper, or finer, backed up with a sanding block.

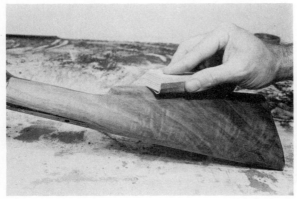

18
A sanding block is used to put the final touches on the buttstock. For a really fine finish, use 280-grit, 320-grit, and 400-grit sandpaper successively.

19
The final polish is laid on the wood with fine steel wool. Note that the wood is so slick and smooth that it seems to be almost glossy—yet there is no finish whatever on the wood yet.

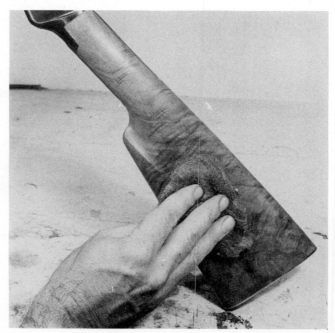

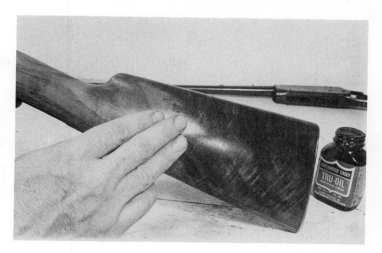

20
The commercial stock finish is smoothed onto the wood with the fingertips. A few coats of this and the job is done.

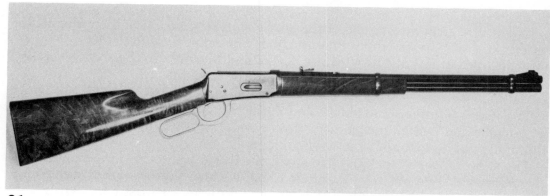

21   The finished product. The wood is Fajen's Fancy grade of American black walnut.

13/

Restocking the Ruger Number One and Other Single Shots

One of the great attractions of the single-shot rifle action is the unlimited variety of stock styles which may be used. The range of styles runs from the straight lines of the military rolling blocks and Martinis to the rococo scrolls and scrabbles of the European schutzens to the graceful utility of the Stevenses, Winchesters, and Ballards used in offhand matches two generations ago.

The Ruger Number One single-shot action, in addition to being a superbly engineered and crafted mechanism, possesses beautiful lines which adapt harmoniously to almost any stock style one might imagine.

The semi-finished stock used to stock the Ruger project in this chapter is the "Classic" style made by Reinhart Fajen. He also supplies other styles for the Ruger, such as his standard field style and the racy "Aristocrat" with rollover cheekpiece.

The only tools needed are a cabinet rasp, a couple of chisels (one straight-edged and one curved), and a few sheets of sandpaper.

The inletting of the Fajen stock is so nearly completed that only minor final fitting is required. This final fitting, however, should be done with considerable care if you want a close wood-to-metal fit. Also, you should take time to examine the recoil surfaces of the action and consider how the force of recoil will be distributed against the wood. You will no doubt be amazed at the remarkably large total area of the recoil surfaces (compared to most bolt actions) and rigidity of the fit. And the "ears" at the forward extension of the inletting, which fit into special recesses in the action, prevent any future spreading or opening up of the fit such as you've probably seen happen to some double-barreled shotgun buttstocks. This is very good engineering!

Though the stock can be fitted without removing the works from the action, it's a good idea to strip everything out completely. The safety, lever, trigger guard, and trigger will very much get in the way during the outside shaping, and sooner or later you'd have to take it apart to clean out all the wood dust anyway. The Ruger instructions on disassembly are very complete and easy to follow.

The entire fitting of the butt can be accomplished with such obvious ease that there is no need here for a play-by-play account of the process. There are, however, a few "don'ts" which should be observed. Because of the close inletting of the stock as it comes, one may be tempted to force-fit the wood by pounding it onto the metal or simply tightening the through-bolt. Such a procedure will put excessive outward pressure on the wood and will cause it to split or crack. It is wiser to slip the stock on a little at a time and scrape away wood along the upper and lower tang channels wherever there are signs of hard contact. Spotting agents such as inletting black or lampblack don't work on these parallel-fit areas. They mark everywhere but don't show where the tightness is excessive. Simply keep the metal clean and dry. Tight spots will appear as shiny spots on the wood where the fibers are compressed. Just shave these away bit by bit.

Of course, inletting black is a good bet for spotting-in and equalizing contact on recoil surfaces and around the curved surfaces at the rear of the tangs.

With the inletting of the buttstock complete and the through-bolt drawn up tight, the next step is fitting the buttplate—that is, if you intend to use a curved steel buttplate such as the Niedner. A special feature of the Fajen Classic stock is that it can be ordered precut and inletted for the Niedner buttplate. (See chapter on fitting curved steel buttplates.) With this work very nearly completed, all that remains to be done is a final bit of spotting-in and smoothing-up for a perfect fit. And make damn sure it is a perfect fit too, or the whole neighborhood will be gossiping about your poor workmanship, not to mention all the moisture that will seep in. Of course if you ordered one of the other styles of butt a plastic buttplate came already fitted.

So now we can fit the gripcap. Here again you can order a stock with a gripcap already fitted or you may prefer one of Fajen's fancy contrasting-wood grips which come preattached. My own preference in gripcaps is the ultra-stylish Pachmayr cap. The Pachmayr cap features a metal inlay available in gold, silver, steel, etc., which covers the screw and makes a mighty handsome-looking fitting with your initials engraved on the plate.

The trick to fitting a gripcap properly is making sure that the wood beneath the cap is perfectly level and smooth. So take a little extra effort here to get it right.

With the buttplate and gripcap in place and the stock fitted to the action, all that remains is working the outside down to final form. As the stock is very nearly finished already, about all the outside shaping amounts to is reducing the wood with the rasp until it is flush with the buttplate, gripcap, and action. Shaping up the panel behind the action may be something new for those of you who are experienced only in rifle stocking, but is old hat for those who have made stocks for good-grade double-barreled shotguns, as described in an earlier chapter.

To be sure, this is a striking feature and offers an excellent opportunity to add some really nice custom features. The panel on Ruger factory stocks is a classic curve. The stock shown on these pages has the panel brought to a point at the rear. *(Text continues on page 106)*

Steps in Restocking the Ruger Number One

1 Before you lay tool to wood, make a careful study of the shape of the inletting and make sure you understand how the wood fits to the metal. This may save costly mistakes later. Pay particular attention to the little ears or extensions at the forward inside edge of the stock. These fit into matching recesses in the receiver and keep the stock from warping outward and splitting.

2

A detail of the Ruger receiver showing the recesses for the stock "ears."

3

The spotting-in operation is similar to any other spotting and cutting technique. The pointer shows where a smudge was left by a receiver and must be shaved away.

4

After fitting the stock to the receiver, work the outside surfaces down flush with the metal. Take care not to mar the metal if you do not plan on having the gun reblued.

5

A fine-cut rasp is used to work the wood down flush with the metal.

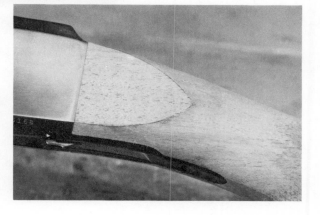

6

The next step is sculpting the panels behind the receiver. If done correctly this adds a lot of grace to a stock. If done badly it makes the stock look quite awkward and clubby.

7

This is the preliminary layout for fitting the gripcap. It is essential that the surface of the wood be worked dead smooth so there will be no gaps between wood and gripcap.

8

Here is a Pachmayer gripcap in place. This gripcap features a metal insert—not in place in photo—of gold Thomas silver or other metal on which you can engrave your initials, etc.

9

The butt being worked down flush with the curved steel Niedner-style buttplate.

10

A cabinet rasp is used to smooth cutting marks left by the Stanley Surform shaper.

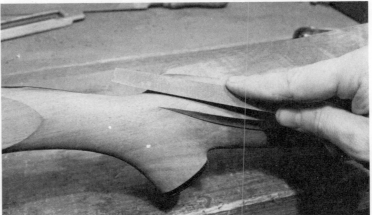

11

A small cabinet rasp is used to do the detail shaping in the flutes at either side of the comb. Properly shaped flutes add a lot of style and grace to a custom stock.

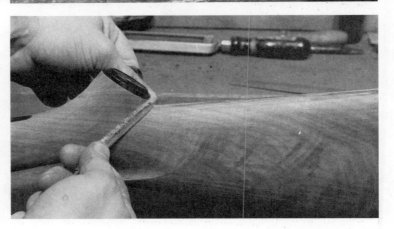

12

A narrow strip of cloth-backed sandpaper is used to sand the difficult niche behind the gripcap. A shoe-shine motion gets the work done fast and easy.

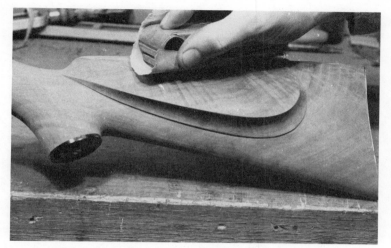

13

A sanding block is used to sand the wood to a glass-smooth, dead-flat surface. Note the "bead" or shallow outlining step around the cheekpiece. This feature is seen usually only on the best custom rifles and is included in the Fajen Classic style semi-finished stock.

14

The underside of the stock after final sanding. Note the graceful way the wood flows into the metal. A harmonious union of wood and metal is a sign of fine stockwork.

15

The inletting as it comes on a semi-finished Fajen stock for the Ruger Number One single-shot. Very little work remains to be done.

16

After inletting the forend, the outer surfaces are worked flush with the metal just as the butt section was.

17

A detail of the recess for the forend retaining screw. Be sure that this is done neatly, and try to keep the outer edges of the recess sharp. Rounded or dished edges indicate sloppy workmanship. The best way to keep these edges sharp is to sand the forend with a sanding block.

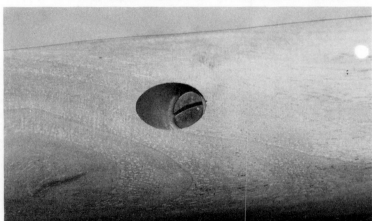

18

Don't forget to finish the inside of the stock as well as the outside. I find that a spray-type stock finish penetrates the inletting recesses quite well and does a superior job of sealing the vulnerable endgrain.

19
Birchwood-Casey's Tru-oil stock finish is rubbed on with the fingers.

20
The silver nameplate in place, after I had my initials engraved by a jeweler. This is what I call a very classy-looking gripcap.

Working the wood down flush with the action surfaces is a pretty tricky proposition, as the barreled action comes with a nice blue. One misslick and you've bought yourself a new blue job. The best technique here is to work the wood down as close as you dare with the rasp, then remove the wood for final sanding.

A wise man once said, "Sanding is a miserable job," and I've never heard this effectively disputed. However, proper sanding technique is so important to the finished product that sanding can be called an art. In fact the difference between a five-hundred-dollar stock by a master stockmaker and a fifty-dollar plug by your local cobbler is largely skill with the sanding block. Therefore it behooves you to give this important step all due attention.

If the rasp marks are pretty deep, start off with 80-grit paper and work the wood smooth and flat. Naturally you want to use a sanding block to keep the surface flat and ripple-free, and by all means sand with the grain! Sanding in tight spots such as behind the gripcap and curved surfaces such as the pistol grip can be handled quickly and easily by using a strip of cloth-backed sandpaper and laying it on with a brisk shoeshine motion.

When all the rasp marks are gone, switch to 120-grit or 180-grit paper and continue the slicking-up operation. A mark of good workmanship is sharp clean edges around the cheekpiece, and in the case of the Ruger Number One stock, around the panel outline. A good way to make sure that these edges finish up sharp is to sand the curved surfaces such as the underslope of the cheekpiece first. This tends to round the edges somewhat, but then you can come along with the sanding block on the flat surfaces and sharpen the edges up again.

Continue with 220-grit and then 320-grit finishing paper until the wood is dead smooth and you're ready for the finish. You probably will want to wait until the forend is finished before applying finish, but now is a good time to apply a sealer to the inletted surfaces. With all the nooks and crannies of the buttstock, applying a thorough coating of sealer could be a problem. The simplest and best way out is to use a spray-type finish such as Birchwood-Casey's spray-on stock finish. The spray gets in everywhere and gives the endgrain a good soaking.

Actually fitting the forend is such a simple task that little needs to be said. The wood is held in place by a screw which angles forward at a 45° angle. Thus, when tightened, it has the effect of jamming the wood both upward and tightly against the action (more good Ruger engineering).

To ensure good accuracy, fit the wood to the action extension as tightly as possible. A tight fit here will keep the wood from possibly rocking around and applying uneven pressure on the barrel. My technique for fitting the wood around the barrel was to fit the wood to a light contact without any pressure points. Thus I hoped for a hairline fit without affecting accuracy. Of course this left the way open to completely free-float the barrel in case performance indicated a change was needed. As it turned out, accuracy was outstanding from the very first, so this method of fitting the forend is highly recommended.

With the forend fitted, all you need to do is work it down a bit and sand and you're ready to rub on some finish.

Despite all the old wives' tales you've probably heard about how much work is involved in getting a really good, durable finish, the truth of the matter is that the modern commercial stock finishes are quick, easy to apply, and a hell of a lot better in all respects than the old "secret" recipes brewed up by the "old masters." The finish on my Number One involved rubbing on three coats of Birchwood-Casey's Tru-Oil, rubbing it into the wood with fine steel wool, then rubbing on two more coats. A final buffing with Casey's stock conditioner brought the finish to a bright, mirror-slick gloss. I'm sorry to disappoint you, old timer, but it just isn't very hard to do. . . .

14

Styling the European Sporter

This classy European-style-stock project is part of a *total* do-it-yourself rifle-building plan which includes a snazzy lever release, hinged floorplate, installation of a graceful shotgun-style trigger guard, and even adding double set triggers. These projects are described in the metalworking section of this book. So, before getting too far along on this style of stocking job, you should turn to the metalworking section to see just how many improvements you can include in one grand enterprise.

Perhaps the most distinctive of all stock designs to come out of Europe is the so-called Mannlicher—so named because of the stocks made by the firm of Mannlicher which extended the full length of the barrel. Thus any stock which extends all the way to the muzzle is unofficially termed a Mannlicher.

Despite the inherent grace of these slender, free-flowing stocks, many do-it-yourself efforts fail to hit the mark so far as styling goes. This is because most stockmakers, both amateur and professional, regard a Mannlicher stock as nothing more than a stock with a long forend.

As a result what they wind up with is a rather clubby-looking affair that has little if any of the original grace of a well-done Mannlicher.

Actually there are a few tricks of the trade required to make this type of stock look really good. To begin with, the Monte Carlo comb is definitely out. This additional height makes the butt section too wide through the profile and throws the entire design out of balance. Even the Mannlicher people themselves were unsuccessful at making a really good-looking full-length stock with a Monte Carlo comb.

Another failing of most "custom" Mannlicher stocks is the shape of the pistolgrip. What is generally considered a "normal" pistolgrip shape curves much too abruptly. This causes a sudden interruption in the flowing lines of the full-length stock, and as a result a certain awkwardness is created.

Instead the gripcap should curve gently and be set much farther back than is usually the case. This feature allows the extra-long line of the forend to change gently and with a more natural grace.

Sometimes we see custom Mannlichers which have been made by stockmakers too bound by traditional rules. In this case the underside of the forend is a straight taper from the front of the trigger-guard assembly all the way to the muzzle cap. This causes the forend to appear too thick and rigid, especially about midway up the barrel. Curved lines look better than straight lines here, so the forend should be a series of subtle curves. The bottom line of the forend profile should be concave, flowing slightly upward as well as outward. A forend thus shaped appears much slimmer.

Though graceful slimness is the essence of a well-done Mannlicher stock, some stockmakers get into trouble, as far as the overall effect goes, by trying to make the *whole* stock too slim. An effect of slimness is largely achieved by *contrasts.* Consider, for example, an original Mannlicher-Schoenauer or the rifle shown on these pages. Notice that the profile is quite thick through the action area. Original Mannlichers, in fact, have a decidedly pregnant look through the magazine section. This contrasts with the forend and makes the forend appear even slimmer than it actually is! If the magazine area is made smaller the forend appears larger and thus less graceful.

Thus when we consider the stylistic features of a well-done Mannlicher stock we realize that the eye does indeed play tricks on us.

For the stock shown on these pages I employed even more tricks. The cute little schnabel halfway up the forend, for example, breaks up the plainness of the forend and thus makes it appear even more compact than it really is. Then too, the concave curve of the schnabel accents the slimness of the forend. Likewise the schnabel at the muzzle, in this case done in ebony, accents the slimness of the stock. Clever? You bet! At the same time I left an additional border of wood around the trigger-guard assembly in order to lend additional boldness through the magazine section.

By now you're probably guessing that such stockwork requires working from a big, rough-sawed block of wood and lots of painstaking layout work. Not at all! The stock shown on these pages is a Fajen Classic-style semi-finished blank with a couple of extra features — the full-length forend and additional wood left in the pistolgrip area. Nothing more.

The extra wood in the grip area allows the curve of the grip to be set back as described above and shown in the illustrations. All in all, the forward edge of the gripcap is approximately ½ inch or so farther to the rear than is "normal" in contemporary styling. (This makes a very comfortable, fast-handling grip, by the way.)

Once you have established the optimum curve of the pistol grip and located

(Text continues on page 114)

How to Style a European Sporter

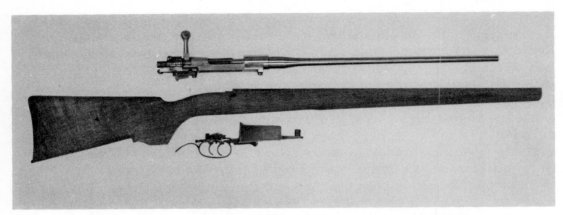

1 Everything you need for a deluxe European sporter with full-length Mannlicher-style forend. The hinged lever-release floorplates, double set triggers, and shotgun-style trigger guard are all projects described in Part IV. The semi-finished stock here is the Fajen Classic style with specially ordered full-length forend. Also, the stock was ordered unfinished in the grip area so that I could give a more European flair to the shape of the grip.

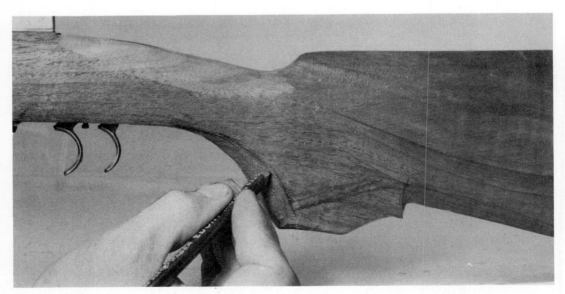

2 A marking pencil is used to draw the smooth flowing line of the Mannlicher-style grip on the stock blank. Note that this type of grip sets farther to the rear than the normal grip, and adds an additional measure of grace to the overall stock lines.

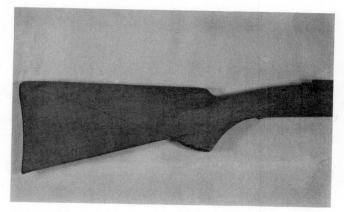

3

A detail of the Mannlicher-style grip after shaping is complete and gripcap attached. Note the two lines drawn on the stock. The gripcap is attached at an angle which is in a direct line to the heel of the stock. The underside of the stock follows a line which would intersect at the rear trigger-guard screw. This is stock styling in the classical mode.

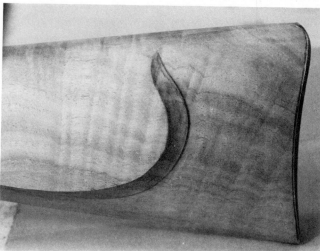

4

This graceful reverse curve at the upper rear reach of the cheekpiece can be carved into the Fajen styling with very little difficulty. It is a very stylish touch.

5

The tang of the Mauser receiver can be corrected so that it is not necessary to cut a groove in the stock for the cocking piece. The Mauser tang is simply filed out or ground down to a shallower profile. This also allows a slimmer, more graceful grip profile. Note that although the metal is inletted to the wood to a hairline fit there is a slight gap of approximately $1/32$ inch at the rear of the tang. This allows for any backing up the action caused by recoil and thus prevents splitting of the wood. This is good stockmaking technique.

111

6

A fine-cut file is used to do some delicate detail work around the ejection port. Delicate contouring such as this adds a great deal of distinction to a stock. Note that this is a considerable improvement, in terms of appearance, than simply leaving the top of the stock flat around the ejection area. It is such little extras as this that really mean the difference between run-of-the-mill and truly custom work.

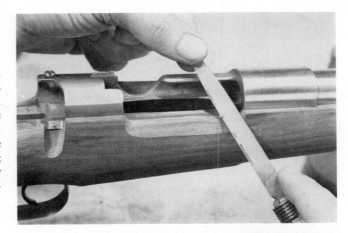

7

A small rasp is used to do the final sculpting of the mid-forend schnabel. This is a distinctive feature and serves to break up the plainness of the long Mannlicher-style forend.

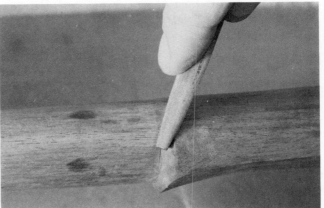

8

The ebony schnabel forend tip. This forend tip was attached in the manner described in the next chapter. The forend tip and the mid-forend Schnabel are sculpted in the same design. This way the lines are compatible. Harmonious lines such as these require a bit of thinking and planning before forging ahead.

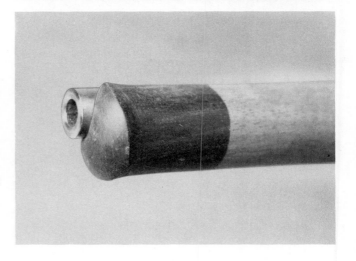

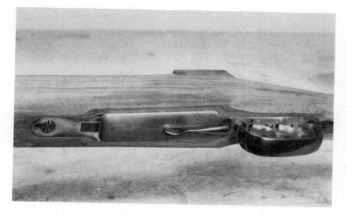

9

Note the highly individualistic styling at the bottom of the stock. Rather than being simply rounded off in the ordinary manner, the stock shape is dead flat in the trigger-guard-assembly area. This gives a distinctive framing effect to the metal parts. The sharp edges around the flat area show off the workmanship of a stockmaker to good advantage and identify him as a highly individualistic stylist.

10

With the shotgun-style trigger guard fitted, both the rear guard extension and the underside of the grip are sanded at one time. This working of both metal and wood together is a good way to achieve even contours. The finishing is done with a shoe-shine motion with a piece of cloth-backed sandpaper. After final sanding and polishing the trigger guard is removed from bluing.

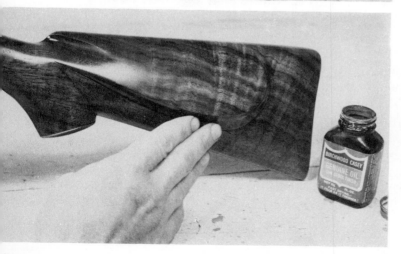

11

The final touch is applying the finish. If the wood is sanded dead smooth, finishing is no problem with the easy-to-use rub-on finishes. Birchwood-Casey Tru-oil is used on this stock. Five coats of finish, rubbed down with very fine steel wool between coats, were required to achieve this rich, satinlike finish.

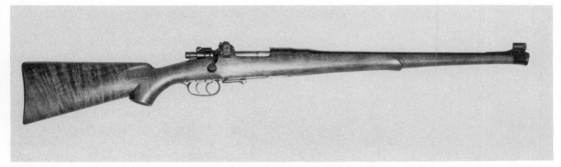

12   The finished rifle. Note how the mid-forend schnabel gives a very distinctive
touch and takes the plainness off the forend. Also, the long, flowing lines of the
grip area make the overall appearance of the rifle trimmer and more graceful.

the general location of the gripcap, draw a straight line from the heel (the top
of the buttplate) to the front lower edge of the grip. This line establishes the
angle at which the gripcap should be mounted. Also draw a straight line from
the toe of the stock (the bottom of the buttplate) to the rear trigger-guard
screw. This line establishes the bottom edge of the butt aft of the gripcap. If
the stock falls below this line it will look paunchy, and if it gets above the
line things start to look a little weird.

With these lines established, the shaping of the butt section goes pretty rapidly. The cross-section shape is pretty much determined by the shape of the
buttplate. (See the chapter on fitting a curved steel buttplate.) Just work the
wood down to the fitted buttplate, then keep the lines flowing straight toward
the grip section.

The Fajen Classic-style cheekpiece is hard to improve on and even has a
step or "bead" edging, which adds even more distinction. The only frill I
added to the cheekpiece was a reverse curve at the upper rear edge.

If you are using a Mauser action for the heart of your custom sporter, you
no doubt became annoyed during the inletting process with the sear groove in
the tang of Mauser actions. This groove, in turn, makes it necessary to cut an
unsightly groove in the stock. How does one avoid this unsightly feature?
Simple—just cut the top level of the tang down until the groove tapers away
at the rear! This way the tang blends into the grip area with no need for an
ugly groove. This is a feature employed by nearly all top-rank custom ri-
flemakers. Ah so! Also, this way the top surface of the tang can be curved so
that it perfectly matches the contour of the stock. In fact, during the final
shaping it is a good idea to shape both metal and wood together. This ensures
a perfect blend.

Through the action area I left the original Fajen contour pretty much as it
was. The ebony forend tip was mounted as described in the chapter on at-

taching forend tips. The bottom side of the forend profile was drawn on the wood, then worked down to final profile with a rasp. Similarly, the side profiles were drawn and cut down to near finished dimensions. This left the sides and bottom flat with a square cross section. The purpose of this procedure is to get all the proportions and dimensions exact before rounding off the edges. It is rather difficult to cut a forend to its final rounded shape and keep both sides symmetrical. Thus it is better in the long run to "slab off" the sides and bottom first, then round it off later.

The mid-forend schnabel was just an experiment on my part; I planned to cut it off later if it didn't look right. As it turned out it added what I considered a very pleasing effect, so I left it intact. The schnabel also acts as sort of a built-in hand stop.

Describing how to do this work of wood sculpturing is like trying to describe what a beautiful woman looks like; you just have to see it to know.

After final shaping, give the entire stock a good going-over with 180-grit sandpaper. By all means use a sanding block, and in most cases sand with the grain. The exceptions to this latter rule are the inside curve of the pistol grip and possibly some of the other rounded surfaces. In these cases try using cloth-backed sandpaper. A brisk shoeshine motion will really raise a cloud of sanding dust. Eventually, however, you will have to do the final sanding *with* the grain.

Next go over the stock with 220-grit or 280-grit paper and erase all the tiny scratches left by the coarser paper. Finally give it a slicking-up with 400-grit paper or extra-fine steel wool.

Finish to your tastes. My stock was finished with five coats of Birchwood-Casey's Tru-Oil rubbed on with the fingers. The finish was given a brisk rubdown with steel wool between coats. The final coat was polished down to the wood so that the grain was filled, but the finish itself was quite dull, European-style. An occasional hand rubbing with boiled linseed oil keeps this finish looking deep and rich.

The next step is to install the sights of your choice, scope or irons. My selection was a Lyman rear peep sight along with the Williams hooded ramp front sight with gold bead. This is a fast-handling combination.

Finally you're ready to blue the metal parts. I used the new Birchwood-Casey diptank cold blue and had remarkable success. Just following the instructions and using the materials that come with the kit I achieved a blue that is a satiny, soul-satisfying, deep black.

Well, dear reader, add sling swivels if you like and add some checkering if you want to try your hand, but by and large the project is over. It has resulted in a handsome sporting rifle that is worth considerably more than the total investment of time and money. But best of all, it's truly a custom rifle with all the nice little extras that make it custom in fact as well as name.

15

Fitting a Forend Tip

A forend tip of plastic or some sort of contrasting wood has become so popular in recent years that practically all custom stocks include this attractive added feature. Even factory stocks by Remington, Winchester, and Weatherby, to name a few, offer a forend tip of plastic or wood on some or all of their centerfire rifles.

To be sure, a well-fitted and well-shaped forend tip adds a certain flair and takes the plainness and "sameness" off what might otherwise be a pretty ordinary-looking stock. And adding a forend tip to your next stock, or perhaps one of your old stocks, isn't at all difficult. Here's how to go about it.

Since you're doing the work yourself, you'll probably be thinking only in terms of some sort of contrasting wood rather than plastic. Plastic is, at best only an imitation of wood, usually ebony, but wood is as easy to attach and looks a lot better. Different types of wood used for forend tips include ebony, walnut, maple, purpleheart, zebrawood, tigerwood, rosewood, cocobolo, and other exotic varieties. Most of these can be obtained in block form from Brownell's, Reinhart Fajen, E.C. Bishop & Co., Herter's, and Frank Mittermeier. The price for a generous forend-size block won't be over two or three dollars even for the most expensive wood, and another buck or so will buy enough extra for a matching gripcap.

In years gone by the permanent attachment of a forend tip presented considerable difficulty because of the generally poor quality of the available glues. Therefore gunsmiths resorted to rather complicated procedures to make sure the forend tip stayed in place after the glue aged and weakened. With today's super-strength epoxy glues, however, a strong, lasting wood-to-wood union is possible with a minimum of time and effort.

The first step is to make sure that the two wood surfaces to be glued together are perfectly smooth and flat. This is essential both for strength and for appearance. An uneven surface, for example, may result in unsightly gaps between stock and tip, and the reduced surface to surface contact will result in a weaker union. One of the best and easiest ways to get the mating ends smooth and perfectly flat is to saw both the stock and tip ends square with a miterbox saw or a table saw. If the saw has small teeth the wood will be cut so smooth there will be little or no need for additional smoothing. If any squaring or smoothing is to be done, be sure to use sandpaper wrapped around a stiff, flat surface such as a large file. This will keep the surfaces flat.

The tip may be attached in the classic right-angle style or at a more modern, racy angle. If you prefer the angle, be sure the angle cut on the stock and tip match perfectly so the grain of each piece of wood will run in a straight line. Otherwise the attachment will look cockeyed.

Though it has been demonstrated that a plain wood-to-wood attachment with the epoxy glues is sufficient to hold the forend tip in place, it is wise and well worth the little extra trouble to install a simple dowel joint. This gives added gluing area and adds considerable resistance to any pressures coming from the side. This is especially important with stocks which are bedded in such a way that there is upward pressure on the barrel at the tip of the stock.

The dowel installation is nothing more complicated than a couple of ¼-inch or ⅜-inch hard-maple dowels side by side and extending about an inch each way into the forend tip and the stock. It would be difficult indeed, without special rigging, to drill perfectly aligned holes which would allow a tight fit in both stock and forend tip and ensure perfectly matching surfaces. Fortunately, however, such perfect alignment isn't necessary or, for that matter, even desirable.

All you need to do is "eyeball" the holes in tip and stock, but make them oversize enough so there will be enough free play to allow the two surfaces to come together perfectly.

If you intend to add thin contrasting spacers of light-colored wood such as maple or holly, now is the time to get it ready, for the final act is coming up. Cut the spacer so the grain runs vertically, drill a couple of holes for the dowels, and you're ready to move on.

For the actual gluing operation, give the dowels a good coating of glue, put more glue into the holes, and spread a thick even layer onto the two mating surfaces. Be sure to get enough glue into the oversize holes to fill up the free space. If this is done correctly the dowels will be locked in place as tightly, or more so, than if the holes had been a perfect fit. Now push the tip on hard enough to squeeze out all the excess glue and bring the two surfaces to a flush fit.

Now comes the problem of how to keep the tip squeezed tightly against the stock until the glue dries. If you have a complete woodworking shop you probably have a set of large bench clamps. Fine—put everything in the clamp and draw it up tight. But what if you don't have a set of clamps? Don't worry—just use a great big rubber band. This means a bicycle inner tube. If you don't have one on hand, just stop by a bicycle-repair shop and they'll probably give you an old one. Just stretch the tube up over the tip and back around the butt. This puts on plenty of pressure.

After the glue dries all you need to do is work the tip down to the same lines as the stock, round off the tip to suit your taste, and the job is all over except for the finish. If you intend to use a gripcap which matches the forend tip, the installation is essentially the same, but this time there is no need for the dowels. Just be sure to get the two surfaces perfectly flat and smooth.

How to Fit a Forend Tip

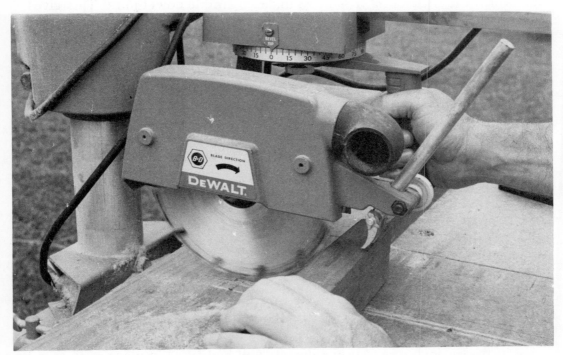

1   A radial-arm saw cuts a square edge on the block of ebony which will be used for the forend tip. Both the stock material and the forend-tip material must be cut extremely smoothly with a fine-toothed saw such as a miter saw, or some other type of saw which will make a smooth, straight cut. If you must cut the wood with a hand saw or other rough cutting tool, the wood can be smoothed up with a rasp or file. The forend tip should be perfectly flush and smooth with the stock.

2

Two dowel holes being drilled with an electric hand drill. The holes are drilled deliberately oversize to allow room for dowel alignment and for the blue mixture to flow well.

3

The hardwood dowels in place, with the forend tip, which has also been drilled.

4

Epoxy glue is poured into the dowel holes.

5

The dowels are inserted into the epoxy. Use plenty of glue so that all the recesses and mating surfaces will be well covered.

6

The forend tip is held firmly in place while the glue dries. The clamping arrangement here is simply an old bicycle inner tube, which applies powerful and even pressure.

7

An assortment of different forend tip arrangements. The forend tip at top has the racy 15° angle cut plus a wide spacer between the tip and stock. At center is a 45° angle tip without spacer, and at bottom is the classic right-angle fitting.

16/

Fitting a Curved Steel Buttplate

If there's anything that rattles my chain it's a beautifully finished rifle in a stock that has nothing over its rear end but a piece of cheap plastic.

Plastic buttplates are all right, I guess—but only on cheap guns, not on expensive or otherwise fine rifles and shotguns. Yet we have become so accustomed to seeing cheap plastic buttplates on all sorts of guns these days that we hardly give it a thought. At least, that is, until we run across a rifle with a gracefully curved, neatly checkered steel buttplate. Then the contrast between cheap plastic and crisp steel suddenly becomes sickeningly apparent. A curved steel buttplate doesn't dress up the butt end of a stock—it dresses up the whole rifle and lends quality to the total effect. In fact, without a decent buttplate, or recoil pad, whenever called for, the only effect is *blah!* As a matter of fact, the only thing that can make a stock with a plastic buttplate look worse is to slip a piece of white plastic between the buttplate and the wood. Now *that*, dear reader, should really make your skin crawl. If it doesn't now, it will as the years give you wisdom.

I'm not saying mind you, that a checkered steel buttplate is the ultimate form of good styling. A trapdoor buttplate, especially if it is nicely engraved, is better, and even better than that is a skeleton buttplate with the wood exposed in the center and nicely checkered. Occasionally one sees a fine English sporting arm with no buttplate at all. The bare wood at the rear looks pretty nice, especially if well checkered, as it usually is, but the whole idea is impractical.

At any rate, a plain checkered steel buttplate will get by in the finest circles provided it is properly (which means *perfectly*) fitted. It will probably come as a surprise to devotees of the plastic buttplate that steel ones are quite inexpensive and not at all difficult to fit.

The Classic Niedner steel plate, for example, sells for less than five dollars and can be fitted in about a hour's time. The Al Biesen steel buttplate is more expensive but is better made and better looking.

The tools you'll need for this project are a drill for the screw holes, a half-round wood rasp, a straight-edged chisel, and a small curved-edge chisel (gouge). In short, if you have enough tools to carry on even the simplest form of gunsmithing you can fit a buttplate. Actually, a pocketknife and nothing more will be sufficient.

Understandably, the buttplate is fitted before the stock is worked down to final shape. In fact the buttplate pretty well establishes the cross-section dimensions and proportions of the entire butt section. I personally prefer to fit the buttplate even before inletting the action. The plate protects the endgrain and corners against any accidental denting, splitting, or splintering during the inletting process.

The first step in fitting the buttplate is determining the length of pull and the degree of pitch that will be required for a properly fitting stock. If you are of about average size and aren't too particular about exact stock dimensions,

How to Fit and Attach a Curved Steel Buttplate

1
When a curved steel buttplate is fitted to a semi-finished stock, as most are, the first step is making a template of a stock shape. This is done simply by placing the stock, butt down, on a piece of stiff cardboard and tracing the cross section.

then the standard-length semi-inletted stock will be close enough. A Fajen Classic style stock with Niedner buttplate, for example, will measure about 13¾ inches for length of pull. Most shooters will find this length of pull about right.

Getting the proper pitch requires a bit more figuring. The "pitch" refers to the angle of the buttplate and, in simplest terms, is usually measured by standing a gun on its buttplate and the top of the action against a vertical surface such as a wall and measuring how far the muzzle extends from the wall. If the bore line is perfectly vertical when the gun is set squarely on its butt, it is said to have zero pitch. Zero pitch, by the way, is good for heavy recoiling rifles of the big magnum class. For light and medium calibers, however—any rifle on which you'd use a steel buttplate—a slight degree of pitch is desirable. It distributes the recoil well and seems to feel most comfortable. A stock that has positive pitch (that is, the toe of its buttplate extends farther out than the heel) wants to slip under your armpit when you shoot it and somehow doesn't look right either. As a general rule, "pitch" means negative pitch.

If you're still confused about this business of stock pitch—and I understand if you are—simply do the following. Lay the stock upside down on a level surface with the top of the forend pressed flat. Now, using a square or the 90° side of a drafting triangle, draw a vertical line across the butt at the point of

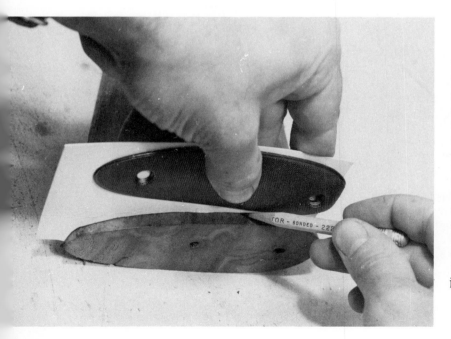

2

When the template is cut so that it fits closely to the shape of the stock, the next step is to trace the curve of the buttplate onto the stock. Hold the buttplate you are going to use against the template so that the template follows the curve. This way the right curve can be closely traced onto the stock. Getting this curve correct at the beginning saves a lot of headaches later. The excess wood is then cut away with a bandsaw, jig saw, coping saw, or rasp.

3

The inside surface of the buttplate is coated with spotting-in preparation. This can be a mixture of soot and oil, lamp soot, Prussian blue, or various other materials. The procedure for fitting a buttplate is similar to that for inletting a stock. You simply touch the blackened metal against the wood and then cut away the marks left by the spotting compound.

4

It's apparent where the buttplate has touched against the wood. At this point the work has progressed to the point where the fit is almost even.

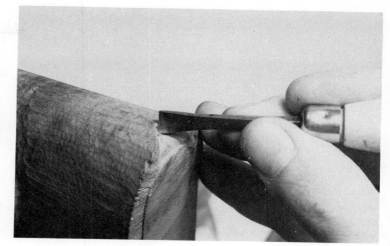

5
A small chisel is used to make tiny slicing cuts in the inletting at the extension of the buttplate.

proper length of pull. Since this line is at right angles to the top line of the stock and hence the bore line too, it represents zero pitch. With the stock on its side again, align the buttplate by "eyeball" alongside the line. Angle the plate so that when the upper curve (heel) is exactly on the line the lower tip (toe) is about ¼ inch *inside* (toward the muzzle) the line. This will come mighty close to being the proper pitch for the average man.

If you're pretty good at this eyeball alignment, go ahead and draw the inside curve of the buttplate on the stock. This will guide your first roughing cuts. If you don't trust your eyeball guessing or want to lay out a guideline that is nearly an exact duplicate of the plate's curve, try this technique. First stand the stock, butt down, on a piece of fairly stiff cardboard and trace half of the cross-section profile as shown in the illustration. Now cut out this outline so that you have a template which closely follows the curve of the stock. Now press the template to the inside curve of the buttplate so that it is bent to the same curve. Holding the buttplate and template in this position, fit the template over the butt of the stock and position it properly in regard to length of pull and degree of pitch. Now all you need to do is trace along the edge of the template and you've got an accurate guideline to follow.

A bandsaw, if you happen to have one, will remove unwanted wood quickly. Even a simple coping saw works fine here. Or, of course, you can simply file away with the curved side of a half-round wood rasp.

Once the stock is shaped so that it follows the curve of the buttplate, the job is well on its way to completion. The next step is cutting an undersize notch at the top (heel) of the butt for the projection at the top of the buttplate. This little inward curving extension at the top of the buttplate is the most

6
A detail of the final fitted butt-plate, before the stock has been worked down to the outline shape of the buttplate. Note the close fit where the upper extension fits into the wood.

troublesome thing about the whole job, but is also what makes a Niedner-style plate look so good.

With this top extension more or less fitted and the buttplate relatively close to its final position, you can go ahead and spot the screw holes and do the drilling. With the plate in position draw the screws up fairly snug and see how the plate lies and how much final fitting there is to be done.

If it is pretty close to a final fit, take it off and swab the inside surface with the spotting agent you use for inletting. The final fitting is a simple "spotting" process. Wherever the metal touches wood and makes a mark is where you cut. Just keep at it until the entire outer edge of the buttplate touches all the way around. The chisel is fine for this job, either as a slicing or as a scraping tool, but for the larger flat areas the rasp moves things along rather quickly.

Really top-flight buttplate fitting is done so that the wood fills the inside curvature of the shell-like plate completely. This is a lot of extra work but will impress the hell out of anyone who sees it. Speaking of impressing some-one, why not write your name and the date on the wood behind the plate.

Think of what a charge some gun collector will get when he takes it off two centuries from now. . . .

Now give all the endgrain several coats of stock finish or some good water-proofing agent. If you don't the wood might absorb water and swell so that the stock extends out past the edges of the buttplate every time it rains. Or, just as bad, dry out and shrink so that the plate is wider than the stock. The idea, you know, is to seal a stock so that no moisture gets in *or out!*

7
An overall view of the buttplate before the wood has been trimmed down to a flush fit.

8
The stock after working the wood down to the shape of the buttplate. A steel buttplate such as this adds a lot of class to a custom sporter. Be sure to apply a coat of stock finish to the wood under the buttplate. This will prevent it from drawing moisture and swelling.

17 / Making and Fitting a Skeleton Gripcap

In my opinion the most stylishly distinctive accessories that can be added to any gun stock are "skeleton" gripcaps and buttplates. They are seen so seldom that relatively few gun fanciers know what they are and even fewer have actually seen either or both.

Skeleton buttplates are most usually associated with high-grade custom rifles and shotguns and were fairly common on the better-grade Parker shotguns. The first skeleton buttplate I can remember seeing was on a CHE-grade 20-gauge Parker. I was only a sprig of a boy then and my desire for fine guns (or guns of *any* kind) outstripped my financial circumstances by a wide margin.

The 20-gauge Parker, long with another half-dozen or so higher-grade Parkers, were owned by a neighbor whom I considered, with good reason, to be the richest man in the world. I used to admire that beautiful little double by the hour. That tastefully engraved and perfectly fitted skeleton buttplate was, and still is, the symbol of the best in stockmaking—at least to my notion.

Perhaps the reason skeleton gripcaps and buttplates are so seldom seen is simply that most gunsmiths and stockmakers don't know how to make and fit them, and even those who do seldom find customers willing to pay for the work.

In truth, skeleton caps and plates aren't all that difficult to make or fit. Considerable care is required, however, and for some craftsmen, both amateurs and pros, this means a heavy time investment. For the do-it-yourself gunsmith, time is usually of no consequence, so mastering the art of making and fitting these accessories is an ideal project and well worth the effort.

Actually it doesn't really take all *that* long. The cap project shown on these pages was completed in one evening, including the time it took for the photography. A buttplate project could take the better part of a day, including checkering the exposed wood.

The skeleton gripcap shown here was made from the Biesen two-screw plain uncheckered steel gripcap. These are available from Al Biesen. Be sure to specify the *uncheckered*, two-screw model.

Though it is best to install the skeleton gripcap on a stock that is in the earlier stages of shaping, it is possible to fit one to a finished stock. This involves trimming the cap down to the shape of the existing grip and carefully plugging any screwholes which may be exposed in the exposed area. If the screwholes are tightly fitted with matching wood and the entire surface then checkered the repair will scarely be noticeable. I've seen a number of skeleton buttplates that have been fitted over butts that had deep holes, 1 inch or thereabouts, drilled in them for the sake of reducing weight. The holes had been neatly plugged and checkered over so that the work was all but invisible.

In this text, however, we will consider only working on unfinished stocks. Even so, the procedure will apply to altering finished stocks.

The first step is to scribe or otherwise mark the area to be removed during the skeletonizing process. This is best handled by coating the surface of the gripcap with machinists' layout blue. Easy-to-see marks can then be made on the blue surface with a scribe. The border of the gripcap should be about 3/16 or so in width, but this is largely a matter of personal taste. I've seen borders less than 1/8 in width, but these are considerably more difficult to work with.

If you have sophisticated shop equipment with which to mill out the center area of the gripcap, fine, go to it. But for those of us who are limited to only a few simple tools, a drill will do the trick. As shown in the illustrations, one simply drills a series of overlapping holes around the inside edge of the border until the center section falls out. This leaves a pretty jagged inside edge, but a little work with a narrow file gets this looking better in short order. A round chain-saw file or even a curved needle file is needed for getting into the rounded corners.

During the drilling and filing operations, be sure not to bend the cap or otherwise get it out of shape. The underside edge of these caps is nice and flat as they come and could be more difficult to fit if it gets bent out of shape.

The next step is to locate the gripcap on the stock and attach it with two screws. Locate the cap first, as you would a solid steel cap. With the cap in place, scribe the inside edge with a sharp, thin-bladed knife. Take care to cut straight down, and keep the outline as close to the edge of the metal as possible. In areas where it is impossible to maneuver the knife, just scribe the outline lightly with a small, sharp scribe.

Now remove the gripcap and deepen the marked outline. The rounded

How to Make and Fit a Skeleton Grip Cap

1

The first step in making a skeleton grip cap is skeletonizing an existing metal or plastic gripcap. Since the layout lines must be permanent it is necessary to scratch them onto the surface of the metal or, better yet, first coat the gripcap with layout blue. This will make it easier to do initial design work.

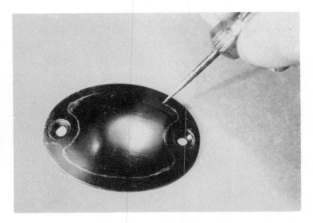

2

The "poor boy's" way of cutting out the center section is simply to drill a series of overlapping holes.

3

The skeletonizing job is very nearly finished with the center section roughed out.

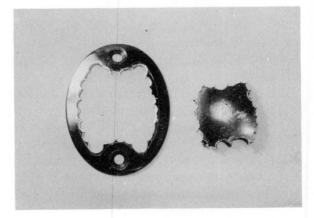

4

The next step is to smooth up the ragged inside surfaces with a file. Small needle files are handy for working in the close curves.

5

Moving on to the inletting, first locate the gripcap screws, then drill and fasten the gripcap where you want it. Next, trace the outline of the cutout into the stock with a fine-pointed, thin-bladed knife.

6

After tracing the cutout section, remove the gripcap and deepen the outline. A curved chisel is used to cut the outline to full depth.

7

The next step is relieving the outside edge of the grip area. This is easily done with a flat chisel. This is an easy job if the chisel is sharp, but a tough one if it's dull.

8

The gripcap has been fitted back onto the stock and the interior wood panel has been filed smooth. Now you are ready to go on with the rest of the stockwork.

9

The finished product. Sometimes the exposed wood is checkered, but in this case the grain was so beautiful that it was left plain.

corners can best be cut to full depth with curved chisels of the appropriate radius.

Though the cap is made of metal about $1/16$ inch or so thick, it is necessary to inlet the cap somewhat deeper than this in order to allow for the curved or "crowned" shape of the finished grip. This means that the cap will be inletted $1/8$ inch or more. Don't try to do all the inletting in one stage, however. It is better to do it in two or three stages in order to "get practice" for the final close fitting.

Actually, all the inletting involves is cutting the inside border edges, then slicing or shaving away the surrounding wood with a flat-blade chisel or knife. In fact, much of this wood can be worked down with a small fine-cut wood rasp. Of course it is necessary to keep this bottom surface flat so perfect metal-to-wood contact is maintained all around the edge of the cap. Any unsightly gaps are absolutely forbidden!

It is a pretty good idea to use some inletting black on the underside of the cap if any fitting difficulties arise. Just keep fitting and cutting until you get a perfect fit all around the edge.

When the fitting is completed and a fair amount of wood extends up through the center of the cap (about $1/16$ inch or slightly more), you can fit the two screws again and contour the "crown" with a smooth-cut rasp or file. Strive to give the wood approximately the same amount of curve or crown the gripcap originally had before you cut out the center section.

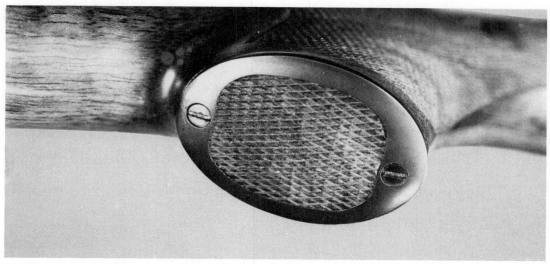

Another skeleton-gripcap design which is somewhat less difficult but nonetheless attractive. The checkered panel gives a very attractive effect.

After this is pretty well cut to shape, finish the job with fine sandpaper on a soft sanding block. During the final finishing sand the wood and metal together. This will give a perfectly flush surface between the two. The brightened metal can be reblued later.

The rest of the pistolgrip can be worked down flush with the outer edges of the cap now or whenever you get to it.

On the job shown on these pages the exposed wood in the center of the cap was finished only, then left plain because of the striking figure and color of the wood. Usually, however, this center section is checkered. This gives a very nice effect indeed. However, it is necessary in most cases to use extremely fine checkering for the best effect. This is usually twenty-six, twenty-eight, or even thirty-two lines to the inch.

Fitting a skeleton buttplate is basically the same process as described here, though the job is more difficult. When you try this skeleton gripcap project, the chances are you'll be so pleased with the results that you'll probably want to do a buttplate sooner or later.

But that's the way gunsmithing is—once the bug bites you've got to keep scratching. . . .

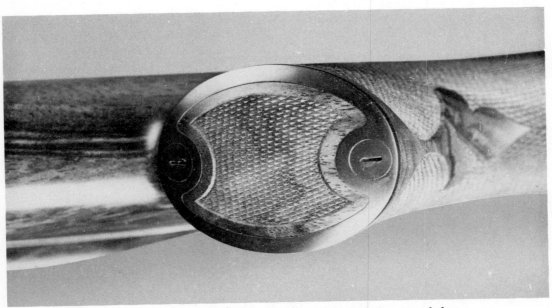

Another skeleton design with a neat border between the checkered area and the skeletonized grip. This is somewhat more difficult but extremely stylish.

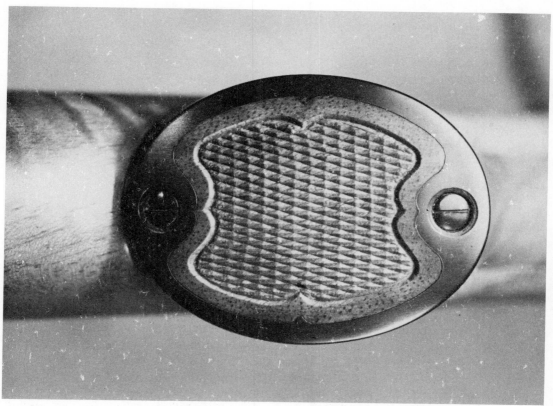

An elaborate and beautiful skeleton gripcap made and fitted by ace stockmaker
Bob Winter. This is magnificent workmanship.

18/

Altering Stocks for Better Fit and Feel

"Be sure your stock fits properly." That's the advice you'll get at the English shooting schools, from wingshooting coaches and from the skeet and trap champions. Yet the very real fact of the matter is that far too many shooters go afield or even enter expensive shooting competitions with a scattergun so grossly misstocked that they are losers before the shooting begins. The tragedy is that many people are suffering from badly fitted stocks without even being aware of it.

The stocks which come on most shotguns are designed for a "man of average build." Though there is no such thing as an "average man," most stocks fit at least reasonably well. This is because most people do a pretty good job of *fitting themselves* to the stock. This is a fundamental mistake. The stock should fit the man, rather than vice versa, and other mistakes will surely follow.

Fortunately, many of these fitting problems can be corrected at home with a minimum of tools and a minimum of effort. All it takes is a knowledge of where and how much to cut plus the resolve to lay a cutting tool to that bright, sleek stock you're so proud of. Frequently the former is less difficult than the latter. But if fear of marring that beautiful stock is all that stands in your way, then please be assured that well-done modifications are usually invisible—only the results are noticeable.

Some folks, especially competitive trap and skeet shooters, don't give a whit what their stocks look like as long as they fit right. This is why you'll see so many stocks at the big tournaments that have been whittled down, taped up, sawed off, and nailed down. These guys are interested in results, not looks. Actually, a little extra time and effort is all that's required for getting a "customized" stock looking like new again, so there is no need for worrying about ruining the looks of a stock for life. At any rate, which is more important — looks or results?

One of the most common problems, and one of the easiest to correct, is a stock that's too short. Traditionally, the length of a shotgun stock is tested by grasping the shotgun's grip with the trigger finger on the trigger and laying the butt along the inside of the arm.

Whichever is necessary, lengthening or shortening, the stock will probably have to be sawed off somewhat. The simplest and most natural-looking lengthening technique is simply to add a recoil pad. This doesn't mean, however, that all you need to do is take the buttplate off and screw on a recoil pad. What may at first seem to be a poorly fitted stock of gross proportions may be corrected by the addition of ¼ inch or less. Thus it is wise to loosen the buttplate screws and add cardboard shims until the fit feels better and your shooting improves. Only then should you attach the recoil pad. But since the additional length required will, in all probability, not equal the thickness of the pad, the stock must be cut off to make things come out right.

So what if the stock already has a recoil pad? Recoil pads come in a variety of thicknesses, so just shop around until you find one thick enough to bring your stock up to the required length. Stocks that are too long tend to feel as though they are much too long. Thus one may be inclined to whack off an inch or so. Actually, the removal of a fraction of an inch may do the trick, so it is best to slice off only about ⅛ inch at a time. Keep cutting and trying until it feels — and shoots — right.

This brings us to the problem of just how to go about sawing a gunstock. Using a common handsaw is asking for trouble. The teeth tend to rip and tear the edges of the cut and give the job a ragged appearance. Also, it is very difficult to make a perfectly straight cut with a handsaw. Instead, use a miterbox saw, a table saw with a smooth-cut blade, or a bandsaw with a fence guide. If you don't have any of these, go to someone who has. As added protection against splintering at the edges, wrap a band of tape (Scotch tape or masking tape) where the cut will be made. You may as well leave the tape on until the recoil pad or buttplate has been worked down to a flush fit. It will help protect the stock from a bad stroke with rasp or sandpaper.

Lowering or thinning the comb can have a dramatic effect on your shooting but requires only a few simple tools and little effort. A shooter with a full face, for example, may have difficulty in properly lining up on the barrel and as a result will tend to shoot to the left of the target (if he is right-handed). A comb that is too high will cause overshooting. Both of these situations can be corrected with a rasp and a bit of sandpaper.

Essentially the technique is a cut-and-try operation: Just shave away a bit of wood and try it for fit. Here again a little cutting goes a long way, so make haste slowly. Rather than cut out a recess just where your face fits, take long cuts which run nearly the length of the stock. This way the alteration will blend into the lines of the stock and be unnoticeable if not altogether invisible. Similarly, blend in the lower and upper borders of the alteration into the natural curve of the stock.

Steps in Altering a Stock

1 This rather full-faced shooter has trouble lining his eye up with the barrel. This will cause his shots to be consistently to the left. Proper eye and barrel alignment can be determined by standing in front of the gun (with the gun unloaded, of course, and the action open), sighting down the barrel toward shooter's eye.

2

The first step in removing excess stock wood is determining how much wood is to be removed and where. A grease pencil is used to mark out the area which needs to be cut away.

3

A Stanley Surform shaper is used to slice away a tiny amount of wood along the comb of the stock. It is best if you can do this with the owner of the gun present so you can cut a small amount and then let him try the gun for fit and feel.

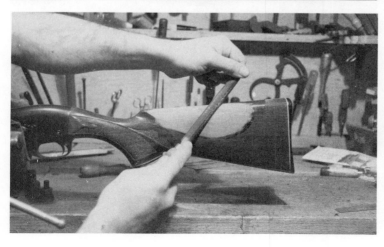

4

After removing the necessary amount of wood, smooth up the cut with a fine-cut rasp or file.

5

The next step is sanding the cut area and blending it into the finish. By tapering, or "feathering," the edges of the cut, you can get the new finish to blend very nicely with the original finish.

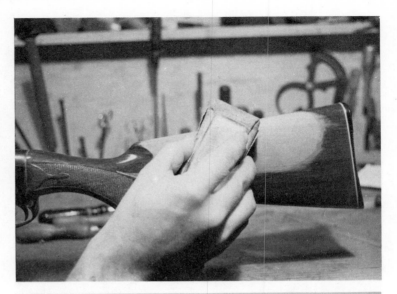

6

A top view of the Model 1100 Remington stock shown in these pictures, showing how the comb has been slightly "dished" to allow the shooter's face to line up more precisely with the rib.

7

A commercial stock finish is rubbed into the smoothly sanded wood. Apply several coats of finish so that the remodeled portion blends smoothly with the original finish. Some staining may be necessary in order to match the original color.

8 Our full-faced friend is able to line his eye precisely over the rib after the modification. Such stock alterations can mean a tremendous improvement in trap or skeet scores or game bags.

For fast wood removal such as hacking off a comb, use a rough-cut rasp, but switch to a fine-cut rasp or even a metal file for smoothing up the surface. Next, being sure to use a sanding block, slick up the work with 220-grit and then 320-grit sandpaper. Always work with the grain, and be careful not to scratch up the stock finish around the reworked area.

As most factory stocks are stained, you'll have a bit of staining to do to get a perfect color match with the rest of the stock. One trick that works well is to use a combination filler and stain such as produced by Birchwood-Casey. If the stain is too light for a color match, try blending in a small amount of darker stain. Liquid shoe polish will do a surprisingly good job if you don't have a darker wood stain handy. Just mix in a drop at a time until the color tone is right.

Though it is a little messy, I prefer to use my fingers to work in the filler/stain on these small areas. This way the depth of color is easier to control, especially around the border areas. Lay the stain on a little richer than the rest of the stock, then when it dries rub it out with a piece of steel wool until the color blends perfectly.

Now all you have to do is put on some finish and the job is completed. To match the new plastic type finishes which come on many factory stocks, use a polyurethane. You can get it in both spray-on and brush-on form. The spray-on types such as marketed by Birchwood-Casey are mighty handy and make it easy to blend the finish with the rest of the stock. For other stocks either a lacquer or the rub-on linseed-oil-type finishes may be best. Finally give the *entire* stock a brisk rubdown with a fine stock-polishing compound. The stock will look as good as new, but more important, the better fit will assure you better scores in the field and at the traps.

The comb of a trap stock is worked down slightly with a rasp. Sometimes these modifications are made at the trap field so the shooter can shoot a bit, later the stock a bit, then shoot and try a bit more.

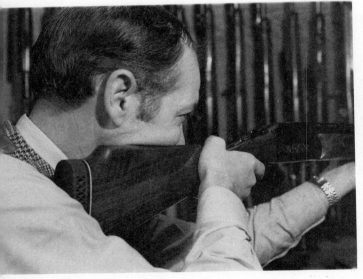

When altering a stock for better fit, you must achieve the desired effect. If too much wood is removed you are no better off, possibly worse, than at the beginning. Therefore, remove wood cautiously and in very small amounts. An alteration of ⅛-inch can cause a significant change in pattern placement. After the comb on this trap gun was worked down only slightly, the shooter's eye is positioned exactly where he wants it.

19 / How to Glass-Bed a Rifle for Better Accuracy

When glass bedding, the concept of bedding a rifle in a plastic or epoxy compound reinforced with glass or metal particles, came on the shooting scene some years back, it was hailed as the final solution to all shooter's woes. After nearly three decades of widespread use we've had ample opportunity to discover that it does not cure all shooting ills. However, the effect of so-called glass bedding on custom gunsmithing, especially in the various areas of target shooting, has been near-revolutionary. "Shifting in the stock," that old bugaboo that hounded bolt-action rifles, especially target jobs, for many years has virtually ceased to be a problem—or at least has caused target shooters to seek other excuses for poor scores.

There is no question that glass bedding adds strength and stiffness to a wooden stock, holds an action more rigidly than bedding in wood alone, and holds up better under both use and abuse. In my rack, for example, there are six glass-bedded big-bore target rifles. These rifles perform reliably month after month in both damp and dry weather. Before glass bedding was available I was forever tinkering with my target rifles—putting shims under the action and "adjusting the bedding" one way or another in the hopes of getting through a tournament without the "bedding going sour." This was a very common phrase in those days.

For hunting rifles, glass bedding has proved effective for stabilizing actions and barrels and thus preventing change of zero due to change of climate and humidity or the action shifting about during travel. Also, the strength of glass bedding has proved adequate, in most cases, for holding big-recoil rifles which tend to batter and pound wood stocks until they splinter and crack.

Among shooting arms, varmint rifles have probably received the greatest blessing of all from glass bedding. Where pinpoint accuracy is a criterion, the solid, nonmoving action bedding is all-important. In fact, glass bedding of one brand or another has become virtually synonymous with fine accuracy. If you doubt this for an instant, just visit a bench-rest tournament for sporter, light-varmint, or heavy-varmint bench-rest rifles and see how many guns you can find *without* some sort of bedding compound. In fact, the most accurate rifles being produced by Remington, their 40-XBR, and by Winchester, their Model 70 Military Match, are glass-bedded at the factory.

Despite the remarkable qualities of these various bedding compounds there are still quite a few fanciers of fine guns and admirers of skillful craftsmanship who tend to turn up their noses at anything but super-close hand bedding. Frankly, I'm one of them. But I do believe that the use of glass bedding can be consistent with fine handwork. An example of this is the target rifles I mentioned earlier. Each of these is completely glass-bedded, but there is no way anyone could guess this without removing the actions from the stocks. From the outside, the wood joins the metal closely and tightly. It *looks* like very fine handwork — and, in fact, it is. This trick was accomplished by first inletting the barreled action into the stock very closely by the traditional manner and then undercutting the inletted recesses and adding the bedding compound. This is the best of all possible worlds, the accuracy of glass bedding and the soul-satisfying "growed around the metal" closeness of fine hand inletting.

Of course there are always those who insist that it doesn't matter what a gun looks like as long as it shoots good. I've long suspected that this is the philosophy only of those who lack the skill, knowledge, or inclination to do a good job. The suspicions are largely confirmed by my observations that rifles that don't look so good usually don't shoot so good either.

My contention is that fiberglass bedding components are not to be looked upon as a substitute for careful handwork but, rather, as an adjunct to it. To better illustrate what I mean, let's see how glass bedding was used to correct a bedding problem in my .224 Clark long-range varmint rifle.

Initially the rifle had been closely fitted by hand, and accuracy had been excellent. After a few months, however, group size kept getting bigger and bigger and was characterized by a stringing that indicated bedding problems. I took the stock off and found that the forend had warped upward and to the right. The warping was so extreme, in fact, that it took considerable effort to force the barreled action back into the inletting. As long as the barreled action was in the stock and the action screws were pulled tight, the forend was forced back to its original straightness. But this put a lot of uneven pressure on the barrel and the result was poor accuracy.

The obvious corrective action to take in this case was to "free-float" the barrel. By scraping out the barrel channel enough of the offending wood was removed to eliminate all pressure on the barrel. Accuracy was restored but the warping had been so extensive that nearly ⅛ inch had been removed from the channel before the barrel was free of contact. Of course, having cut this much wood from one side of the channel I had to cut an equal amount from the other side to get things evened up and looking right. Fortunately, the stock has a wide beavertail forend, so there was plenty of wood to cut on. Since the rifle now shot straight I didn't worry too much about the ugly gap between stock and barrel.

Within a month or so I noticed that the forend was continuing to warp. In fact, the wood had moved almost an ⅛ inch and was about to come in hard contact with the barrel again. This is where glass bedding became the solution, it just might help you in a similar situation.

If you are making a stock from either a semi-inletted blank or a solid block of wood and intend to glass-bed the action or complete barreled action, the first step is to inlet the metal into the wood as closely as possible. This, I realize, shatters your illusions about the labor-saving advantages of using a bedding compound. It really doesn't take that much longer anyway, and in the long run you'll sure be glad you went to the extra effort.

When the barreled action is fully inletted, as close as you can manage, begin clearing out room for the bedding material by enlarging the inletted recess *below* the upper edge. I find it's best to leave the top ⅛ inch or so as is so the wood will remain in close union with the barrel and action.

If you intend to use the bedding compound only to reinforce the area behind the recoil lug, don't make the common mistake of just cutting out some of the wood immediately behind the lug and replacing it with compound. This does very little good, because the recoil is still distributed over a very small area. The proper technique is to enlarge the inletting all around the front receiver ring and back along the sides of the action as well as behind the lug. This way the force of recoil is transferred to a large mass of compound which in turn is firmly attached to the stock over a wide area. Even the wood in *front* of the lug gets to lend a hand in absorbing the recoil!

When "hogging out" the wood to make room for the compound, be sure to leave a couple of strips of wood supports under the action flats and behind the recoil lug. These will hold the action in proper position while the bedding compound is hardening. If you don't, the whole works will sink too deep into the stock and you'll have to do it all over again.

Just how much wood you clear away for the compound depends largely on how thick the sides are. With thick target stocks you may be able to clear out ³⁄₁₆ inch or so around the sides and even more under the action and around the recoil lug. With slim sporter stocks try to get about ⅛ inch around the front ring and about ¹⁄₁₆ inch along the sides. Take out a bit around the recoil lug.

This "hidden bedding" technique, by the way, takes some special planning and preparation of escape routes for the excess compound. The close contact of wood and metal prevents the excess compound from squeezing out along the top of the inletting. This problem is easily solved by cutting a small groove or two from the recoil-lug mortise to the magazine well. This bleeds off the excess compound as the action screws are pulled up tight and allows the receiver to bottom properly. As a general rule, there is no problem anyway, because the inletting is undercut enough to allow an escape route either through the magazine or up the barrel channel. If the barrel is to be glass-bedded too, just allow enough clearance under the barrel at the tip for the excess to squeeze out.

Glass-bedding a finished stock takes care, because you don't want to mess up the outside. But the procedure is essentially the same. By using this technique with factory stocks it is possible to do a complete glass-bedding job without altering the outside appearance in any way. We've all seen glass-bedding jobs "committed" on factory rifles where wood was axed out of the inletting, thus leaving a wide, irregular band of compound showing between wood and metal at the top edge. This is not only unsightly but considerably lowers the value of the gun.

Of course there are times when the compound cannot be hidden. A case in point is my .224 Clark varmint rifle. Since the barrel channel had been opened up to float the barrel, a fairly wide gap already existed. If you're wondering, with good cause, what benefit there would be in glass-bedding a free floating barrel, it was to help stiffen the forend and, I hoped, arrest the warping. The bedding compound was extended from behind the receiver ring all the way out the barrel channel. Here's how I went about it.

Since the barrel channel was already oversize, there wasn't any need for additional enlargement. However, I did rough up the wood a bit by wiggling a curved chisel back and forth up and down the channel. Roughing up the wood this way makes a better gripping surface for the compound and thus ensures a more positive bond. The action inletting was opened up about 1/8 inch or so around the front ring, and the barrel channel was deepened even more for about an inch and a half in front of the receiver. Even when a barrel is to be free-floated, I like some solid support ahead of the receiver for the first inch or two. (This support helps reduce stressing of the action.) Here again the wood was roughly cut so as to ensure a good bond.

Also, in order to make sure the excess compound had an "escape route" a groove was cut across the "floor"—the flat area just behind the recoil lug mortise. This allowed the excess material to flow out into the magazine well.

Since bedding resins can play mortal hell with a nicely finished stock, I put a layer of masking tape all around the forend and everywhere else I thought it

How to Glass-Bed a Rifle

1

One of the main concerns, and therefore the first step in glass-bedding a bolt-action rifle into a stock, is properly preparing the recoil-lug area. Poor accuracy is frequently caused by a poorly fitting lug which shifts in the stock as the rifle recoils. Therefore the recoil lug must be cut back so that a considerable amount of glass will fit immediately behind the lug. The sides of the recoil-lug cut should also be cut away so that there is reinforcement in the entire area.

2

A small flat-bladed chisel is used to scoop away the wood which fits immediately under the receiver behind the recoil lug. Cut away a fair amount of wood here, but leave some supporting edges on either side so that the stock will not sink too deep into the fiberglass material while it is in a soft form. Do not bother to make the cut smooth, because the fiberglass resin will adhere more tightly to rough cuts.

3

The pointer indicates one of the supporting ridges left to hold the receiver at the proper position while the fiberglass resin hardens. A small supporting member can be seen on both sides. Note how the wood has been scooped away in a very rough manner so as to allow maximum adhesion between the fiberglass resin and the wood.

4

The barrel channel is enlarged with a scraping tool. As in the receiver area, do not bother to make the barrel channel cuts particularly smooth.

5

A wax release agent brushed onto the surface of the metal. It is essential that all the metal parts receive a very thorough coat of release agent so that the barreled action can be removed when the fiberglass compound hardens. Epoxies are powerful glues, and if a release agent is not used the metal parts will be permanently bonded into the stock. Take care to see that the screw threads, etc., are well protected with release agent.

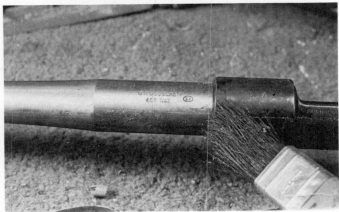

6

In order for any fiberglass-epoxy compound to be effective it must be prepared in a very precise manner. Instructions that come with the fiberglass compounds are very precise and must be followed to the letter.

7

The wood is coated with a thin layer of epoxy before adding the fiberglass compound. A thin coat of pure epoxy, without the fiberglass floc, helps ensure better adhesion of the fiberglass to the stock. After this step is completed, mix the fiberglass floc into the epoxy compound until it reaches the right consistency, then spread it throughout the areas that are to be glass-bedded.

8

When the metal parts are fitted into the stock and the screws are tightened up, a good bit of excess bedding compound will be squeezed out along the sides. Wipe away some of this immediately if it becomes too messy. After the compound has hardened to a rubberlike consistency it can be trimmed off with a sharp knife as shown here. It is essential that the barreled action not be removed at this time.

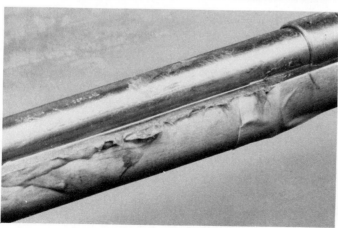

9

The stock after the excess squeezed-out compound has been trimmed away. Note that the stock has been covered with a layer of masking tape. This is essential to protect the finish of already completed stocks. When semi-finished stocks are glass-bedded this is no problem.

10 A small straight-edged chisel is used to trim the fiberglass material close to the metal. This rifle is a .458 Winchester Magnum. The fiberglass will help ensure that the heavy recoil does not split the stock. The inletting on this rifle was prepared so that the fiberglass compound was actually under the stock line and therefore almost invisible. Note that the wood seems to go right up to the metal even though the action is actually fiberglassed. This is the best possible fiberglassed technique.

might be needed. Also, I layered strips of tape on the barrel to a thickness of about 1/32 inch. This is a good technique for free-floating barrel in glass bedding. After the bedding hardens, the tape is peeled off and you have a neat, uniform space between the stock and the barrel. For big-bore target rifles, however, it is better to have a gap of about 1/16 inch. This allows the air to circulate more freely and cool the barrel more efficiently.

The bedding compound used was Brownell's Acraglass, but instead of using the release agent that comes with the kit I just brushed on a coat of paste-type floor wax. This is easier and faster to use than anything else I've tried and works fine.

It is important to get a coat of release agent on the guard screws, guard assembly, magazine box, in all the screw holes, and even inside the action, especially in the locking-lug wells. This latter is necessary because some of the compound will probably squeeze up through the front guard-screw hole and get in the action.

Always mix the bedding compound *according to instructions* and stir thoroughly. But don't whip! The whipping fills the compound with tiny air bubbles. When it hardens it will have a honeycomb structure and not be nearly so strong as it could be. Stir it gently instead. When the resin and hardening agent are thoroughly blended, but before the fiberglass is added, smear a light coat on the inletted surfaces to be glass-bedded. The thin resin matrix will seep into the wood and ensure a better bond. Now add the floc and stir it well. I prefer to add the floc a bit at a time. This way I can be sure that it is properly mixed, and I can also work the blend up to the desired consistency with less likelihood of getting it too thick. If the compound is used too thick (meaning too much fiberglass floc) it will not be as strong, and there will be white spots where the resin squeezes out of the floc when the action is held in the stock under pressure. On the other hand, a compound that is mixed too thin is hard to work with and runs too much. A mix that is the thickness of light grease is about right.

Completely fill all recesses such as the recoil-lug mortise and other nooks and corners with bedding compound. Even though much of this will be displaced when you drop the action in, it is good insurance against voids or open spots in the bedding when it hardens. Keep an eye on the escape routes. When the action is placed in the compound and the guard screws are pulled up tight, quite a bit of compound should squirt out. If it doesn't, it means that you aren't using enough compound or possibly that the escape routes aren't working and that the compound is trapped with no place to go. In this latter event the action simply won't go all the way down.

When the bedding has set firm, usually after a few hours, remove the barreled action and see if everything went right. This is a good time to trim out excess bedding at the magazine and other places where it shouldn't be. At this stage, the bedding cuts like soft plastic and is a lot easier to work with than after it has had a couple of days to set up hard. If there are any voids that need filling, this is as good a time as any to do it. Filling the smaller voids really isn't necessary unless you just want a nice neat-looking job. If you do any filling it is essential that there be some means of venting off the excess material. Otherwise the excess will bleed out where it shouldn't and pretty well get the whole works out of kilter.

Whether you repair any voids or not it is important that the barreled action be given another coat of release agent and put back in the stock for a day or so while the compound cures and reaches its final hardness.

Occasionally a barreled action will stick tightly in the stock and require considerable effort to remove. I've even heard of stocks that had to be chopped away from the metal with a hatchet. If a solid whack or two on the underside of the barrel doesn't shake it loose, don't panic. Just put the whole works in the deep-freeze for an hour or two. After this treatment the metal will virtually fall out.

Another trick worth knowing is that some of the compound should be cut out of the recoil-lug mortise so that there is some clearance below and in front on the lug. This has been found to improve accuracy — sometimes to a considerable degree — but this is supposed to be a secret, so don't tell anyone that I told you. . . .

III

Stock Decorations — The Stylish Extras

20 / Beginning Checkering

The construction of a gunstock can be divided into three major phases: (1) inletting and shaping, (2) applying the finish, and (3) checkering. A great number of amateur craftsmen have demonstrated considerable skill at the first two phases, even on their first attempt, but generally do not fare so well at checkering or, as is usually the case, do not even have a go at checkering their stocks. Most beginners hesitate to tackle a checkering job, and, quite frankly, there is good reason for such trepidation.

It would be unwise and unfair to state that checkering is a simple task which can be mastered in a few moments. However, it would be equally unwise and unfair to state that checkering is a difficult skill which can be mastered by only a few. Actually, checkering is a skill which can be mastered by almost anyone who is willing to take the time and effort required to learn the fundamentals. For some this learning period may be longer than a single evening of practicing on a block of wood. For others it may require a week of evenings before enough confidence is gained to start checkering on a valuable stock.

Regardless of how long it takes to develop that certain "feel" for the checkering tool there is little doubt that it is one of the most useful—and profitable—"basement skills" one can learn. Few amateur (or professional) gunsmithing skills will attract as much admiration as good hand checkering. In this rush, rush age we're living in it seems that fewer and fewer people are willing to take up checkering. But this makes it all the better for those of us who do take the time to learn the checkerer's art. The amateur can thus be even more proud of the stocks he has checkered himself, and if he does a bit of checkering on a professional basis he can always pick up plenty of profitable work. *What's more, it costs very little to get started!*

To get started checkering all you need is a single-line V-cutter, a double-line spacing cutter, a border cutter, and a thin, flexible straightedge such as a plastic ruler. Later, as you become more advanced, you may add other tools, but for now let's just stick with the basic tools listed above.

Checkering is really just rows of V-shaped grooves cut closely enough together so that the tops of the ridges come to a point. The trick is to get the grooves evenly spaced and of a uniform depth. With this in mind, let's take a step-by-step look at the checkering process.

Using the single-line V-cutter, a single, straight line is cut across the area to be checkered. Usually the area is somewhat curved, such as on the forend or grip of the stock, but following the curve and still keeping the line straight is no trouble with the flexible straightedge. The groove should be about $1/32$ inch deep. Another groove is then cut which angles across the first groove. (The correct angle will be discussed later.) These two grooves form the *master lines* which establish the directions of the grooves for the entire panel. The master lines are now used as a guide for cutting more grooves. This is done by tracing the master groove with the spacing cutter. One edge of the cutter follows the groove, while the other cuts a new groove. The spacing tool is then stepped over a notch, and another, then another, groove is cut.

These grooves are not to be cut full-depth but only deep enough to guide the spacing cutter for the next cut. After all the grooves have been cut in one direction, you switch over to the other master line and cut all the crossing grooves. This forms the outline of the diamonds but does not, of course, bring them to a sharp point. The "skill" to be acquired with the groove-spacing cutter is the "feel" which allows the tool to stay in the proper groove and thus keeps the lines equally spaced. Beginners have a tendency to try to guide the spacing cutter rather than let it guide itself. As a result, lines become unequally spaced or begin to curve noticeably. With a bit of practice, however, you'll learn to let the tool do all the guiding.

The actual cutting action is a gentle back-and-forth sawing motion. Don't bear down too hard, and don't try to cut too fast. Some tools cut only on the forward stroke, and some cut coming and going. After you have become more proficient in the basic checkering skills, you'll want to try two or three different tools and select the one which seems best to suit your personal technique.

With all the spacing lines cut, it is time to pick up the single-line V-tool and cut the grooves to full depth. The cutting motion is the same as with the spacing tool. Only one line is cut at a time. Here again you should strive for an even depth of cut, but the grooves are *not* to be cut to full depth. About a third of the final depth is about right. After going over the entire panel, start over and take the grooves down another third. On the final pass, the diamonds will be brought to sharp, even points. For an extra-nice-looking job, another once-over-lightly will trim up what few diamonds aren't perfect. A good checkering job is one in which straight rows of grooves, each diamond is sharply peaked, and there are no run overs at the edge of the pattern.

These run overs at the edge of the pattern are caused when the cutting tool "jumps" the edge line and can be cured only by slowing down your stroke as you near the end of the groove and also by developing good tool control. This will come with practice. Small nicks around the edge will be hidden by the border cutter. In fact, the principal use of the border is just to cover up run

How to Begin Checkering

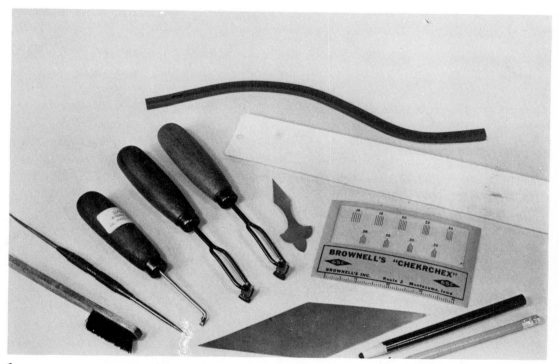

1 With these few checkering tools and accessories one can do everything from beginning checkering to the most sophisticated designs. The three basic tools shown are two Brownell's fill-view handles and a Brownell's short-angle tool. The Brownell's full-view tool utilizes replaceable blades so that the same handles can be used for all checkering widths as well as fine and coarse V-cutting tools. Also shown is a flexible "straightedge," a straightedge made from a length of venetian-blind material, a plastic "Chekr chex" sold by Brownell's, a 3½-to-1-ratio angle guide, a scribe, brush, a grease pencil, and a pencil.

2

The elementary checkering process is demonstrated on a piece of plain wood. Practicing on scrap wood such as this is a good way to get the feel of your checkering tools. The first step: scribe a straight master line, using a straightedge as a guide.

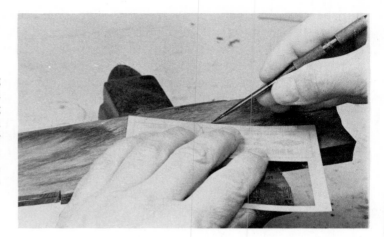

3

The next step is to scribe the intersecting master lines, using the angle guide to determine the proper angle. Of course you can use any size and shape diamond you like, but 3-to-1 or 3½-to-1 usually is about best.

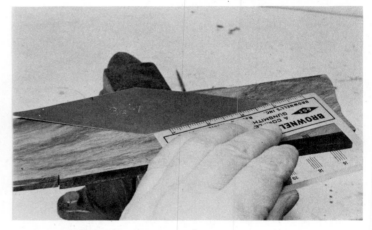

4

After the two master lines have been scribed, they are cut a bit deeper with the V-tool, also called the single-line cutter.

5

The spacing cutter doing the spacing work. These lines are not cut to full depth but only deep enough so that the tool can "feel" the previously cut line. Most spacing tools cut two lines at a time, but they are available with three and even four spacing lines. For right-handed workmen the spacing usually proceeds from right to left and vice versa for left-handed workers.

6

After the intersecting spacing lines have been completed, the lines are then deepened one by one with the V-tool. Do not try to cut the groove to full depth with one pass. Use two or three passes, cutting progressively deeper each time.

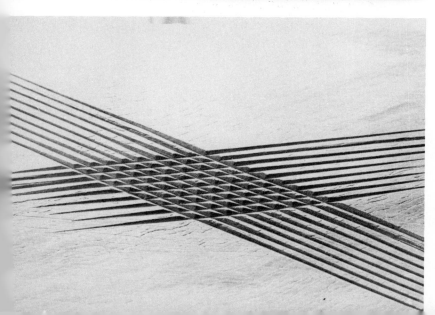

7

This is what your practice checkering should look like. Strive for even spacing, keep the lines straight, and deepen the lines with the single-line cutter until each diamond is uniformly sharp and perfectly shaped.

overs. This is why highly skilled stockmakers delight in showing off their borderless checkering.

This brings us to the matter of laying out the checkering pattern at grip and forend. Beginners should stick to simple "point" patterns until enough skill and confidence is gained to try the more complex designs. The best way for beginners to lay out a pattern is by using cardboard patterns traced from checkered stocks. The outline is lightly scribed or cut with the single-line cutter. The single-line cutter will follow gently curving outlines such as at the grip, but for sharply curving lines on the more complex patterns a small V-chisel or veining tool will be needed.

Brownell's offers a variety of full-size decals of checkering patterns which are applied directly to the stock. These decals eliminate the layout problems and considerably speed up the overall operation.

Before beginning on a valuable gunstock, do a bit of practicing on a discarded stock or on a plain piece of walnut or maple. Mistakes made and lessons learned here will ensure a better job on your first for-real effort. Also, this is a good place to practice laying out the master lines. The angle of the two crossing lines should be such that the finished diamonds will be about three to three and a half times as long as they are wide. A simple guide for laying out the master lines can be made by cutting a cardboard of thin plastic template to these dimensions. Make the template about 3 inches long.

When the checkering is complete, give the pattern a good scrubbing with a toothbrush. This clears out the bits of chips and wood fuzz and pretty well polishes up the work. Now brush it in a bit of stock finish, and the job is done except for running out to the clubhouse to show off your newly found skill.

21/

Checkering a Target-Rifle Stock for Better Control

The weekend of the 1968 National Long Range Championships may well go down in history as the hottest ever recorded in the vicinity of Oak Ridge, Tennessee. Sweat flowed so freely that gripping a rifle's pistolgrip was not unlike squeezing a wet bar of soap. My rifle, like the trophies which I eagerly sought, just seemed to slip out of my grasp, and I expect the same sensation was experienced by quite a few of my fellow competitors. A checkered grip, I decided, was the only answer.

Of the dozens of dozens of magnificent target rifles which graced the firing line, the great majority were equipped with fine custom stocks. Yet only a handful bore any sort of checkering. Doubtlessly the reason for this was that very few shooters are willing to tackle the checkering operation. To be sure, the checkering of gunstocks is an exacting task and more than a few amateur craftsmen have come to grief when first taking checkering tool in hand.

The type of checkering described in this article, however, is far less exacting. The checkering on the grip of a target rifle, on the other hand, is rather coarse for best effect and need follow no line other than the outline of the hand. As function, not appearance, is the only consideration, there is no need to worry if the job is less than perfect.

To do a first-class checkering job on your target rifle, all you'll need is a checkering tool, a V-chisel, and a grease pencil.

Begin work by placing the firing hand on the grip in the normal manner. Trace around the contacting areas with the grease pencil. This, of course, will result in a rather irregular outline but is, nonetheless, the basic pattern. Dress up and simplify the pattern by converting the irregular lines into more appealing border lines which complement the design of the stock.

Using the V-chisel, cut the border into the wood about ¹/₁₆ inch deep. This will form the permanent edge of the checkering pattern and should be carefully done. Just make sure the chisel is razor-sharp, and take your time. For the beginner, cutting such lines is more difficult than it may appear, and this alone is good reason for keeping the design simple.

One cannot just pick up the tool and start cutting. A bit of preliminary "figgerin' out" is required if there is to be any system to the pattern. Thus two intersecting master lines are cut to indicate the direction of the other grooves. These master lines will determine the proportions of the diamonds as well as their directional arrangement.

The arrangement of checkering on sporting guns is usually such that the points of the diamonds tend to point along the line of the grip and forend. For a maximum nonslip effect on the grip of a target rifle, the diamonds should run vertically. This looks strange at first, but the "grab" of such checkering is terrific.

For a checkering pattern which continues around and under the grip, the master lines must be laid out in the center of the forward underside of the grip. If the master lines were begun on either side, the curvatures of the stock

Checkering the Grip of Target Rifle Stock

1
The only tools you'll need to complete this project: a grease marking pencil, a brush to clean out the checkering, a veining tool to cut out the outline, and a checkering tool. The Brownell's checkering tool shown has replaceable cutting heads.

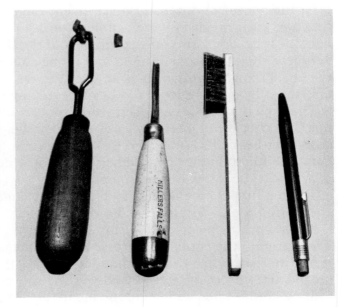

might cause the angle of the lines to shift considerably by the time you checkered around to the other side. Scribe the master lines lightly into the wood, using a flexible straightedge as a guide. The angles of the master lines should be such as to result in diamonds which are about three times as long as they are wide. Too, for the best nonslip grip, use a checkering tool, which spaces the grooves about sixteen to eighteen to the inch. With the border and master lines in place, all that remains to do is fill in the space with checkering.

Checkering is nothing more than cutting a series of straight, parallel V-shaped grooves from one side of the pattern to the other. A second series of grooves, angled to cross the first series, forms the diamonds. The checkering tool, in case you've never used one, is a simple tool with a double or triple row of cutting teeth. One row of teeth cut a new groove, while the other row follows the previously cut groove. This way the grooves are kept straight and evenly spaced. The diamonds are made neat and sharp by progressively deepening the grooves until the tops of the "ridges" become sharp. It is easier to do this by deepening the grooves with a single-line cutter, or V-cutter. Usually about three separate passes are required to bring the grooves to full depth.

The checkering tool shown on these pages is the Brownell "Full View" tool, which features removable cutting heads. Thus the spacing cutter and the V-cutter may be used on one handle. Other types of tools may require a separate tool for each operation. Take your pick—they all work fine if used with care.

When the checkering is worked up to neat, sharp points, give the job a good brushing with a toothbrush to remove sawdust, then complete the project by brushing in a good coat of stock finish.

2
Begin work by drawing the outline of your desired pattern on the target stock. Make quite a few sketches if necessary until you get a design that is both pleasing in appearance as well as functional. The grease-pencil marks are easily wiped away.

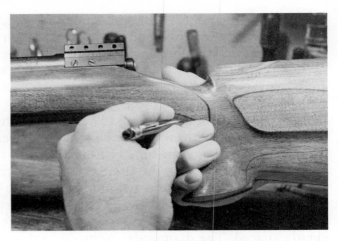

3

A tracing is made around the gripping hand in order to make sure that the checkering pattern is adequate.

4

After sketching the desired design on the stock, cut the outline to about ¹/₃₂ inch with the veining tool.

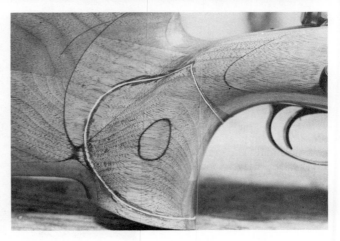

5

Here the outline has been cut to depth and the pattern is ready to take the checkering.

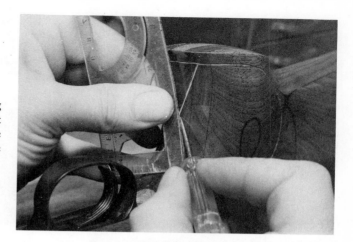

6

Since this is a wraparound checkering pattern the master lines are laid out at the center of the grip. A flexible rule is handy to follow the curve of the stock when laying out these lines.

7

A detail of the master lines. Note that the diamonds run lengthwise up and down rather than in the more usual horizontal direction. Vertical diamonds give a very good gripping surface for target stocks.

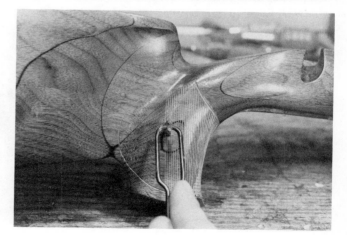

8

The checkering tool is used for spacing the lines. For target stocks, sixteen to eighteen lines per inch is very functional for a good grip.

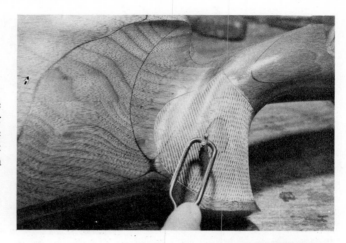

9

After the spacing is completed in one direction it is completed in the other direction. After the diamonds have been completely laid out the next procedure is deepening the lines with the V-tool.

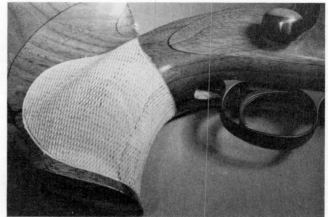

10

Both sides of the grip after "pointing up," or cutting to full depth with the V-tool. The next step is brushing some stock finish into the freshly cut checkering. This will not only toughen the checkering but will make it more attractive as well.

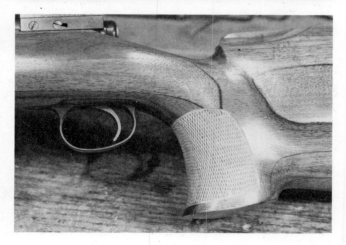

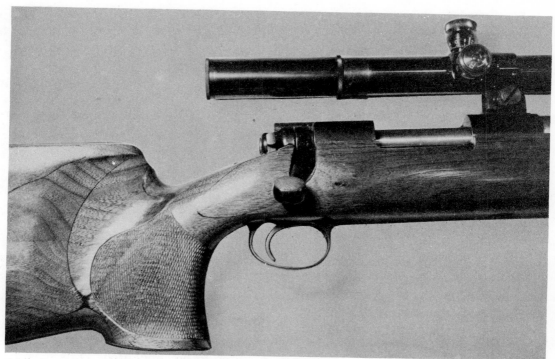

11   Here is the finished checkering job. This rifle is a Remington Model 40-XB in .300 Winchester Magnum caliber with a special laminated-walnut stock. I use the rifle in 1,000-yard competition.

22 / Fancy Checkering

The preceding chapters have begun with a few sentences describing the ease with which a project can be accomplished by a rank amateur with only a fistful of tools. To begin this chapter with such a proposition would be to pull your leg, and not very gently at that. True, a few checkering tools is all you need, but there just ain't no way this project can be described as easy.

Or perhaps that's not a completely fair description. By and large, checkering is just checkering, and the difference between an "easy" checkering pattern and a difficult one is usually the size of the area to be checkered. Thus it is basically a matter of time required to complete the pattern. So instead of saying that this project is difficult, let's just say it requires a fair amount of time to complete.

As for the degree of checkering skill and experience required for this particular project, I'm going to hedge a bit further. The reason for this is that the natural talent and determination of some otherwise inexperienced individuals never ceases to amaze me. Good checkering, like everything else, is largely a matter of knowing what you want to do and then having the intestinal fortitude to see it through to completion.

And of course there are always those who question the purpose of so complex a pattern. They reason that checkering above and beyond that which is required for a nonslip grip is purely superfluous. If one is willing to accept this point of view one must also decline figured or well-colored wood for stocks, all engraving, well-finished surfaces, and just about everything else of aesthetic value. In my experience, however, the principal critics of ornate checkering are those who are unable to master the art themselves.

In this vein it has often been said that the only person truly able to appreciate the work of a master gunsmith is another master gunsmith. Not being a master gunsmith, I cannot offer any opinion as to whether or not this is true, but after completing a number of checkering projects such as the one shown on these pages, I find myself increasingly able to understand why the services of top-notch stockmakers are not available at bargain-basement prices. Even at that it is no secret that top-notch stockmakers could probably make more money elsewhere and only follow the gun crafts out of sheer love for the art.

The work illustrated here was done on an A-series Model 52 Winchester .22 rimfire which has been refitted with a sporter-weight barrel. The nicely textured French-walnut stock is the semi-finished Reinhart Fajen Classic style with only slight modifications.

The checkering pattern was copied, with some modifications, from an original Al Biesen rifle. The fleurs-de-lis, in fact, were traced from the Biesen pattern. I hasten to add that the modifications mentioned above were not an attempt to improve the original pattern but only to adapt it to this particular stock.

The checkering is twenty-six lines to the inch. Much has been said about the relative merits of coarse-line versus fine-line checkering, and I do not intend to continue the argument here. However, the neat, delicate appearance of fine-line checkering lends itself much better to decorative patterns such as this one. And, too, well-done fine-line checkering is a nice showcase for the stockmaker's talents. It has been pointed out that that fine-line checkering of, say twenty-two or more lines to the inch is not practical on a hunting rifle because it takes much abuse and general scuffing around. Again, I can't take sides in this argument, for though I have hunted with rifles having both fine and coarse checkering, I've made it a point not to abuse either.

I do know for a fact, however, that scuffed fine-line checkering is easier to restore than coarse checkering. A few passes over the battered area with a V-tool (single-line cutter), and the fine-line checkering looks as good as new. Coarse checkering takes a lot more cutting to bring the diamonds up to point again, and as a result, the pattern gets a "dug-out" look.

True, it takes a bit longer to do fine-checkering, and no doubt it's harder on the eyes. However, some of the extra time spent on the line-spacing part of the project is made up for when it comes to cutting the rows to full depth. Fine checkering actually involves the removal of less wood than does coarse checkering.

The tools made on this job were the "Full View" type made by W. E. Brownell, of Vista, California. I can't say that these tools are better than any other type, but they seem to suit my technique, and, most important I suppose, I'm used to them. A person always seems to do his best work with familiar tools. Also, it is important to add that if you've been doing poor checkering with one brand of tools, don't expect a miraculous improvement by changing brands.

One of the principal features about this pattern is that it is slightly inset.

That is, the pattern, even the tops of the diamonds, is about a $\frac{1}{32}$ inch lower than the surrounding wood. This involves shaving, or relieving, the entire surface of the area to be checkered before any checkering is done.

I can already hear the gasps of disbelief at the prospect of all this extra work. Actually it doesn't take all the much extra time, and there are some very definite advantages and compensating factors. The first and foremost of these is the simple fact that it makes the job look a whole lot better. The higher level of wood has a framing effect that gives added emphasis to the pattern. The fleurs-de-lis, rather than appearing flat, stand up through the sea of checkering and have a distinctly sculptured effect.

From the standpoint of actual technique, it is much easier to avoid disastrous runovers because the "walls" at the edge of the pattern offer a fairly substantial and positive stop at the end of the line. This is not an invitation to give the edges a good battering, nor is it a surefire prevention against runovers, but it does help.

Begin work on the checkering layout after the final sanding is completed but before the finish is applied. Actually, it won't make much difference if some of the filler coats have been applied, but as we shall see later, there is a good reason for applying the final finish after the border lines are cut and the relief cutting completed. One of these reasons is simply that it's easier to draw on bare wood. Layout of a pattern of this sort sometimes takes a bit of jockeying around, so if it doesn't suit you or come out where it ought to, it is a simple matter to scrub out the pencil mark with a bit of fine steel wool and try again.

Though it is convenient to trace a pattern onto the stock, most stockmakers usually improvise a bit in order to make the basic pattern more harmonious with the lines of a particular stock. For instance, the pattern may be shortened or extended to cover a flaw in the wood, or to expose an especially nice streak of color or figure.

It may come as a pleasant surprise to learn that curved-border patterns such as this, where the lines and grooves of the checkering do not form any of the borders, actually take less "figgerin' out" than does a complex point pattern where all the lines and points have to come out exactly right.

Also, you will discover that this pattern doesn't have any tight areas where there isn't enough room to work freely with a full-sized checkering tool. The usually cramped area around and behind the fleur-de-lis, for example, has been eliminated by giving the fleur a longer stem than usual. It not only looks nice this way, but gives plenty of room to scratch around with your tools.

After the pattern has been laid out to your satisfaction, the next step is to trace the outline with a veining chisel (V-chisel) or a simple slender-bladed knife. Brownell's offers a dandy little incising-knife kit that sells for about two-fifty complete with extra blades of various shapes. It's just about perfect for this sort of work.

For cutting sharp curves such as the outline of the fleurs-de-lis, the best possible tool is a curved chisel which notches the curve. This way all you have to do is put the edge of the chisel on the wood, give it a press or tap, and there is your curved outline, as neat and perfect as can be. In fact, it's a good idea to take inventory of your curved chisels before doing your preliminary layout work. This way you can design the curves in your pattern to match the variously curved chisels you have on hand. Very clever.

During a recent visit to the Rifle Handloader offices, Lenard Mews, the world-famous stockmaker, showed us a pair of chisels he'd made, which were shaped like half a fleur-de-lis. When the tool chisels, or outline cutters, I guess they are, are held together, they form the complete outline. Two taps and the fleur is completely outlined on the wood. What's more, all are exactly alike. He didn't mention how long he worked on the tools, but my guess is quite a while. Like all of Mews' work they were perfect and beautifully made.

With the outline incising done, the next step is "insetting" or removing the 1/32 inch or so of wood in the pattern area. This is done with simple flat-bladed chisels. It doesn't make a lot of difference if you cut with the grain or at right angles to it. In fact, you'll cut every which way before the job is done. One thing you'll learn for sure is not to cut with the grain when it angles down into the stock. This tends to lead your knife deeper and finally causes a chipped-out place in your otherwise smooth surface. Also, you'll learn right quick, if you don't already know, the value and purpose of a razor-sharp tool.

My technique is to do the area all around the borders first. One is usually fresher and has more enthusiasm for the job at the beginning and is less liable to make a boo-boo. So after the delicate border area is inset you can relax a bit and go after the open center areas in a reasonable free-wheeling style. For large areas such as the forend pattern I use an inch-wide chisel and make a single slice from one end of the pattern to the other—just like peeling a cucumber.

If you take long, smooth cuts there will be little need for additional smoothing up when you finish with the chisels. The surface doesn't have to be perfectly smooth, because the checkering will level it out nicely. It should, however, be smooth enough for the checkering tool to move smoothly.

I smooth up the area with a small pad of 220-grit sandpaper but make no effort to get a dead-flat surface; just enough to take out any humps, dips, or ridges left over from the insetting operation. During this sanding operation the sharp, square edges of the border are somewhat rounded and smoothed off. These borders should be sanded as nicely as the rest of the stock with a nice, uniform radius curve down into the recessed area. Remember, all of the border will show and is, in fact, the checkering's "frame." Any irregularities will stick out like a skunk in the strawberry patch. A final polishing with fine steel wool completes the job. Also, more than likely, the rest of the stock will, by this time, need a once-over-lightly with steel wool to get rid of the oily fingerprints and smudges which have accumulated while you've been at work.

Now go ahead with your normal finishing routine and completely fill and finish the stock as you normally would. All of the recessed area is finished right along with the rest of the stock. One of the main reasons for doing the

How to Proceed with Fancy Checkering

1   The first step of any checkering pattern, be it plain or fancy, is laying out the pattern. Since this stock was unfinished at the time of checkering a soft lead pencil was used. If the stock is already finished it is better to use a grease pencil, which leaves a distinctive mark but is easily wiped away. When you're drawing on unfinished wood with a soft lead pencil the best eraser is a bit of steel wool. Draw and redraw until the pattern is harmonious with the stock lines. For distinctive features such as the fleurs-de-lis used on this stock, it is best to use a template which can be traced. A template made of plastic, thin aluminum, or even thin cardboard works well. By using a template you can make the fleur-de-lis shapes uniform with relative ease.

recess carving before applying the finish is to have the inset area filled and finished before checkering. The stock finish penetrates the wood and makes it checker more cleanly. The diamonds are sharper, tougher, and less likely to chip or break off while you're checkering or later in the field.

I will not go into the basics of checkering for the simple reason that those who will be most tempted to give this type of project a try will more than likely have had some checkering experience. The earlier chapter on basic checkering will help those who need it.

Since this is an over-the-grip pattern, special instructions are in order. Rather than laying out the master lines at the side of the grip as is normally done, you must start at the top of the grip. This gets the rows of diamonds in proper order so they will flow down either side of the grip in perfect order. If

2

The outline of the pattern is fully incised and ready for the next step, which will be slicing away the wood inside the pattern.

3

The incising is done with a thin-bladed knife. The cut should be about ¹/₃₂ inch deep. In tightly curving areas where a straight-bladed knife is difficult to control, a curved chisel makes very neat, vertical cuts, especially around the fleurs-de-lis. As a matter of fact, it's a smart move to design your curves so they will fit the curve of chisels you have on hand.

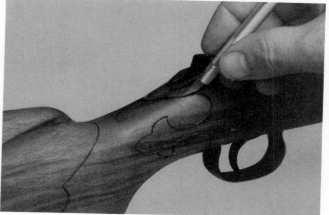

you get the master lines laid out evenly to start with, and don't get the lines too crooked along the way, you'll be pleasantly surprised at how neatly the rows come back together down under the grip. They won't rejoin perfectly so as to form a continuous pattern, but the angles will converge neatly and look very, very professional.

The borders will look a trifle battered, but with care and reasonable luck there should be no runovers. The battered look can be eliminated by tracing around the edge with a narrow checkering rifler (available from Brownell's) or even shaving a fine slice away with the incising knife. If the knife is razor-sharp, the edges will be perfectly smooth and will require no further work.

Now give the whole job a good going-over with a toothbrush. Don't just brush away the sawdust and quit. Bear down and give it a good scrubbing. The stiff bristles tear away the loose fibers that make checkering look fuzzy. Also, the bristles tend to burnish each diamond and gives the entire pattern a nicely polished look. Now brush in a couple of coats of oil base stock finish and you're home free.

4
A razor-sharp flat-bladed chisel is used to shave the wood out of the pattern. I prefer to do the delicate edges first, then slice away the less difficult open areas. Be sure to make the cuts as smooth and flat as possible. For a good checkering job the recessed area must be quite smooth, so be careful at this stage.

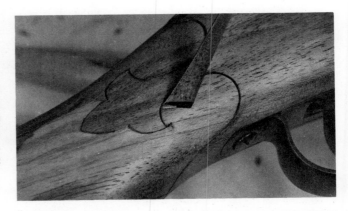

5
The recessing is completed and almost ready for the checkering to begin. Note how smoothly the wood has been cut away. Very little additional finishing will be required.

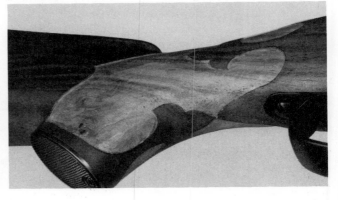

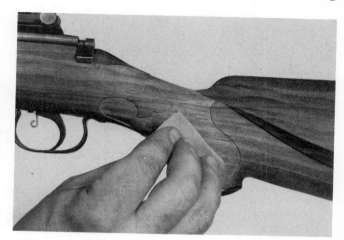

6

A small pad of fine-grit sandpaper is used to smooth the background and round off the corners somewhat. Note how the border of the fleur-de-lis has been rounded so that it stands up in distinctive relief. A wad of fine steel wool adds the final polish.

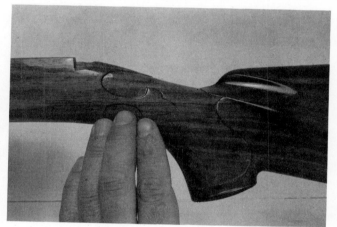

7

After recessing the pattern, but before checkering, the stock is finished as normal. Be sure to put plenty of finish in the recessed areas, as this will toughen wood and aid in checkering.

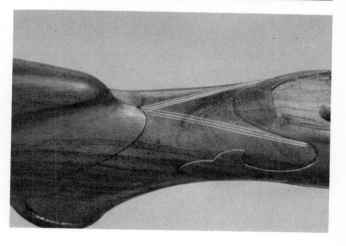

8

The trick to over-the-grip checkering patterns is starting the master lines at the top of the grip. The checkering then proceeds down both sides of the grip in the normal manner.

9

A Brownell's full-view checkering tool is used to space a checkering of twenty-six lines per inch. Note the slightly battered borders, but lack of runovers. The step at the edge of the border tends to prevent runovers, but you still have to use considerable care. After the checkering job is completed the battered edges are trimmed up with the incising knife.

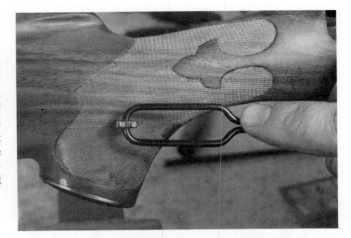

10

The checkering is complete and the borders have been trimmed. The next step is rubbing stock finish into the checkering with a stiff brush, such as a toothbrush. Note the framed efect given by the recessed checkering. This is particularly evident in the way the fleur-de-lis design stands above the surrounding checkering.

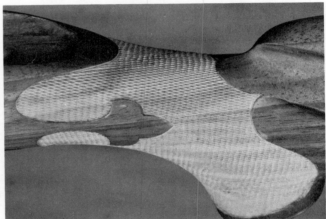

11

The underside of the grip area after the checkering was completed. The technique for the forend is exactly the same. This cute little stock is for a Winchester Model 52 .22 rimfire.

23 / How to Use Electric Checkering Tools

Despite all the bad things gunsmiths and professional stockmakers say about checkering (when they have to do it), the plain truth of the matter is that it's downright habit-forming. Once you master the basic checkering skills you'll be tempted to try more and more impressive patterns. Some amateur gun tinkerers even pick up some spare cash by checkering stocks made by other amateurs and even by professional gunsmiths.

When this happens the craftsman has to think of ways to reduce the time it takes to complete a checkering job. The greatest tools ever to come down the pike for honest "production" checkering are the electric-powered checkering tools manufactured by Micro Machine Tools and by Dem-Bart Electric Checkering Tools. The MMC tool and accessories are distributed by Brownell's and the Dem-Bart tools are sold direct by Dem-Bart.

These units are hardly cheap, with the MMC going for $305.50 in 1977 and the Dem-Bart for $298. But these prices are for the complete setup, with motors, flexible shafts, and foot-operated speed controls. And they might be considered a bargain when you consider the time savings and keep in mind that the motors and shafts have many other gunsmithing uses, such as grinding, polishing, and drilling. If you already own a Foredom or similar dental-type motor with flexible shaft, the MMC and Dem-Bart checkering heads can be bought separately for $203.50 and $170 respectively.

The hand-checkered stocks on Ruger rifles are done by women using Dem-Bart tools. One of these gals can completely checker a Model 77 bolt-rifle stock in *less than a half-hour!* With ordinary hand tools the same job would take several hours. Yet, there is no way to tell the difference between work done with hand tools and that done with electric tools. The beautiful and complex checkering patterns we admire on stocks made by our best stock-makers are often done with electric tools!

Though it is possible to start out on the basics of checkering using only a power tool, I think it best to master the fundamentals with hand tools. With skills gained by completing other checkering projects discussed in this book it is a lot easier to master the electric tool. In fact, you have to learn to *like* checkering before you'll want to invest in an electric tool. But if you do, you'll find that you can checker *at least* as well as with hand tools.

The Dem-Bart and MMC tools are used in the same way. Spacing is accomplished by a bladelike guide which has adjustments for both depth and spacing of cut. The click-ball spacing adjustment may be set anywhere from sixteen to twenty-two lines to the inch. With a special narrow cutter, checkering as fine as thirty-two lines per inch is possible.

A flexible shaft connects the cutting head to the motor. With the motor suspended somewhat above and to the rear of the operator, the cutter can be manipulated with complete freedom and ease, though the feel of the tool is somewhat awkward at first for those accustomed to hand tools.

One's first experience with an electric checkering tool can be either pleasant or terrifying—depending on what you are expecting. I had never seen the tools demonstrated previously, and I was terrified. After laying out a nice straight pair of master lines, I pressed the rheostat foot pedal and carefully laid the tool against the wood. The result was an angry snarl and a shower of powdered wood. This is ridiculous, I thought; who can do precision checkering with something scaring the hell out of him? A few more passes, however, and I felt in total control.

One of the first concerns you might have about using a power tool for such work is that the cutter, in the manner of many saws, might tend to chatter, dig out soft spots, or lead with the grain. Such, however, is not the case. The Foredom motor produces up to 14,000 rpm, and at such speeds as this the tiny buzz saw of a cutter is totally oblivious to the texture of the wood or direction of the grain. The tool head simply glides along on its path with a minimum of effort on the part of the user. In fact, the real trick in learning to use the tool is learning to let it, not you, do the work. Once you get the feel of the tool, checkering can become a real pleasure.

Laying out a pattern to be checkered with these tools is done exactly the way you would do layout work for conventional tools. The outlines are scribed or marked, then the master lines are marked and cut with a single-line cutter or V-tool or, better yet, use a layout tool or "riffler" such as is available from Brownell's. A pleasant alternative to the tedious and sometimes downright annoying job of laying out the pattern is simply using checkering decals, which are available in a wide assortment of designs from Brownell's.

With the master lines cut, you simply step on the rheostat and the power head buzzes to action. Spacing with electric tools is the conventional right-to-left, line-by-line process, only this time you start the tool at one border and push or pull the tool along in one smooth, continuous motion to the opposite border. The line is cut several times as fast as with a hand tool, and also, the groove can be cut full depth!

With a little practice you can come extremely close to the edge of the pattern. So close, in fact, that a final touch-up around the edges by hand may not even be needed. A good technique for cutting a trim borderless edge without runovers is to scribe only a light line around the pattern, then on each lining pass run the tool up so that it only lightly nicks the scribed line. When the panel is fully checkered, deepen the edge line with a V-tool or riffler. This removes the nicks and leaves a neat edge with no runovers and clean, full-depth checkering running right up to the edges.

One's first judgment of the maneuverability of electric tools might be that they would be all right for broad, flat patterns but would have to be augmented by hand tools in tight corners or on treacherous contours. Actually, the opposite is more true. A typical example is the inside curve of the pistolgrip on "down and under" patterns. Unless the master lines are at the right bottom corner on the right grip panel (which is impractical), you will soon be faced with a situation where you have to cut spacing lines from left to right, an awkward task for many. Coming in from the other side is impossible because the stock gets in the way. But with an electric tool you just tilt the tool a little higher and checker, right to left, to a fare-thee-well.

When you're first becoming acquainted with a power checkering tool, you have the impression that you cannot feel the wood as you can with hand tools. This is true only to the extent that you cannot feel the effort required to plow through the wood. With a little experience, however, you will develop a surprisingly sensitive feel and "ear" for the tool. When the wood toughens up and rpm begin to drop, your foot seems automatically to press harder on the rheostat. Likewise, you learn to judge the cutting pace best suited to the wood.

The ideal depth of cut is one that will bring each row or ridge just to a sharp crest. Cutting the grooves too deep will cause the crests to be lower than they should and low spots will result. On the other hand, not cutting the grooves deep enough will cause the ridges and diamonds to be flat-topped. The beginner may prefer to make the ridges slightly flat-topped, then bring the diamonds to a point with a once-over pass with the hand tool. This is a safe way of doing it, and perhaps a pretty good idea during the learning period. With practice, however, you can cut perfect rows of perfect diamonds with only one pass. This is where checkering gets to be fun, and if you're in the business for extra cash this is where the profits start to climb.

According to the manufacturers, maintenance is virtually nil except for re-sharpening cutters. The fine bearings in the MMC are packed with a special lubricant which lasts several years. When the lubricant shows signs of failing (if it ever does) you return the tool to the factory, where the gearbox is re-packed and the whole tool given a thorough going-over. The Dem-Bart tool comes with a supply of special lube which you inject as needed.

The cutters will become dull after a certain amount of use (depending on type of wood and stock finishes) and must be returned to the factory for resharpening. One sharpening lasts for at least five complete jobs, usually many more. Just how long it might take to recover the initial cost of these tools depends, of course, on just how much checkering you intend to do. However, a fairly complex pattern which might cost seventy-five or a hundred dollars (one that could ordinarily take the better part of three days) can be completed in a single working day with no sweat. With this in mind, you can

Checkering with Electric Tools

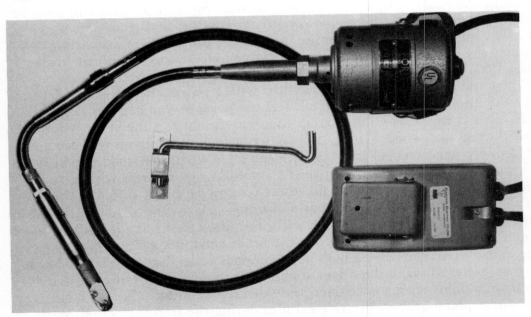

1 The complete Micro Machine Company (MMC) checkering tool as sold by Brownell's. Foredom electric motor with flexible shaft, checkering head, foot control, speed control, and a hanging bracket.

see that the initial cost is overcome in five to ten checkering days. From there on out, the time saved is all gravy.

While the home hobbyist is not necessarily concerned with profit, he is concerned with his time investment, and these tools can certainly save you a lot of time which can be usefully spent in the shop or out at the range showing off your checkering. In addition to this, there is the pride and pleasure that come from owning and operating a fine piece of precision equipment.

So just how fast are these checkering tools? The only careful time log I kept on a fully checkered panel is a wrap-around forend panel involving some 26 square inches of checkered area and *seventeen* points. Checkering was done twenty-two lines to the inch. Total time elapsed from time tool touched wood until oil was brushed into checkering was *one hour and fifty-five minutes!*

2

A closeup of the MMC checkering tool in action. The cutting wheel is like a tiny buzz saw which rips its way through wood. The tool is guided somewhat like a hand tool; it has an adjustable spacing guide which follows the previous cut. The tool can be either pushed or pulled, though I prefer the pulling technique.

3

Some practice work done on scrap wood with the MMC tool. Note that the checkering was cut right up to the border with no runovers whatever. No tools except the electric checkering tool were used.

4

Though a prior knowledge of checkering is not necessary when you're learning to use electric checkering tools, it is indeed helpful. Also, before attempting your first stock job with an electric tool it is a good idea to practice on some scrap wood. The entire surface of the practice block shown here was checkered in only a few minutes. This is the Dem-Bart checkering tool.

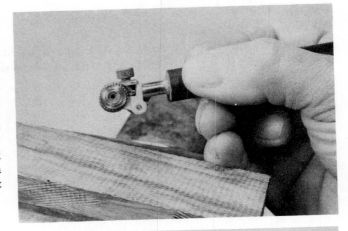

5

A bit of fancy practice checkering on a piece of scrap wood. Note how close the checkering comes up to the border without runovers. Only a small amount of handwork is needed to complete this difficult pattern.

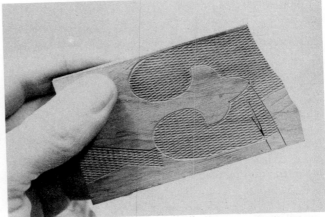

6

For right-handers the best spacing procedure is from right to left, just as with hand tools. The MMC tool is used on a classic point pattern which goes over the top and under the grip. After you gain a measure of control with electric checkering tools it is possible to cut each line to full depth.

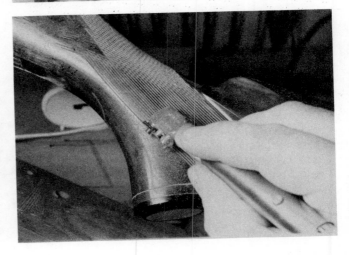

7

The checkering lines "coming back the other way." This checkering pattern was cut only to partial depth and finished with hand tools. However, it was my first attempt with an electric tool, and since then I have learned to do a finished job on the first pass.

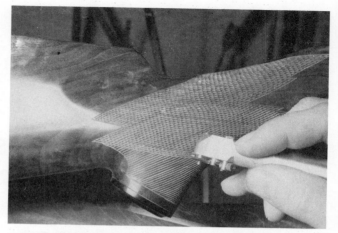

8

Electric checkering tools are especially handy and flexible in cramped areas such as under the grip.

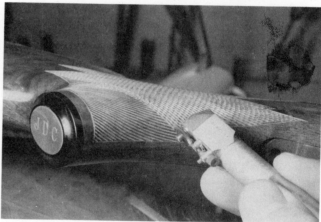

9

The finished job—my first attempt with the MMC electric checkering tool. The checkering is quite nice with no runovers or badly spaced lines. The time required to complete this grip panel was approximately one-quarter what it would take to do it by hand.

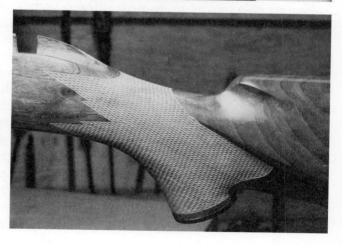

24 / Converting Impressed Checkering to Hand-Cut Checkering

Impressed checkering, no matter how fancy the pattern, is still impressed checkering, and quite a few of us old-timers are having more than a little difficulty learning to live with it.

I'm not implying that all impressed checkering is ugly and all handwork beautiful; on the contrary, we've all seen skimpy, poorly done hand checkering, and impressed checkering that is surprisingly handsome except in the eyes of diehard traditionalists.

Back when all the manufacturers were producing guns with hand-checkered stocks, many shooters "cleaned up" the factory checkering to improve its looks. But most have been hesitant to attempt a similar operation on impressed checkering, primarily because it often looks as if it can't be done.

But all checkering types now offered by manufacturers can be converted to hand checkering, with excellent results and a minimum of tools and experience. In fact, the most difficult parts of checkering (layout, pattern outlining, and line spacing) are already done, which makes it an ideal project for the beginner—though experience has taught me never to say "foolproof."

Basically, there are two types of impressed checkering. One is the "positive" type such as is found on the Browning lever rifle. "Positive" impressed checkering looks most like hand checkering; the diamonds are shaped more or less in the traditional form. However, they are not sharply pointed and the edges and corners tend to be rounded rather than perfectly formed.

The other type is the "negative" checkering used by Remington and Savage. It doesn't have projecting diamonds, but, rather, indentations in the wood that look like diamonds in reverse. Hence the name "negative."

Impressed checkering is accomplished by stamping or rolling the stock with a hot die that "impresses" a pattern on the wood. Though the die is quite hot, the process is completed so quickly that the wood does not burn or even scorch. The hot die or stamp literally melts the wood's lignin (nature's own plastic) and, in effect, molds the wood under high pressure. Were it not for this technique, stamped checkering would look like a mass of crushed and bruised wood.

For our purposes this process is significant because it compresses the wood into a dense, almost plasticlike form that takes hand checkering as well as hard, close-grained walnut. Basically the only tool required for the conversion operation is a single-line checkering tool, preferably one with fine teeth so the grooves are "filed" rather than cut. A tool with a rather long cutting head, such as Brownell's, tends to cut a straighter groove and feels its way along better. A shorter cutting head, however, such as that on the Dem-Bart S-1 tool, is somewhat more flexible in that it allows working in tight, close areas and is maneuverable enough to follow fairly sharp curves. Such a tool is also handy for trimming up around the edges of the checkered panel. Either is adequate, especially for a beginner.

One other tool, the two- or three-line spacing cutter, while not necessary, will considerably speed up the conversion operation. With it you can open up two or three grooves at once. Using a multi-groove cutter, however, requires special care and the beginner will do well to stick to the single-line cutter. Of course, if you use a two- or three-line spacing cutter it must match the groove spacing of the impressed checkering.

Since converting the positive-type impressed checkering is less difficult, let's discuss this first. Using a single-line checkering tool, trace each of the grooves in the panel. Two light passes over each set of grooves will sharpen up the edges of the diamonds and bring them to a point. A side benefit of this

Some pressed checkering is done in a positive form which more nearly resembles hand checkering, but the diamonds are not so sharp or well shaped. The lighter-colored half of this pressed panel of positive pressed checkering has been gone over with a single-line cutting tool. Note that the diamonds are much more sharply pointed and finely shaped than those in the dark area. This is very easy work and incidentally is a good way to learn the basic skills of checkering, since the guide lines are already there.

touching-up operation is that while you're tracing out the checkering, you are also removing the finish from the checkered panel. Impressed checkering, as you'll notice, is stained the same color as the rest of the stock. If you lighten the color of the checkering, it becomes more distinctive and contrasts better with the rest of the stock. Also, the shine of impressed checkering is gone, leaving the flat tone of authentic hand checkering. Best of all, however, is the feel—those sharp little diamonds bite into the fingers as only hand-cut checkering can. Now give the recut checkering a good brushing to get rid of sawdust, brush in a coat of stock finish, and this job is all done.

The procedure for converting the negative-type checkering is nothing more than cutting into the already-existing grooves and removing the partitions which suggest the negatively formed diamonds. This will leave uninterrupted rows of grooves and sharp-topped ridges. When the operation is duplicated on the intersecting rows, the ridges are divided into the diamond-shaped pyramids of true hand checkering. Though these grooves may easily be cut full depth on the first pass, it is very important that the first one-way series of grooves be cut only half way. Otherwise, the guide grooves for the second series, or crossing lines, will be completely obliterated. These crossing grooves may, however, be cut full depth without harm. Next, return to the half-cut grooves and complete the final depth.

With a single-line cutter you don't have to worry about an error being transmitted to all following lines, as with regular checkering, but any misalignment will show up in uneven diamonds when the job is completed. If you do cut a crooked line, immediately straighten it up with the edge of a flexible straightedge. Finally, keep the tool head perpendicular to the surface so the diamonds aren't lopsided.

My first efforts at recutting negative impressed checkering were done with a 90° single-line cutter. Though the results were highly satisfactory, I noticed that even after the diamonds had been brought to a sharp point, there were still some signs of the original stamping; a tiny pinprick mark remained in the grooves at the corner of each diamond. This, of course, is of no real consequence and can be detected only by close inspection. It is the only evidence that the stock had ever been impressed-checkered. Switching to a Brownell 75° cutter, I was able to remove this last vestige of the original stamping.

Impressed checkering is somewhat inset (i.e., below the surface of the surrounding wood), and the panel edges form a positive end-of-the-groove stop for the checkering tool, particularly if a single cut is made around the border to square the shoulder. Runovers are almost entirely eliminated by this feature, but by job's end, the borders may have a somewhat battered look, which is why finishing border cuts should be left until last. Here a short maneuverable cutter, traced lightly around the panel's edge, will remove most nicks and irregularities.

Steps for Converting Impressed Checkering to Hand Checkering

1

This Remington Model 700 rifle stock is a typical example of pressed or inverted checkering. The gripping surface is not as good as that of positive-type checkering, and it certainly is not as attractive.

2

The job of converting negative checkering to positive hand-cut checkering is underway. A Brownell's full-view checkering tool with single-line cutter is used to plow through the pressed lines and establish a series of grooves. A spacing cutter is not necessary because the checkering tool will follow the pressed lines.

3

A short angle tool is used to work the narrow spaces. In this photograph the line deepening has been done in both directions and the pointing up of the diamonds is very nearly completed.

4

The short angle tool is used to work close to the border. It is necessary to take care in order to avoid runovers, but they are less likely with pressed checkering because the checkered panel tends to be a bit below surface of the wood and forms a natural abutment at the end of the pattern.

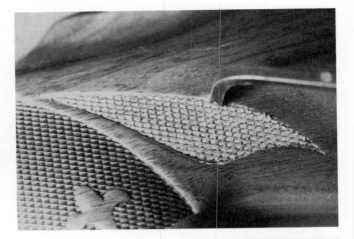

5

The completed panel. Note the contrast with the larger panel, which is still undone.

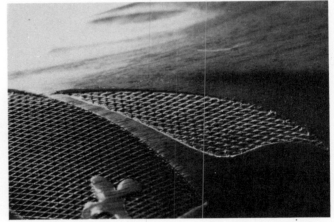

6

Work about halfway completed on the main panel. The improvement in appearance is very much evident when the two styles of checkering are so closely contrasted.

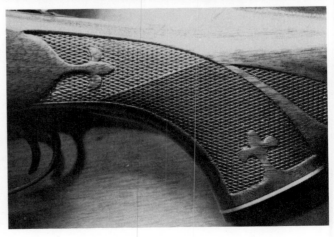

7
A closeup showing the difference between positive and negative checkering afetr being converted with ordinary checkering tools.

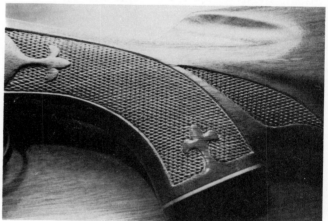

8
The completed recheckering job. Now the checkering looks like top-quality handwork.

When you discover how well the checkering conversion works out, you'll probably want, as I did, to do something about the borders on the fancier patterns. With straight-edged point patterns all you need to do is trace out the edging with the single-line cutter and you're home free. But with the more elaborate patterns, such as on Remington rifles and shotguns, the problem is considerably more difficult. Not because of the curved borders — these are easily dealt with — but because of the molded simulated carving and, worse yet, the crushed and cracked condition common to these moldings.

My efforts to eliminate, or at least hide, this condition were not altogether successful because the cracks simply run too deep in many cases. In the case of some older Remington 700 BDL rifle stocks, for example, there is a ribbon about ⅜ inch wide running upward through the grip panel and dividing the checkering into two sections. The effect is handsome enough, to be sure, but my unsuccessful efforts to remove the slight cracks, caused by die crushing, involved relieving the wood ¹/₁₆ inch. The fissures were still evident.

In another effort to improve the appearance of the molded border, I used a veining tool and narrow gouge to carve detail and add dimensional character. This had the effect of giving the border a true hand-carved appearance but, again, the cracks and fissures caused some unsightly but unavoidable chipping. About the only thing that can be done under these circumstances is to use razor-sharp tools, take it slow and easy, and hope for the best. Of course, if you happen to have a stock without any of the above-mentioned flaws (I deliberately selected a stock with pronounced flaws), there is no reason to expect anything but good results—discounting, of course, errors on your part. All in all, the best advice I can offer, based on my own experience, is to leave the borders alone unless you are an experienced wood carver and/or the wood is in good condition.

Converting only the checkering is a tremendous improvement, and it looks quite good with the molded border. In fact, it's difficult to describe just how much better an impressed-checkered stock does look—and feel—as a result of this relatively simple two-evening project. It goes a long way toward making a standard factory rifle look like a custom sporter!

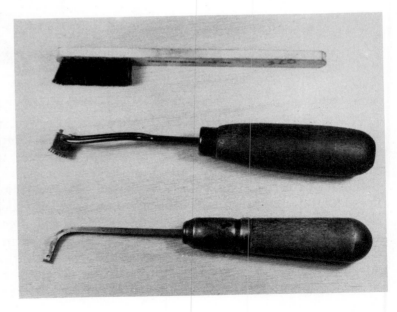

The only tools needed to complete a pressed-checkering conversion job: a small brush to clean sawdust from the work area, an ordinary checkering tool with a single-line cutter, and a short angle cutter used to get into the tight areas.

25 / Decorative Carving on Rifle, Pistol, and Shotgun Stocks

An average workman, using only simple tools, can do a very impressive job of carving pistol grips, rifle and shotgun stocks, and other items. The money expended for tools (if you don't already have them) will amount to no more than two dollars, and a single evening's work will complete a job.

The only cutting tool you need is a 75° veining tool. This is a simple tool which can be obtained at most hardware, hobby, or woodworking-supply stores. Like all cutting instruments, the veining tool must be kept extremely sharp for best results. A dull tool will cause lack of control, uneven depth of cut, and a generally rough appearance. Best control over the cut, especially on close curves, can be had by driving the veining tool with short, quick taps of a light hammer. Pushing the tool by hand is possible but is much more likely to result in uneven scrollwork. The beginner will do much better to use a hammer. This is, incidentally, the method used by most professional engravers.

The pattern can be laid out to suit your own taste. Use a grease pencil to experiment with designs. These marks can thus be easily wiped off and rearranged without marring the finish on the wood.

At first, designs may be difficult to draw, but you'll find it easier with a bit of practice. Study pictures of engraved and carved guns for ideas. In addition to the usual scroll patterns, cattlebrands, initials, family crests, and other designs are appropriate and may appeal to individual taste.

The carved pattern is greatly enhanced by stippling or "beading" in the background. This gives an effect of depth or relief. A small punch with a concave surface at the point is best for this. The common cabinetmaker's nailset, with its concave point, is a perfect tool for the job. Experiment on a scrap piece of wood to find the right pressure of blow to give a well-defined but not

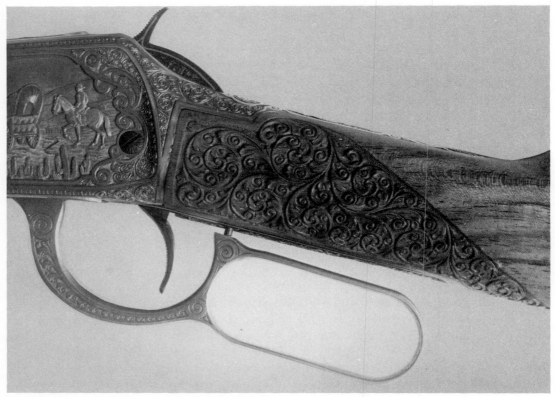

An example of advanced carving done by Pachmayr.

too deep "bead," then apply an even background with short even taps of the hammer.

Any of the commercial oil-based stock finishes are excellent for finishing up your work. Using a rather stiff brush, force the finish into all the cuts and smooth up the surface with light finger strokes or as recommended. If the cuts are of a lighter color than the surface of the grips, they may be darkened by simply adding a bit of stain to the finish.

With reasonable care, even the most unskilled beginner will be quite surprised and pleased with the professional appearance of his work. A simple design is best for beginning, but with only a little practice, you can do intricate patterns with relative ease.

Decorating a Revolver Stock

1 A Ruger Blackhawk single-action revolver with plain finished wooden grips. Guns of this type with plain grips are ideal candidates for attractive stock carving.

2
The only tools that will be needed for a complete stock carving job: a scribing tool, an inexpensive veining tool from your carving-tool set, a carpenter's nailset which is ideal for doing the bead or matted background effect, a grease pencil for drawing the preliminary design, and a light utility hammer to propel the veining tool.

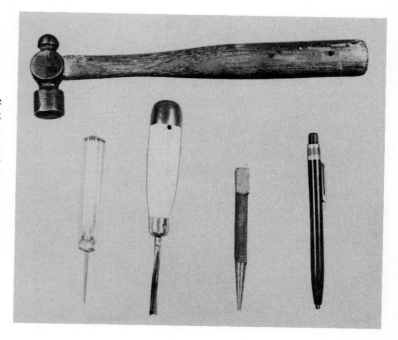

3

The grease pencil is used to sketch some design ideas on the pistolgrip. If the design is not suitable it can usually be wiped away with a soft cloth and you can begin again. The grip is held fast in the vise by means of the grip screw, which is simply clamped in the vise jaws.

4

The carving design has been drawn on the pistolgrip and the initial incising or veining cuts are being made. When the chip curls up from the cuts in a long continuous curl, your tool is good and sharp.

5

Hold the veining tool like this when you're carving by the hammering technique. Simply guide the tool, don't try to push it, and gently tap the butt of the carving-tool handle.

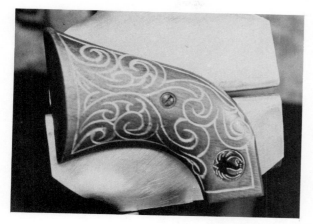

6

The finished incising job before the background matting is begun.

7

The matting, or background beading is accomplished simply by tapping lightly with a carpenter's nailset. This makes a circular design which has a pleasing overlapping matting effect. When striking upper or lower ends of grip, turn it so they are over vise for support.

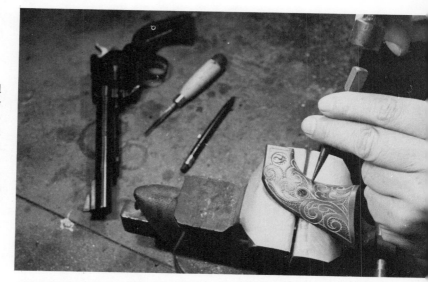

8

Stock finish is rubbed into the freshly finished carving.

9 The same Ruger Blackhawk after completion of the carving job. Design below is adapted to work around the Sturm Ruger logo on the upper part of the grip.

RUGER BLACKHAWK
SINGLE-ACTION

Some suggested patterns for different kinds of pistol grips. Note that the Colt .45 auto grip design has a center panel for carving your initials.

S.& W
SMALL-FRAME
DOUBLE-ACTION

POCKET
AUTOMATIC

COLT .45
AUTOMATIC

26

Basketweave Carving

A very eye-catching substitute for checkering is the so-called basketweave carving. It provides a nonslip surface at least as effective as checkering and is certainly something out of the ordinary as far as stock decoration goes. Since it is a form of carving, most folks assume that it requires special skill and fancy tools. This assumption is bolstered, no doubt, by the fact that basketweave carving is usually found only on very expensive custom-grade rifles and shotguns.

Actually, there's nothing very difficult about basketweave carving, and you need only the simplest of tools. Frankly, I consider basketweave carving much easier than checkering, and there's no question that it takes less time and experience for equal coverage.

Toolwise, all you need is a veining tool (V-cutter) for cutting the outline of the pattern, a scribe for marking the basic master lines, a narrow blade chisel, a blocking punch, and a stippling punch, which you can make yourself.

Timewise, a complete four-panel job on a rifle or shotgun takes about one evening. Of course, it goes without saying, basketweave carving will look great on pistol stocks and gives a really terrific gripping surface. Here's how you go about doing an eye-catching job of basketweave carving on *your* gun!

The first step is designing and laying out the panels or areas to be carved. If you wish you can follow the more or less traditional patterns such as used for checkering on the pistolgrips and forend. This is the so-called "four-panel" job and simply means a carved pattern on each side of the grip and forend.

Or, if you have an artistic flare, let your imagination run wild and create something new and different. Try drawing different designs with a grease pencil. If the design doesn't suit you, just rub it off with a cloth and try again. Try using subtle curves that complement the natural curves of the stock. Also, if the wood is nicely figured you may want to try a design that accents the natural beauty of the wood. The only limitation is your imagination, and as basketweave carving covers large areas in a relatively short time, there isn't much danger of biting off more than you can chew.

After you have drawn a pleasing pattern on the stock, the next step is to cut the border edges with the V-cutter. If the V-tool is good and sharp you should be able to follow the drawn-out line with little difficulty. If you're a stranger to the V-tool it might be a good idea to make a few practice cuts on scrap wood. In most cases the little cutter can be guided and powered by hand pressure alone. If you feel less than confident with this technique, try propelling it along with quick taps of a light mallet, engraver-style.

When the outline is completed you can move on to scribing the master lines. These master lines, as shown in the illustrations, are about ¼ inch apart and intersect at about a 45° angle. Actually there is much latitude here, and the lines can be spaced and angled according to your personal whim. Frankly, the pattern shown here is rather bold and somewhat oversize for the sake of photographic clarity. The pattern will appear somewhat more dainty if the bands are about ³/₁₆ inch wide with about ⅛ inch, or slightly less, spacing between. Just keep in mind that the narrower the bands, the longer it takes to complete the project.

With the master lines all laid out, the next step involves marking every other spacing, which is to be cut in deep relief. This space is lowered below the level of the surrounding wood by about ¹/₁₆ inch. This can be done by cutting the outline with a narrow chisel and slicing out the wood. If the grain runs flat, the whole chip can be "popped" out in one piece. At any rate, the bottom of the cuts will be rather ragged and uneven. If these bottoms had to be smoothed out individually by hand, the task would be onerous and time consuming. But wait, there's a better way!

Simply make a diamond-shaped punch which exactly fits the bottom of these spaces. Fit the punch into the cut, give it a light whack with a mallet or light hammer, and, lo, the bottom is pressed smooth and clean with nice sharp corners. These punches, by the way, can be made out of about anything; mild steel, brass, or aluminum. Anything that is easy to file—make it easy on yourself.

With all the relief sections cut out and neatly punched, you're ready for the main order of business—carving the basketweave effect. This takes a bit of thought at first but after you get the hang of it the job moves along rather quickly. Just keep in mind that bands go "over" then "under" each other in alternating fashion.

If your chisel or knife is good and sharp (and it should be), four deft cuts will complete a whole segment—up, over, and down—of the weave. Just make a downward angling cut from both sides of the "on top" position, square up the ends, and the section is completed. After you get the hang of it, it's a lot of fun and hard to make a mistake. The realism of the woven effect is so remarkable that you'll probably catch yourself saying, "Over it goes and under it goes." With the carving completed, all you need to do is slick off the bands and round the edges slightly with some 280-grit sandpaper. Not too much sanding—just enough to burnish the wood. Too much sanding tends to flatten out the pattern.

Carving a Basketweave Stock

1

The panel design is marked with a china marking pencil or grease pencil. This way if the pattern doesn't suit you, you can rub it off with a soft cloth and try again. After the border outline is drawn to your liking, it is traced with the veining tool. Cut the border to a depth of about $1/32$ inch. A veining tool is much easier to use if it is kept razor-sharp.

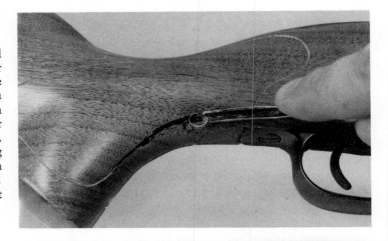

2

The master lines are drawn with a straightedge and a scribe. Here a thin plastic straightedge is used because it is flexible enough to bend around the curves of the stock. The bands or "strands" are about $3/16$ to $1/4$ inch wide, and the spaces between are $1/8$ inch or so. In this pattern the spacing was made especially wide for the sake of photographic clarity.

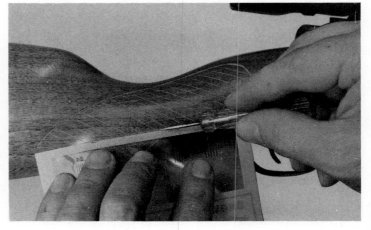

Next add a bit of contrast between the "woven" bands and the "in between" areas by lightly stippling the bottoms of the in-between cuts. When the finish is applied, the stippled area becomes darker and gives an even greater depth or "relief" effect.

For a stippling tool you can use a nailset, which makes a tiny pattern of overlapping circles, or make a stippling tool by cutting tiny rows of checkering on the tip of a ⅛-inch or so punch. The checkering is cut with a knife-edge needle file. Don't worry if the checkering isn't perfect—it'll make a great impression on the wood nonetheless.

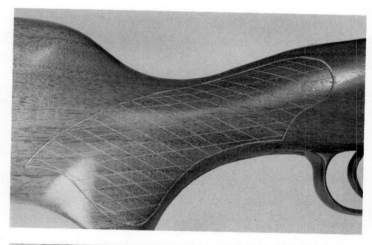

3

The border complete with the master lines laid out.

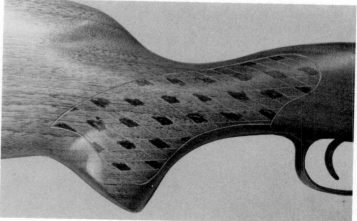

4

The spacing at every other line width has been marked with a grease pencil to show just where the relief cuts will be made. These relief cuts are, in effect, the space between the bands, and they are cut to ¹⁄₁₆ inch depth or so to give the pattern a deep-relief look.

5

A narrow chisel is used to cut the outline of the areas to be cut in relief. When the four edges have been cut to depth the wood chip can be more or less popped out.

6

A wood chip has just been cut out and a homemade punch is being used to flatten the bottom of the relief cuts. This makes the bottom smooth and flat and adds sharpness to the bottom edge of the cut.

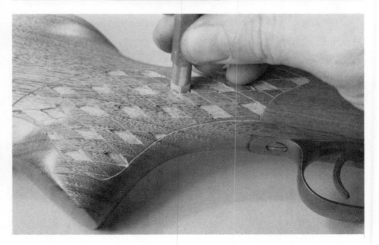

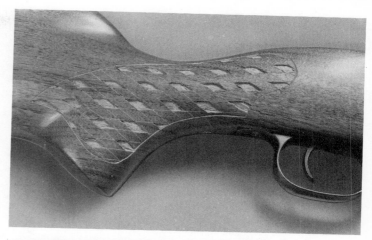

7

The entire panel has been cut and punched and is ready for the basketweave carving.

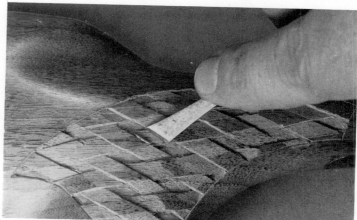

8

A sharp chisel is used to do the carving. As you can see, the bands, or "strands," of the weaving are cut down one side and in the same way down the other side to give an over-and-under lapping effect.

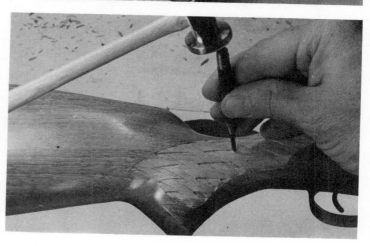

9

A stippling punch is used to mat the background in the relief-cut areas. This gives an additional effect of depth.

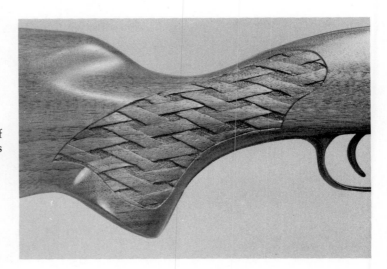

10
Stock finish is hand-rubbed into the carving.

With the background stippled you're almost to the stopping place. Now all you need to do is apply the finish. A coat or two of Tru-Oil liberally spread on with the fingers does the trick. Be sure that plenty of finish runs down into the recessed areas.

Now there's only one more thing to do. Run upstairs, outside, or wherever and show your wife, sweetheart, or fellow gun fancier the remarkable bit of artistry you've wrought. Try to be modest. . . .

11
The finished product. A panel of this general size requires less than an hour to complete.

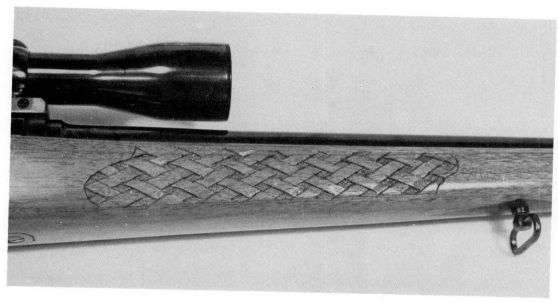

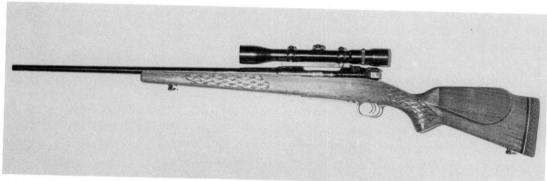

The complete basketweave-carving job on forend and grip.

27

How to Fit Stock Inlays of Exotic Wood

Inlaid patterns of rare and colorful woods are one of the most distinctive forms of stock decoration. As a general rule, however, this type of stock artistry is seen only on the more expensive custom firearms, probably because the *apparent* difficulty of such work scares off amateurs and more than a few professionals.

In truth, other than a little care, there is no great difficulty involved, and the whole operation requires only a stark minimum of tools. Timewise, much depends, of course, on the individual craftsman, but to give an approximate idea of the time investment the completed inlay shown on these pages took slightly less than three hours *including time for picture taking,* so it is fair enough to say that our three-piece design is a one-evening project.

Inlay materials include a variety of woods such as holly (white), ebony (black), cocobolo (multi-hued), vermilion (red), purpleheart (purple), osage orange (yellow), and other exotic types. These are available from Brownell's in a goodly assortment of shapes and sizes. Costwise the inlays run from thirty to eighty cents each, so the total investment for materials can hardly be called prohibitive. Materials for our project, comprising three large inlays, totaled $2.40.

As for tools, you could actually make do with a pocket knife, but a thin-bladed chisel is best. Also, a handy little $2.50 incising knife kit offered by Brownell's is perfect for cutting outlines and shaving edges for a perfect hairline fit. The replaceable blades are razor-sharp.

If you are interested in getting the job done in a hurry or plan on doing a lot of inlay work, the Dremel Moto-Tool with router attachment will cut work time by more than half. With a little practice you'll be able to work right up to the edges with the router, leaving only the corners and point areas to be finished with hand tools.

The first step is designing your pattern and arranging it on the stock. To help with the design layout and to get an idea of what the finished job will look like, simply stack the inlays and look straight down on the pattern. This technique allows you to space the individual pieces to suit your taste and also to substitute different colors of wood until you get the desired effect. Also, this is your guide to what order the individual elements are to be inlaid. The pieces on the bottom are inlaid first and then on up the stack.

Holding the inlay firmly in position, trace the outline with the incising knife. Naturally you want to keep the incision perfectly flush with the outline of the inlay, because the name of this game is perfect fit!

After marking the outline, use the incising knife to deepen the cut to ⅛ inch or so. Don't press too hard with the knife, or you'll bungle the whole thing. You'll have better control if you retrace the outline with a series of light passes rather than one or two heavy passes with the knife. Now you can start removing wood with the chisel or Dremel router. Take your time here and keep the "excavation" neat and even. When necessary, use the incising knife to deepen the outline until you've reached full depth.

The inlays are about ¼ inch thick and when fully in place should extend above the surface of the stock only slightly—1/32 inch or so is about right. When fitting the inlay you'll be tempted to try it often to see how the fitting is going. Be careful not to force the inlay in if the fit is too tight. You might find, to your utter dismay, that the inlay won't come out, or when it does it jerks a big hunk out of the surrounding wood. So be on the lookout for tight spots and keep them shaved away with the incising knife. A properly fitted inlay not only fits perfectly but is never so tight that it must be pounded in, it's only snug at the most. Overly tight inlays might, at some future date, absorb a little moisture, and not having anywhere to expand, they will buckle upward. This is cause for tears.

With the modern resin and epoxy glues now available, anchoring the inlay permanently in place is no problem, but a word of caution is in order. If the inlay fits as it should, there is no way for excess glue to flow out of the inletted cavity as the inlay is pressed in place. Therefore it is important that only a thin coat of glue be applied to the mating surfaces.

When the glue has set, all that remains to be done is to work the inlay down flush with the surface of the stock. For this, use a fine-cut rasp or even a metal file. If you are working on a finished stock you'll naturally want to avoid marring any more of the finish than is necessary—that is, unless you are planning a complete refinishing job anyway.

After all the elements of the design are in place and worked down flush with the stock, give the whole thing a smoothing up with 220-grit, 280-grit, and then 320-grit finishing paper. If the stock was originally stained, you'll probably have a bit of touching up to do on the area around the inlay in order to get the stock color matched up again. Now smooth on a few coats of stock finish and you're home free.

Of course you may be wondering just how much this minimal investment of time and cash has increased the value of your gun. A three-element pattern such as we used is worth, on the average, about twenty-five dollars. In the high-rent districts the figure may very well go three times that much! This naturally brings us to the final question: Just what good is an inlay anyway? Aside from the undefinable qualities of just owning an example of fine workmanship and beautiful woods, there is the very real value of inlays for covering up damaged areas on your stock, knot holes, and various other blotches.

1 A sampling of the precut exotic-wood inlays available from Brownell's. They come in rosewood, holly, ebony, purpleheart, and many other woods. Or you can cut your own shapes from a variety of attractive woods.

Steps in Creating a Wood Stock Inlay

2

With an assortment of inlays in hand you can do a bit of experimenting to determine what combination of inlays looks best. Here a few inlays are stacked on top of stock to get an idea of how it will look when finished.

3

After the inlay pattern is determined the first step is to trace the outline of the inlays with a sharp thin-bladed knife. Make several passes with the knife, cutting deeper on each pass.

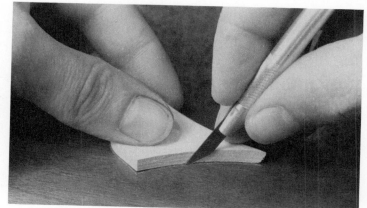

4

After the edges of the inlay have been cut with the narrow-bladed scribing knife, a chisel or mini-router can be used to cut away the wood inside.

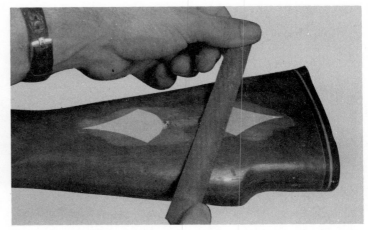

5
The two outer elements of the inlay have been fitted and are being worked down to surface of stock with a cabinet rasp.

6
After the two outside elements of the pattern are smoothed off the center section is placed in position and traced with the knife as before.

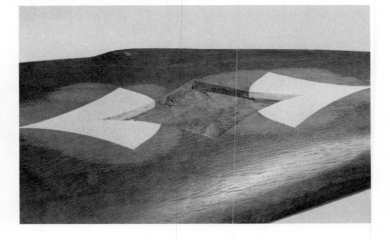

7
The inletting cut completed.

8

The ebony inlay is fitted into the inletted recess. The outer elements of this inlay are white hollywood, which contrasts very nicely with the ebony.

9

The inlays are held securely in position with a tight bonding cement such as epoxy. Epoxy is probably the best possible kind of bonding cement to use for inlays.

10

After all the inlays are in position the surface of the wood is smoothed down flush with a fine sandpaper.

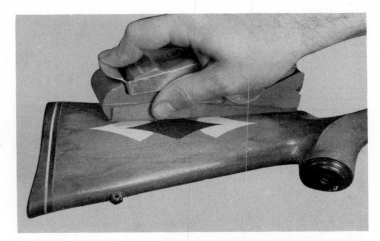

11

A closeup of the inlay, showing the close fitting. Such perfect fitting is not difficult if you take your time and use sharp tools.

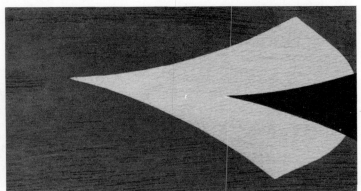

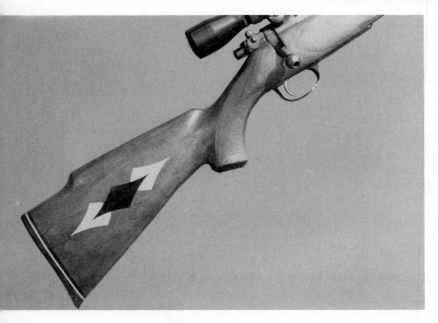

12

The finished inlay job. Note how it lends a highly distinctive custom effect to the otherwise plain buttstock.

28/

How to Fit a Monogram Inlay

There are few, if any, custom accessories that will add as much "class" to your shotgun or rifle for as little cost and effort as a monogram inlay engraved with your initials. A simple item, to be sure—hardly noticeable, in fact. But a small oval of gold or silver inlaid in your stock and engraved with your monogram adds just that something extra it takes to make your shooting pals turn a satisfying shade of envious green. And the really good thing about this monogram-inlay project is that it is a really high-return project. That is to say, it doesn't cost much, it's an easy one-evening project, but yet it adds greatly to the overall appearance of a sporting firearm.

There are several ways of attaching a monogram inlay, and, frankly, one or two are easier than the method described here. My technique, however, is the "English Classic," and for whatever reason, snobbishness perhaps, this is the technique preferred by fanciers of fine guns. In effect, all the technique amounts to is simply nailing the inlay in place with six tiny silver or gold nails. Too—and this is a curious point—*the nails must not be so well fitted as to be invisible!* If the outlines of the nails don't show, there's no proof that the "English" method was used. Therefore the work will not be so highly esteemed! Ah, vanity thy name is gun nut.

Though several different metals such as gold, silver, steel, brass, copper, and aluminum can be used for inlays, brass, gold, and silver are the most commonly used. Naturally, gold is the most desired as well as the most expensive. Nonetheless, the total cost for enough solid 14-karat gold sheet and wire for one inlay shouldn't run over ten dollars. Silver and brass, of course, are much cheaper.

The sheet gold and gold wire used for my project was of 1mm thickness and diameter, but this is actually somewhat thicker than necessary. A more ideal thickness would be 21-gauge metal (.0343 inch) and wire. A square piece of sheet some 1 × 1½ inches will make a nice-size oval, and 3 inches of wire will make you six ½-inch nails.

Gold or silver wire and sheet can be purchased in some jewelry shops, but a better place to look is hobby shops specializing in jewelry crafts. If these materials aren't available locally, order direct from a jewelry supply house. Southwest Smelting & Refining Company (see Appendix for address) is one such outfit.

The trick to cutting a perfect oval is to simply fold a piece of paper then double it again. Then, at the corner of the double fold draw one quarter of an oval and cut out with scissors. When the paper is unfolded you have a perfectly symmetrical oval to use as a pattern.

Glue this pattern to your inlay material and cut the inlay to shape with tin snips, scroll saw or jewelers' fret saw, leaving just enough margin to smooth up with a file.

After trimming and filing the inlay to the desired shape, centerpunch the six nail holes and drill with a No. 66 bit. Though this size drill is only .033 inch and the wire diameter is .043 inch (21-gauge); the fit will be about perfect after you get through shaping the nails. Now lightly countersink the holes and you are ready to make some nails.

The wire is simply clipped into six ½-inch lengths and the end of each piece is sharpened. Getting a sharp, tapering point on these tiny pieces of wire can be pretty tedious, but it helps if you hold the wire in a small vise and file a taper on six or eight sides.

Forming a head on the nail requires only a few taps with a light hammer. The trick, however, is gripping the wire securely while the head is being formed. A three-jawed chuck, I found, is about perfect.

Getting a smooth stock-fitting curve on the inlay is easily accomplished by simply placing it in a rounded channel, placing a ½-inch rod on top, and striking the rod a few good licks with a hammer. This way the inlay will come out smoothly curved and unmarred. For a forming channel, I used the barrel channel of a discarded stock.

Begin the inletting by temporarily attaching the inlay to the stock and tracing the outline with a slim-bladed knife. The traditional location for a monogram inlay, by the way, is about 3 inches forward of the buttplate.

With the outline cut to full depth, remove the inlay and, using a small chisel, shave away the wood where the inlay is to fit. Not much cutting is required here—only about ³⁄₆₄ inch or so will do. Upon repositioning the inlay you will find that it does not fit properly even though the inletting appears perfect. This is because of the curvature of the stock. Further cutting is required along the "downhill" sides of the inletting to allow for the "gain" as the inlay is lowered into its slot. Here you'll just have to use the good old cut-and-try technique. *(Text continues on page 219)*

Steps in Fitting a Monogram Inlay

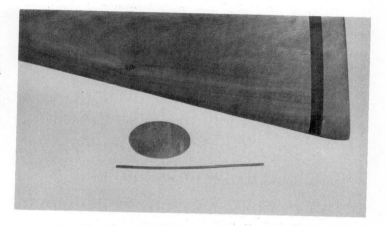

1

All you need to complete this project is a small monogram oval, which can be easily filed or sawed from a number of materials such as silver, gold, copper, brass, German silver, etc. You will also need a length of matching wire.

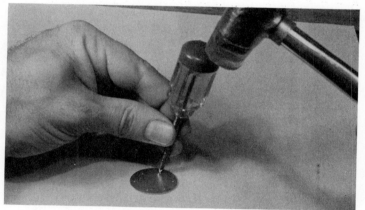

2

The first step, after cutting out the oval (see text) , is to center-punch four to six spots where holes will be drilled.

3

The drilling operation. An electric hand drill is an easy way, but the job can be done with a hand-powered crank drill.

4

After drilling the holes it is necessary to countersink each one slightly. Countersink the holes to a depth of about half the thickness of the inlay material.

5

The first step in making the retaining pins is to sharpen the edge of the wire. It is easiest to sharpen the wire to a point with a file, then cut the retaining nail to the necessary length and continue sharpening the next length of wire. This is easier than cutting all the nails to length before sharpening.

6

A fast and simple way of holding the nails for the "heading" operation is to grip them in a three-jawed drill chuck. Hold the wire sections firmly in the chuck with about 1/16 inch protruding. Tap the protruding tip lightly with a small hammer until a flat head is formed.

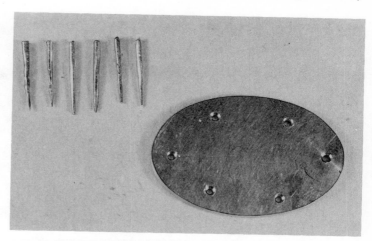

7

The finished monogram inlay with six handmade nails.

8

The next step is bending or curving the monogram inlay so that it will closely follow the curvature of the stock. A trick is to place the monogram inlay, face down, in the barrel channel of a discarded stock, then carefully tap the inside with a rod. This will give the inlay a smooth, even curvature.

9

After the inlay has been bent to approximate shape, attach it to the stock with only two nails. Do not drive the retaining nails full depth, as they will have to be removed later.

10

With a small, narrow-bladed knife, trace the edges of the inlay into the stock.

11

When the inlay is removed, a cleanly cut outline is left.

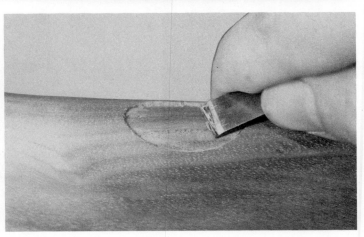

12

The next step is simply slicing away the wood inside the traced boundaries. Though this part will be covered by the inlay it is a good idea to cut it smooth and flat so that the inlay will be well supported and will not rock back and forth as sometimes happens.

13

The monogram inlay is in place with the nails driven flush and the overall surface finished roughly. The wood and metal are polished together with progressively finer sandpaper and steel wool.

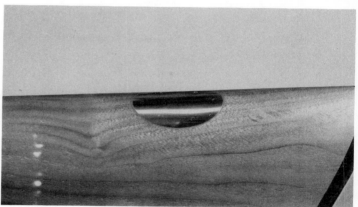

14

The finished and polished inlay. If you have engraving talents you can carve your own monogram or have it done at a jewelry shop.

With the inlay fully in place, at last you can begin driving in the nails. A few light taps on each nail head flows the metal into the countersinking and helps ensure a really close fit. However, don't try to hammer the nail heads flush with the inlay or all you'll do is bend the inlay.

The nail heads are filed flush with the inlay and the inlay is worked flush with the stock. Gold and silver cut so easily that a bit of finishing paper wrapped around a file cuts fast enough as well as leaving a flat, smooth surface. For final polishing use extra-fine steel wool.

If there isn't a gun engraver in your neighborhood who can cut your initials on the inlay, just visit your local jewelry store. They'll probably have someone who is pretty good at engraving nice monograms. Cost usually runs about a dollar per letter.

IV

Metalsmithing: The Professional Look

29 / Styling Trigger Guards

Aside from a bit of elementary drilling and tapping for sights and scope mounts, the average amateur gunsmith or do-it-yourselfer seems instinctively to shy away from cutting or otherwise altering the metal components of a firearm. Some craftsmen will whittle and rasp a stock to a fare-thee-well, but never consider laying a tool on a piece of gun steel.

In this section we will discuss some basic (and not so basic) metalsmithing projects which will add a lot of style and grace to otherwise prosaic or downright ugly metal parts.

We'll begin with one of the simplest, best-looking, yet least attempted metalsmithing projects—the restyling of an ugly military trigger guard into a graceful, classic guard bow. You've no doubt seen any number of do-it-yourself military-to-sporter rifle conversions which were nicely fitted with a sporter-style stock but still didn't look truly custom because the military guard and floorplate were left as they had always been.

Amateurs are not the only offenders in this area; far more than a few experienced professionals seem perfectly willing to render a military Mauser or Springfield '03 trigger guard no service other than a buffing and bluing. Perhaps this lack of attention to detail is a matter of economics, or perhaps it never occurred to many folks that the line and form of a trigger guard was a definite part of the overall artistic effort. Judging from the decidedly unsightly trigger guards that may even be found on commercial rifles, I suspect the latter condition is generally the case.

Whatever the cause may be, it certainly isn't because reshaping a military trigger guard is too much hard work. Nor is it because expensive, hard-to-use metalworking tools are required.

One hour's time, a small half-round file, three sheets of sandpaper, a wad of fine steel wool, and you can turn a prosaic military (or commercial) trigger guard and floorplate assembly into a strikingly graceful fixture which will do justice to any well-turned sporter.

First of all, take a long, close look at the trigger guard you've decided to streamline. Chances are this is the first time you've ever noticed just how ugly the thing is. You'll notice that the guard bow is of uniform width and also of the same width as the rearward extension. This "sameness" is graceless and monotonous and from the standpoint of guarding the trigger totally unnecessary. It got that way because of manufacturing expediency. Fortunately, however, the wide, thick guard bows have plenty of metal, which allows plenty of reshaping for modern or classic styling. Too, the guards are of a rather mild, even-textured steel which is fast-cutting and can be finished to a high polish using only hand tools.

Begin work by scribing a line along either side of the guard assembly at the stock line. The trigger-guard bow will be reshaped, so that it slopes slightly inward from this line. If the line is accurately scribed and the cutting precise, the effect will be that of the bow curving away from and in harmony with the stock. This is much more graceful than the right-angle appearance of the issue guard.

With the guard held firmly in the vise or clamp fixture, cut two grooves about 1/8 inch deep and 1/2 inch wide on each side of the bow near the scribed lines. This is easily done with a half-round wood rasp. The rounded side cuts just about the correct curvature for the groove, and the mild steel cuts pretty easily with a good grade of wood rasp. Let the edge of the groove flow right up to the scribed lines, but be sure to keep the edge or shoulder formed here sharp and straight.

Now work the other side of the groove outward around the bow so that a gracefully curving edge is formed completely around the edge of the bow. The effect thus achieved is of the bow sloping to a narrow width just below the stock, then flaring out as it curves below the tip of the trigger. The width of the bow should be reduced so that at the widest point it is narrower than the guard strap. (The strap or rear extension is the portion inletted into the stock.) You may find that the overall effect is even better if the rear of the bow is cut even slimmer than the forward part of the bow.

Now, as shown in the illustrations, use the rounded side of a small, half-round rasp or a round file to begin cutting flutes around the outer edges of the bow near the strap. Cut and smooth the flutes so that a gentle curving surface seems to flow inward and upward into the bow. The sculpturing should flow to an edge formed by the inside curve of the bow.

The forward edge of the bow on some military models has an unsightly structure which must be ground, filed, or sawed away. The hole through the forward-portion bow presents no problem, for there is still plenty of metal remaining after the surrounding portion is cut away. With this chore completed, proceed to sculpture the forward edge of the bow like the rear.

A trick worth learning is to follow the lead of the natural curve of the rasp. Let this cutting surface do the work, and the concave surfaces you're shaping have a way of coming out smoothly cut and gracefully curved. In other words, don't fight your tools—let them do the work.

When the base points of the bow are fully shaped, begin cutting around the outer edges of the bow. Curve the edges downward until they almost meet the inside edges. The curvature should be cut so that the outside surface of the bow curves gently from one side to the other.

Now, going to the inside of the bow, file a slight curve from side to side. This curve is much more shallow than the contour of the outside surface. However, the degree of curvature should increase near the base of the bow on both ends. Don't worry about the edges around the bow being too sharp; you'll dull them down during the polishing operation.   *(Continued on page 229)*

How to Style a Trigger Guard

1

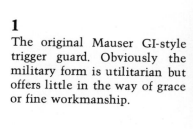

The original Mauser GI-style trigger guard. Obviously the military form is utilitarian but offers little in the way of grace or fine workmanship.

2

The first step in refurbishing the trigger guard is to scribe a straight line establishing the upper edge of the trigger-guard bow. The stock line meets this line when the trigger-guard unit is fully inletted. Therefore the restyling and reshaping should not extend beyond this line.

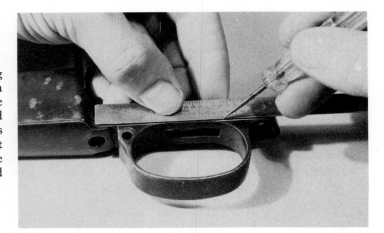

3

The next step is thinning the trigger-guard bow near the rear extension. Here a coarse-cut file is used to get rid of excess metal in a hurry. Trigger-guard metals are usually quite soft and not difficult to file.

4

A detail of the work immediately after thinning or "pinching" the trigger-guard bow.

5

A half-round file is used to begin the sculpting or contouring of the trigger-guard bow. Note how the square edges of the trigger guard have already been rounded off.

6

The shaping has been completed with the rough-cut file. From here on out it is simply a matter of finishing and polishing the trigger guard.

7

The file marks are easily worked away with a bit of sandpaper wrapped around a file. Start off with a 120-grit paper and then work down to 220-grit and on to 400-grit finishing paper.

8
Don't neglect the inside of the trigger-guard bow; a good finish on the inside is a sign of careful workmanship.

9
Final polishing is a good scrubbing with fine steel wool.

29-10
The polished and reworked trigger guard prior to bluing.

11
This trigger guard is being reblued with a quick cold-blue preparation.

12
The finished trigger guard after resculpting. This is a fast job but adds style and beauty to a military conversion.

Use 400-grit wet or dry finishing paper wrapped around a dowel for the concave surfaces, and a soft sanding block for the outside surfaces. By this time you're probably pretty tired of sanding and polishing, but here's where it really pays off. Of course, if you have a buffing wheel just buff it to a bright polish and you're home free. If you don't have a wheel, however, just pick up the paper and keep working. Inspect all surfaces, inside and out, for any signs of file or sanding marks. Also run the finishing paper around the edges of the guard bow. A fairly sharp edge looks best, but of course you don't want it sharp enough to cut or scrape anything—especially your finger. Now give everything a brisk rubdown with a wad of super-fine steel wool.

If you are planning to reblue the remainder of the trigger-guard assembly and floorplate it is a good idea to give these surfaces a brisk once-over with finishing paper and steel wool. Chances are the floorplate has some nicks and scratches, but these can easily be worked with finishing paper.

When all polishing is completed, secure the assembly in the vise so that all surfaces to be blued are exposed. Now give the whole thing one more brisk rubdown with clean steel wool to remove all fingerprints. Metal which is somewhat warm tends to take cold blue better, so don't be afraid to generate a little heat with the final rubdown. I apply the bluing solution immediately after the rubdown. Whatever your brand of bluing, follow the application instructions printed on the bottle or tube.

Two or three applications with rubdowns between may be required to get the desired depth of color. The mild steel usually used for trigger-guard assemblies tend to take a deep rich bluing which is impossible to tell from hot-bath bluing. You will, of course, have to follow directions for best results. Most of the failures experienced with cold bluing solutions are caused by improperly preparing the metal or not following instructions.

Once the bluing is completed to your satisfaction, give the guard a coat of oil, put it back in the stock, and take a long, admiring look at the fine work you've done.

Another restyled trigger guard in place on a sporter rifle.

30 / Making a Hinged Floorplate with Lever Release

After a day or two of admiring your nice work on the trigger-guard project you're going to begin looking at the rest of the trigger-guard assembly and wondering what more can be done to take away the plainness. Most military floorplates attach by means of a tongue-and-groove catch which was originally designed to operate by depressing the release catch with the point of a bullet. When released, they jump loose like a jack-in-the-box. Such a Mickey Mouse arrangement might be OK for a military weapon but certainly not for a fine sporting rifle.

Fortunately, the existing floorplates on these surplus military rifles can be converted to a hinged model with classy lever release with surprisingly little effort. The final result is a lot like those featured on those beautiful Mauser sporters from before World War II which cost so much these days.

Since a hinged floorplate is a feature usually found only on the more expensive guns, one might assume that there is considerable work involving intricate machinery. Such, however, is not the case. As the illustrations show, the only tools needed are a couple of files, a drill, and a torch. Timewise the whole project fits very nicely into a single evening.

Begin work by inspecting the floorplate you wish to convert. Notice how it clips into the trigger-guard assembly and is held in place by narrow lips which fit into slots at either end of the magazine well.

The first step is to file these lips off. Do not cut away the molding where the lips were, as the front molding will serve as a hinge support and both the front and rear moldings help align the floorplate with the trigger-guard assembly.

The hinge bar shown in the illustrations was made from a piece of ⅜-inch keystock about an inch long. I chose Key stock because it is nice and square, is easy to file, and blues nicely. Mostly, however, I chose it because there happened to be a piece handy when I started work on this project. Actually, most anything will do so long as it is about ¼ inch square or a bit larger. Just select something that is reasonably tough but is easily filed and will blue properly. If there is any question about the bluability of any given piece of metal, try a drop of cold blue. If the cold blue works OK, you can figure it will take hot blue also. But for that matter, cold blue will do fine for this project anyway.

Next file a notch in the lip molding for the hinge bar. If you center the notch carefully you'll save yourself alignment difficulties later on.

Upon fitting the hinge bar into the notch, you will find that while the bar rests squarely on the flat edge inside the floorplate, some extra support is needed. Thus the hinge bar itself should be notched until there is an extension of "foot" extending down into the milled-out recess on the inside of the floorplate. Be sure to cut the forward edge of this notch square and sharp so that it fits against the forward edge of the floorplate without any sign of a gap.

The next step is to solder the hinge bar to the plate. My technique was simply to sandwich a thin piece of ribbon silver solder between the two parts, clamp everything together, and then heat the whole works until the solder ran. Actually a good union with cold (lead-and-tin) solder would be strong enough and is less trouble. Keep in mind, however, that hot-bath-type bluing will play hell with cold solder. Cold bluing causes no problem.

A possible alternative to silver solder is Force-44 solder such as is sold by Brownell's. Force-44 melts at a relatively low temperature but still resists hot-bath bluing.

With the hinge bar in place, the next step is to cut a recess for it in the forward extension of the guard assembly. Though this is mainly a task for the files, a lot of excess bulk can be gotten out of the way in a hurry with a ¼-inch drill. Simply drill a couple of holes, side by side, where the hinge bar will eventually fit, then drill a third hole angling up through the magazine wall. This takes care of opening up the slot and leaves only a bit of dressing up with the files.

After squaring up the corners of the slot and evening the walls, you can start fitting the hinge bar. Naturally, the closer the fit the better the finished product will look, so take it slow and easy here.

Fitting the hinge bar into the slot is nothing more complicated than the good old-fashioned cut-and-try method. Simply open up the sides of the slot until the bar can be wiggled into place. Don't worry if it seems a bit too tight —it'll loosen up with a bit of use. Just try to make the fit as snug as you can manage.

Along about here you'll probably find that the hinge bar is a little too long for the slot you've cut. So, cutting only a little at a time, trim back the bar until it fits perfectly in the slot when the floorplate is in the full forward position. With everything fitting snug and flush here, we're ready to move on to drilling a hole for the hinge pin.

You must take care to see that the hinge bar is fully inserted in its slot and that the floorplate is perfectly positioned in the trigger-guard assembly. Also it is important that the hole be drilled at a near-perfect right angle to the edge of the guard. If the pin goes in at a crooked angle, the floorplate will not swing so freely—if at all. So take care with the drilling operation. Of course if you have a drill press it's easy.

The size of the hinge pin is up to you. You can use whatever sort of pin stock you happen to have on hand. About 3/32 inch or thereabouts is fine, and the shank from a broken drill bit makes a perfect pin because it is good and hard.

With the pin in place you have a sho'nuff for real hinged floorplate and you can flop it up and down to your heart's content. However, there is still work to be done. The top of the hinge bar has to be worked down flush. This is a simple job with the file, but be sure to keep your work smooth and level. When the bar is flush, wrap a piece of 220-grit finishing paper around the file and continue to smooth up the surface. At this point sand lengthwise with the guard assembly. Next switch to 320-grit paper, or finer, and wind up the polishing with steel wool.

Making the release lever is just as easy. What could have been the sticky point—undercutting the trigger guard for the lever catch—has, in fact, already been done for us on Mausers, Springfields, and 1914–17 Enfields. We simply make use of the milled undercut just forward of the trigger-guard bow originally intended for the floorplate catch lip.

Though any sort of mild steel will do, a piece of 3/8-inch or 1/2-inch cold rolled key stock about 4 inches long will do fine. Actually the finished lever will only be some 2 inches long, but the additional length makes a nice "handle" for holding the lever in a vise during the shaping process.

Begin work by tracing the profile of the lever on the key stock. Arrange the pattern so that both the lever arm and the pivot shank will be single piece. It takes a bit more filing this way, but the added strength and simplicity are worth the effort. Also by doing it this way you get one up on the old-world gunsmithing wizards who made the lever arm separate from the shank and then had to hold the two parts together with a screw *that showed from the outside.* Our way keeps the outside parts free of screws and is thus much better-looking.

(Text continues on page 238)

How to Make a Hinged Floorplate

1

The first step in making a hinged floorplate is sawing or filing away the original floorplate catch mechanism, which is similar on Mauser, Springfield, and Enfield rifles.

2

Also the lip which hooks into the front of the trigger-guard assembly is filed away. File the lip only so that it is perfectly flush with the shoulder.

3

The rough-filed hinge bar. The notch is necessary so that the hinge bar can straddle the molding at the front of the floorplate. There is also a rim at the front of the floorplate which must be notched itself in order for the hinge bar to fit properly.

4

The hinge bar clamped onto the front edge of the floorplate. Heat is being applied with a butane torch to apply the solder.

5

The hinge bar after being soldered to the floorplate but before being cleaned up. Note how the hinge bar fits neatly into a notch filed into the forward floorplate rim. The soldering technique used here is that described in Chapter 5.

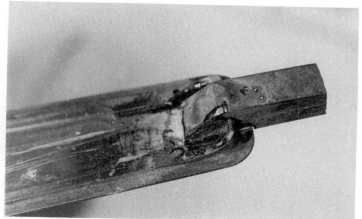

6

Moving on to the trigger-guard assembly. The opening for the hinge bar is being hogged out with an electric drill.

7

After excess metal has been hogged out with a drill bit, the sides of the cut are smoothed up with a file. This cut must be very carefully made so the hinge bar fits snugly without gaps.

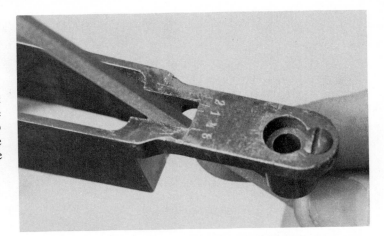

8

With the floorplate properly held in position in the trigger-guard assembly, the hingepin hole is drilled.

9

The fitted, hinged floorplate before final finishing. The next step is to file the hinge bar flush with the rest of the trigger-guard-assembly front extension.

10

After final finishing the hinged floorplate should work like this.

11

The next step is beginning work on the release lever. Any type of mild steel can be used. I selected key stock material for this project because it blues nicely and it is quite easy to file. Tough steels are not necessary. In this photo the rough shaping, which is done almost entirely with a file, is underway.

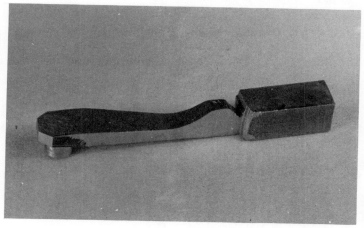

12

The rough-shaped release lever. Note that the top and side profiles have been cut to shape but the lever has not been rounded as yet. By establishing both the side and top shapes first it is easier to contour the lever uniformly. Note the "tail" or excess stock still attached to the lever. This bit of excess metal makes it easier to hold the part in a vise during the preliminary shaping. It can be removed later.

13
The post piece which extends through the floorplate is first filed square and then octangular. This makes it easier to file into a precisely round shape.

File the profile to shape, but make no attempt to contour the lever for the time being. If you establish both side and top profiles first it will be much easier to get smoothly flowing symmetrical contours later. Also be sure to leave the "handle" attached.

Filing the pivot shank to a near-perfect cylinder may seem a formidable task but is, in fact, quite simple. The square form is first cut to an eight-sided shape, which then is rounded off. The proper diameter of the shank is determined by the size of the hole which already exists at the rear of the floorplate. A little cut-and-try here will get you a perfect fit.

After the pivot shank and the side and top profiles have been filed to shape, you are ready to move on to working the lever down to final shape. Also, this is as good a time as any to cut the lug off the inside of the floorplate. These are always of mild steel and easy to cut with a hacksaw. Use a file to dress the inner surface smooth and flush.

Frankly, it is difficult, if not impossible, to describe how to shape a form by words alone. Therefore your best guide will be the illustrations shown on these pages. Note how the contours flow gracefully with no sharp edges or slab-sided surfaces.

Most of the shaping can be done with a simple six-inch three sided file or even a round chain saw file. A set of needle files, if you have one, is very helpful but not really necessary.

During this final shaping is where you really begin to appreciate that "handle" fastened to the rear end of the lever. If it were not for this you'd really have a job trying to hold on to the small lever and file on it too. You'd file as much skin as steel.

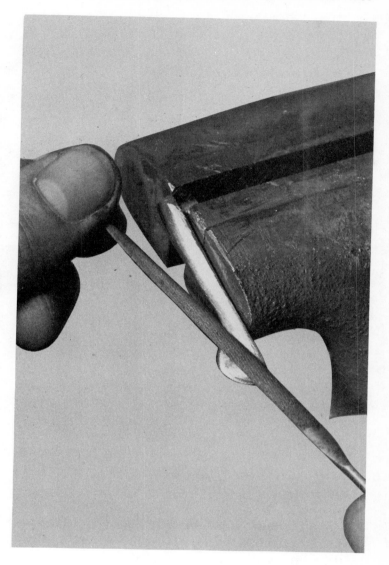

14
Needle files are used to achieve the delicate shape you want for a graceful lever.

For final finishing wrap a strip of 220-grit or 320-grit finishing paper around the file and work out the tool marks and scratches made by the filing operation. When the lever is smooth you can cut off that handy little handle and then smooth up that last little scar. Now you're ready to install the lever.

The floorplate is locked in place by a small latch arm which pivots laterally, entering into that milled recess in the trigger guard we discussed earlier.

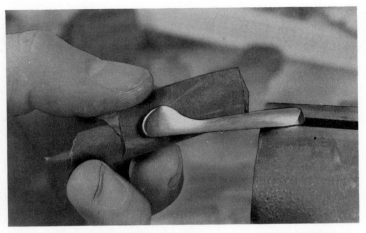

15

The nearly finished lever is smoothed with a small pad of fine-cut sandpaper.

16

The release lever, showing the catch tab, which is held in place by a screw. The tab is held in place simply by tapping the underside of the release-lever post and fitting a screw.

    Since the latch must fit rather snugly and be in positive alignment with the lever, it is necessary to attach the two parts in such a way that any slipping will be impossible. This is accomplished easily enough by a simple tongue-and-groove union with the two parts held together by a small screw running down though the latch piece and threading into the lever shank. A 6-48 screw is fine for this job, and just about everyone who tinkers with guns has a 6-48 tap.

    The latch piece should be about ½ inch square and about ¼ inch or so thick. Don't worry too much about the shape at the beginning, because it will undergo a good bit of reshaping before the job is done. For openers, cut it down just enough so that it will fit in the lug well—the hole in front of the

17

The catch tab in place in the trigger-guard unit. When the lever is turned to the side the tab swings clear of the catch notch and allows the floorplate to open.

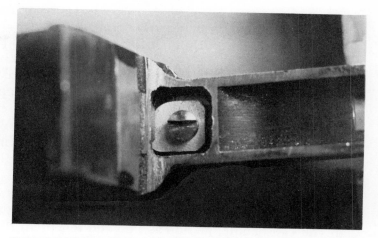

18

Another detail of the catch tab showing the tab in the closed, or locked, position. The catch tab fits directly into the original recess in the trigger-guard unit.

trigger guard bow—when the lever is in the full open position (at right angles to the floorplate).

The next step is cutting down the edge of the latch so that it will slip into the locking slot when the lever is moved to the "closed" position. Since this is a "blind" operation, there is no other way to go about it except to cut a little, give it a try, and cut some more.

A handy hint here is to cut a bevel on the leading edge of the latch arm so it can slip into the slot easily. Once the edge catches in the slot it is an easy matter to file the rest of the latch to the correct shape. It is a good idea to bevel the entire surface of the latch slightly so that it wedges tight as the lever is moved to closed position. This gives the floorplate an extra-tight closure.

Repeated use over a period of time will probably result in some wearing of the locking surfaces, which could result in looseness. This can be avoided by heat-treating the latch. Holding the latch piece by a piece of wire through the screw hole, heat it to a cherry red, and quench it in oil. Test the surface with a file to see if the proper degree of hardening occurred. If not it may be necessary to heat it again and quench it in water. It all depends on the type of steel you're using.

All that remains is to blue the floorplate lever. Cold blue will do fine if the lever is polished clean and is free of oil and fingerprints. Repeated applications of the cold-bluing solution will darken the blue until it matches the rest of the guard assembly.

The trouble with these little do-it-yourself projects is that all your shooting pals want you to do the same on their guns. So if you don't want more work than you can handle, just do as I do and tell them that the work was done by your little old master gunsmith deep in the Black Forest.

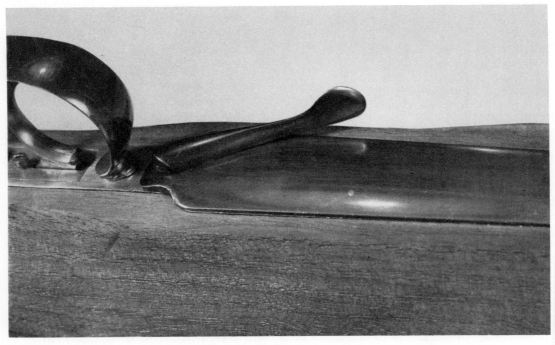

19 The finished release lever in the open position. When the lever is pushed to the side the floorplate springs open because of the follower spring contained inside. The release lever and catch tab should be closely fitted and adjusted so that the release lever remains snugly in position when the floorplate is closed.

31/ Installing a Shotgun-Style Trigger Guard on a Rifle

Did you ever look at the gracefully curving trigger guard on a fine double-barreled shotgun and wonder why rifles don't have such nice features? Well, as a matter of fact, there's no reason why *your* rifle can't. The job calls for getting rid of the existing guard, a little drilling and tapping, and a tiny bit of inletting metal into wood, but you can complete the whole project in one evening with only a few simple hand tools.

The first step is finding a suitable shotgun-type guard. Gunsmiths usually keep a stock of salvage parts on hand, and a search through their junk might turn up just what you're looking for. Of course you can always buy a new guard. The guard shown on these pages is an original Mannlicher-Schoenauer rifle trigger guard ordered from Stoeger. Price is in the neighborhood of ten dollars. If you order the Mannlicher guard, be sure to specify the *set trigger* model. Other fine guards available include those for the Browning and Charles Daly over-and-unders, Stoeger's Zephr, and the Winchester Model 21 double.

Begin work by getting rid of the existing trigger guard. This is easily accomplished by holding the guard assembly in a vise and cutting the bow off with a hacksaw. Next file down the "stumps" until the guard plate is smooth and flush.

The next step is to find the proper position for the new guard. In the case of double set triggers, be sure to allow enough room behind the rear trigger for it to be "set" or cocked and enough room for a finger in front of the forward trigger. Most double-barreled-shotgun guards as well as the Mannlicher guard were designed for double triggers, so there is plenty of room. However, rifle double set triggers tend to be a bit longer than shotgun triggers, and it could be that the guard bow may not be deep enough. This can be corrected by rebending the bow until the triggers have ample clearance all around. If your rifle is a single-trigger model there is even less to worry about. Simply position the guard where it looks best.

My guard was attached to the plate by drilling and threading with a ¼-inch 28-thread tap. The shank on the Mannlicher guard came threaded in a metric pitch, which I converted by simply running into a ¼-inch 28-thread die. This is a makeshift procedure but works fine. Of course, if you've found an American-made guard bow, all you have to do is match the existing thread when you tap the hole in the guard plate. It could also be that you'll be using a guard with a larger or smaller shank. It doesn't matter what pitch thread you use, but it is best to use as fine a pitch as possible.

Two examples of finished shotgun-style trigger guards.

The reason for this is that when the guard is screwed in place it probably won't line up properly when it hits bottom. This is corrected by filing a small amount of metal from under the flange just at the base of the shank. With a fine-pitch thread it doesn't take much of this filing and fitting to bring the guard around to proper alignment with the rest of the guard assembly. Be careful not to force the guard into position. Too much pressure will only strip the threads and then you'll be in a *real* mess.

With the metalwork completed, you're ready to inlet the bow extension into the stock grip. First you will have to bend the extension, or tang, so that it matches the curve of the grip. Next, with the tang held close to the grip, trace or scribe the outline into the wood. The tangs on shotgun-style guards usually have a slight inward bevel to facilitate inletting. If your guard doesn't have this bevel it is a good idea to file a bit of an angle before you begin the inletting. A square (nonbeveled) edge is more apt to cause chipping or splitting as the metal is repeatedly removed from the wood during the inletting process.

After cutting the outline to full depth with an incising knife, start removing the wood with a narrow, sharp chisel. A wide chisel takes out more wood faster, of course, but a narrow chisel of about 1/8-inch width is much easier to control. And since you're working in a rather cramped area anyway you need all the control you can get.

When the tang is inletted full depth, fit the tang screw and you're about home free. With luck and careful workmanship it could very well be that no additional work will be required on the stock (that is, if you were working on a finished stock). But on the other hand it may be necessary to file or rasp the metal and wood to get a perfectly flush fit. Then for a really flush fit, sandpaper the wood and metal together and you won't even be able to feel where wood starts and metal stops.

With the rear extension of the trigger-guard assembly filed down, the rear action screw will probably protrude somewhat. If it sticks up enough to be unsightly the cure is simply to file it down flush with the rest of the plate. If necessary the slot can be deepened with a needle file so your screwdriver won't slip and make the head look messy.

Now all you have to do is polish everything nice and bright with finishing paper and steel wool then dab on a bit of cold blue.

Looks great, doesn't it?

How to Install a Shotgun-Style Trigger Guard

1

The original Mauser trigger-guard bow is sawed off with a few strokes of a hacksaw.

2

After the bow of the trigger guard has been removed the rear extension is filed flat with a smooth-cut mill file.

3

The rear extension after filing is finished. The double-set-trigger housing discussed in the next chapter is in place here.

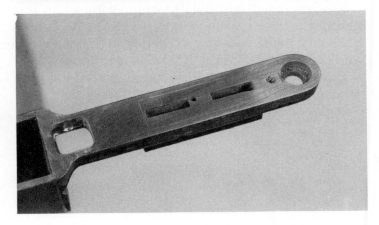

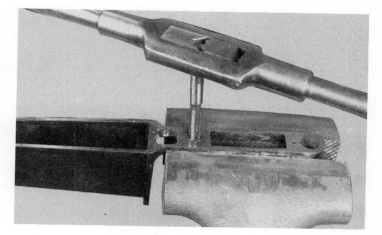

4

After the shotgun-style trigger-guard bow is positioned, the rear extension is drilled and tapped in position.

5

With the trigger-guard assembly in place in the stock, the stock is worked flush with the upper surface of the extension.

6

While holding the rear trigger-guard-bow tang in the proper position against the grip, scribe or mark the outline with a sharp scribe.

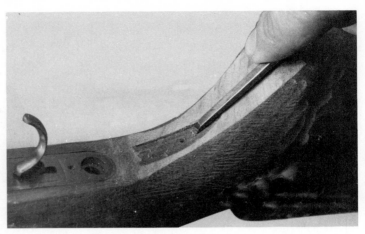

7
Next, the trigger-guard tang is inletted into the grip with a small chisel.

8 After inletting the trigger-guard tang, drill the appropriate-size hole and fit the trigger-guard screw. Here it is in final position before the stock is shaped around trigger guard.

32 / Installing Double Set Triggers

Back when I was just discovering the joys of varmint shooting, one of the chief problems with which I had to contend was trying to squeeze off a 300-yard shot at a crow without muscling the crosshairs off the target. Finely adjustable single triggers with pulls that measure in ounces were unknown then, at least to me, and the factory original triggers on my Mausers and Springfields left a lot to be desired.

Clearly, what was needed was a trigger mechanism that would fire at the slightest touch, but the only triggers of this sort I'd ever seen, aside from vintage "Kentucky" rifles with "hair" triggers, were the double set triggers on finely made European sporting rifles. These triggers could be adjusted so fine that only a whisper of a touch would set them off. This type of trigger, I reasoned, would be perfect for long-range varmint potting. Alas, however, the only rifles I could find equipped with double set triggers were of foreign origin chambered for weird-sounding cartridges which were hard to come by and no good for varmint shooting anyway. So, taking the only route known to me at the time, I traded dearly for a set-trigger-equipped German sporter and sent it to be rebarreled for the then wildcat .22/250 cartridge.

When the newly rebarreled rifle arrived it was suddenly a whole new ball game. Busting varmints and assorted other critters way out yonder was ridiculously easy. I'd just cock the rear trigger, line up the crosshairs on old Mr. Crow, gently stroke the front trigger, and there'd be nothing left but fog and feathers.

I immediately wanted more rifles with set triggers, but the big problem with this was that European-made rifles with set triggers were mighty expensive, even in those days. Thus the only other choice I had was to equip my collection of rifles with double set triggers *of my own manufacture*. Or, at least, I thought this was my only alternative. After some days of sawing, filing, pol-

249

ishing, and fitting, I had succeeded in making and installing what might have been termed set triggers (but they did work). But in the process I also reached the decision that my first set of handmade set triggers would also be my last.

As luck would have it, about two weeks after my attempt at making set triggers I came across an ad for ready-built, ready-to-install set triggers. The price, as I remember, was something like six dollars. My immediate reaction was complete elation at having located a source for ready-made triggers and utter despair at all the time and effort I'd wasted only a couple of weeks before. At any rate, within a short time I'd installed these ready-made triggers not only on all of my own varmint rifles but on those of my shooting buddies as well.

Set triggers not only eliminate much of the bad shooting caused by poor trigger control or "jerking," but also tend to lend a certain flair and distinction to a sporting arm.

Working time is only about one evening, and the only tools you'll need are a drill with a small bit, a couple of files, and a scrap of sandpaper or steel wool. A hand-held grinding tool such as the Dremel Moto-Tool is mighty handy and speeds things up a bit if you happen to own one. Of course you'll also need the set-trigger mechanism and parts for the conversion. These are available from Brownell's. The conversion kit, complete with all the parts you'll need, sells for about fifteen dollars. Though these triggers are commonly available for '98 and FN Mauser only, they can, with a little modification, be made to work on the Springfield, the Model 14 and Model 17 Enfields, and a few other makes and models.

Virtually every Mauser you're liable to find, be it military or commercial, will have a milled channel in the inside surface of the trigger guard's rear extension. The purpose of this channel is to remove weight. For over half a century and regardless of manufacturer the dimensions of this cut have remained remarkably uniform. This is very fortunate for our purposes, because the presence of this channel eliminates most of our work. All we have to do is enlarge the channel enough to make room for the set-trigger mechanism.

The first step, after disassembling the trigger mechanism, is to measure the width of the channel to see how close the trigger body comes to a perfect fit. As a rule the trigger body or housing will be a trifle wide in order to make allowances for variations in the width of the channel in different rifles. This is easily corrected by either slimming down the trigger body itself or widening the channel.

Also the slot for the original trigger will have to be widened to the full width of the channel. This is done easily enough by inserting the tip of a file into the slot and "having at it." The guard bow will restrict your work with the file somewhat, but as the guards are made of mild steel the work goes pretty quickly. You can protect the inside of the guard bow from banging and scuffing by wrapping it with a layer of tape.

With the trigger slot cut to full width and the channel widened (or the trigger body slimmed, as the case may be), you can begin fitting the mechanism into the guard. In most cases the trigger slot will have to be extended both fore and aft, and you will also notice that the trigger mechanism is beveled on the rear edge. This makes it necessary to cut a corresponding angle at the rear of the slot. Make haste slowly here, as you don't want to cut too much and have an unsightly gap between the two parts. Just cut a little, try the fit, and cut again.

When the mechanism is fully inletted, secure it in place by small pins in each end. Simply drill a $1/16$-inch (or thereabouts) hole through the side of the guard extension right on through the trigger body, but be sure to keep the holes at the extreme ends so as to miss the moving parts of the trigger mechanism. Now make a couple of pins out of small nails, welding rod, or whatever you can find and drive them into the holes. Dress up the sides with a file and it will look real good.

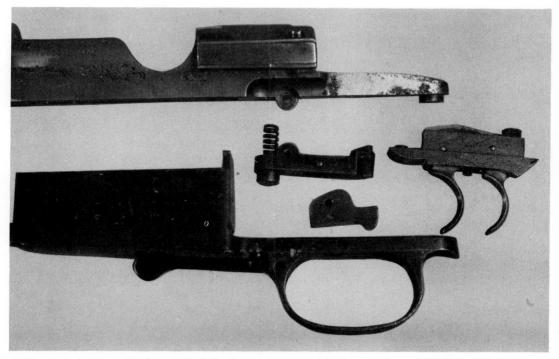

A Mauser receiver with the original single trigger removed, the double-set-trigger replacement unit with parts, and the trigger-guard assembly.

The contour of the underside of the trigger mechanism is designed to match the inside curve of the trigger-guard bow and usually matches up for a pretty close fit. A little dressing up may be in order, however, to get the two parts perfectly matched. A slightly rounded needle file is fine for this, but even a narrow flat file will do in a pinch. Next wrap a piece of 220-grit sandpaper around the file and give the inside of the bow a good polishing. You'll be surprised at the close metal-to-metal fit—only a faint hairline. Now lay on a final polish with a bit of steel wool, apply some cold blue to the bright areas, and no one will ever know this isn't a factory job.

How to Install Double Set Triggers

1
The first step in fitting the double set trigger is enlarging the trigger slot in the trigger-guard assembly. This is easily done with a simple hand file. It can also be done with a grinding tool if you have one available.

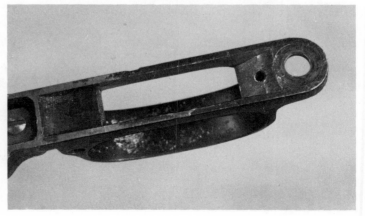

2
Here is the trigger-guard extension after the trigger slot has been widened to accept the double set trigger.

3

The double-set-trigger unit in place and being filed flush with the counter of the trigger-guard bow. Usually the double-set-trigger unit fits quite closely, with minimum of final fitting.

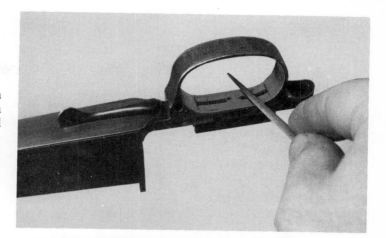

4

The double-set-trigger housing is in place and a retaining-pin hole is being drilled. Perfect alignment is ensured by drilling while the unit is in place in the guard assembly, but make sure that it is fully positioned.

5

The assembly attached with the two retaining pins.

6
Another view of the assembled double-set-trigger unit in place in the trigger guard.

7
The sear adaptor is easily fitted into the original trigger mechanism simply by driving out the original pin, removing the original trigger, and then fitting the adaptor in place.

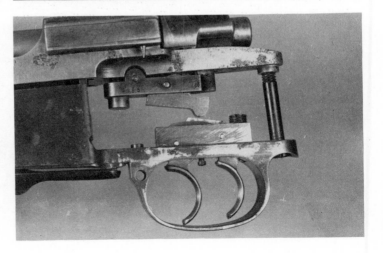

8
This photo shows the proper alignment of the double-set-trigger unit in conjunction with the sear mechanism.

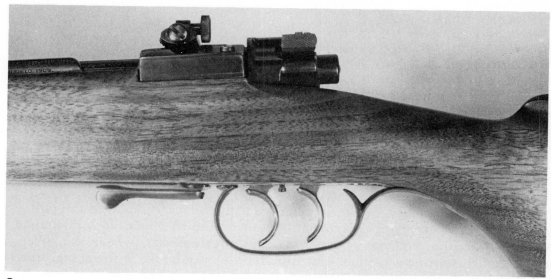

9   The do-it-yourself European sporter described in these pages. The double-set-trigger unit is in place, complete with a shotgun-style trigger guard, hinged lever-release floorplate, etc.

Now remove the pins, take out the trigger body, and reassemble the complete mechanism, being sure to clean out all the dust and grit that has accumulated in the slots and contours of the trigger body while you were at work. While you're at it, you may as well adjust the triggers; the small screw between the triggers is the adjustment for weight of pull. Turn it in (clockwise) to lighten the pull, and back it out for a heavier pull. Some folks tend to adjust the triggers to too light a weight of pull, and as a result trigger function is unreliable and even unsafe. It is best to adjust the triggers so you can distinctly "feel" the trigger as you touch it off.

Next step is installing the "kicker" arm. Simply remove the original trigger and install the kicker in its place. This is done by driving out the pin that holds the trigger in place; nothing else is changed. Make sure the kicker is operating freely, without any bind. With the rifle cocked, press upward on the kicker arm. The firing pin should release and fall. If there is any tendency to bind, it can be corrected by removing the kicker and polishing or stoning the sides a little.

Now check the operation of the entire mechanism by attaching the complete trigger-guard unit to the action and securing it in place with the action screws. With the bolt closed and cocked (rifle unloaded, of course), set the rear trigger and touch off the front one. If everything is working right the rear trigger arm will fly up and strike the kicker, which, in turn, will release the sear and allow the striker to fall. If it fails to work, try again, but this time observe the trigger arm to make sure it is hitting the kicker. If not, check for foreign material in the mechanism which may be blocking the movement. Also you might check again to make sure the kicker arm is working freely.

If both the mechanism and the kicker seem to be operating properly but the rifle still won't fire, it is probably because the trigger arm is too close to the kicker arm. This is corrected by filing away some of the hump on the lower extension of the kicker arm. This hump, by the way, is made oversize to allow for this final adjustment. Keep in mind, however, that when the action and trigger guard are in the stock they will be separated by $1/16$ inch or so, and this may be just the amount of clearance needed.

A final word of caution is in order before using set triggers. Since the pull required to fire set triggers may be only a fraction of an ounce, they take a bit of getting used to. Practice by dry-firing. It is not necessary to cock the bolt to dry-fire with set triggers, since they function independently of the actual firing mechanism. If you simply pull the front trigger the rifle will fire as if it were equipped with an ordinary single trigger. This is helpful if you're wearing gloves or times when single-trigger function is best.

One does not carry a rifle with the triggers in the set position. Only after the sights are on the target should you move the rear trigger to the set position. If a shot is not fired after the triggers are set, they can be disengaged by first opening the bolt and then releasing the mechanism.

Once you get the hang of set triggers and find that you are free of the old trigger-squeeze burden, you'll have to think up some other excuses for those misses. But maybe there won't be any more misses.

33/

Checkering Metal

The checkering of steel is one of the least-discussed facets of the gunsmith's trade. This no doubt stems from a dearth of information among even professional gunsmiths. Very few practicing gunsmiths, it seems, ever do any fine checkering on safeties, bolt stops, or bolt handles, have any real idea of how to go about it, or, for that matter, even own a checkering file.

Perhaps it is this very scarcity of skilled checkerers that helps add distinction to a neatly checkered bolt knob. And too, of course, there's no getting around the fact that a sharply checkered surface greatly increases the gripping qualities. If you doubt this for an instant, compare a brightly polished bolt knob with one that has been checkered *by hand.* (The reason I emphasize "by hand" is that the current Remington 700 series of bolt-action rifles feature checkered bolt knobs, but in this case the checkering is done as part of the investment-casting process which forms the bolt handle. To be sure, it looks good and is nonslip—but it's not nearly so sharp as hand checkering.)

The nonslip properties of checkered steel are even more apparent when you're wearing gloves. As you've probably noticed, it's pretty hard to manipulate a slick bolt handle with gloves, especially if they happen to be the bulky cold-weather variety. With a sharply checkered bolt handle, however, the gloves seem to snag the checkering and hang on almost by themselves.

Aside from the practical side of checkered steel there is also the aesthetic side. Neatly done handwork is always attractive, especially when the craftsmanship is a few cuts above the ordinary. Thus you can appreciate checkered steel for the functional service it performs, its decorative value, and the careful handwork it represents. So for all of these reasons we should do a bit of metal checkering on the European-type sporting rifle we've been working on.

As far as equipment goes the only thing you'll need is a checkering file and a sharp-edged needle file. As a matter of fact, it is possible to do a pretty fair

Steps for Metal Checkering

1

A metal-checkering file in use on a Mauser safety. Note that it is cutting a series of parallel grooves. In order for metal checkering to be neat and precise, the file must be held at a constant angle and not allowed to override previously cut lines.

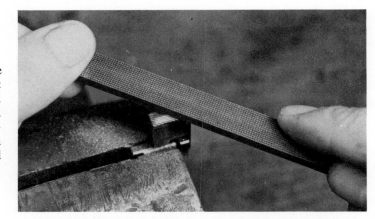

2

The first step of the metal-checkering process is completed. All the grooves going one way have been cut to full depth. Next the file is used to cut grooves in an intersecting right angle.

3

The checkering complete, with the diamonds fully formed.

4
A stiff wire brush is used to clean and polish the checkering.

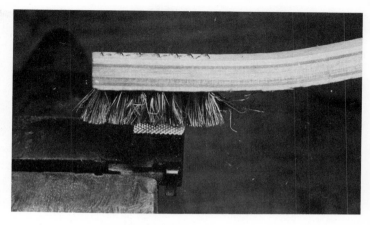

5
The job is finished by applying some touch-up cold blue.

job of checkering with nothing more than a needle file, but this means spacing the lines by eyeball. It's a lot easier and faster to use a checkering file, and they don't cost much anyway. Brownell's stocks checkering files in cuts of twenty, thirty, forty, fifty, and sixty lines to the inch. Prices run from three to ten dollars each, with the price getting higher as the cut gets finer. In case you don't already have a set, Brownell's also has needle files for about seven dollars per twelve-piece set. Get the *fine-cut* model.

Essentially, all a checkering file happens to be is a tool with rows of fine teeth that cut close rows of grooves separated by a narrow, sharp-topped ridge. When two sets of rows are cut so that they intersect each other at an angle, the ridges are divided into individual diamonds with sharp peaks. These sharp peaks, of course, are what gives checkering on wood or steel its nonslip characteristic and handsome appearance.

Needless to say, a checkering file is not used like an ordinary file. The trick to neat metal checkering is being able to keep the file in perfect stroke-after-stroke alignment while the grooves are being cut to full depth. This in itself isn't all that difficult, but it's rather tedious to keep the file working in a straight line and work around a curved surface, such as a bolt knob, at the same time. For this reason it's best to practice on a small, relatively flat surface before tackling the harder jobs.

The first step is to decide on the layout of the checkering. All this involves is establishing the angles of the lines to be cut so that the diamonds will form rows that are more or less harmonious with the lines of the rest of the gun. Keep in mind that the rows should intersect at a 45° to 60° angle. Practice with different angles until you find the one that suits you, or the work you'll be doing, best.

The outside surface of a bolt knob is being checkered.

The small needle file is used to put the finishing touches on a bolt-handle checkering job.

Another application of metal checkering is on the bolt-release tab of Mauser rifles.

My technique for cutting smooth, even rows is, first of all, getting myself and the piece to be checkered into a position that is as uncramped and comfortable as possible. Since it is essential that the tool stay in the groove, it is important that your hand and arm move in a smooth, natural motion. If you try to cut from an awkward angle, you can't feel the position of the tool as well and you're more likely to lead it astray.

When you begin cutting, don't lift the tool from the work to see what kind of a mark you're making. This changes your arm's position and makes it hard to find the groove again. So keep the file pressed down firmly on the work and cut back and forth until the grooves are cut to full depth. You'll know when they are full depth because the tool stops cutting when the ridges come to a point. In other words, it's impossible to cut too deep, because the checkering file won't let you.

If the area to be checkered is wider than the file, simply set the file over about half or two thirds of its width and continue with the pattern. By not setting the file over to its full width you can feel some of the previously cut grooves and thus keep the spacing and angle perfect. The file is most likely to skip and "loose its place" on the first few strokes, so take it easy until you feel the file riding in the grooves.

This skipping about can be especially troublesome on hard surface metal. Many rifle actions, especially older Mausers, have been heat-treated so that there is a thin but extremely hard surface. At first the file will want to slip around on the glass-hard surface, and progress will be slow. But when it breaks through, the going will be a lot easier, because the underlying metal is usually pretty soft. Or, if you prefer, you can buff off the hardened surface on the area

Another bolt checkering job, showing large, coarse diamonds which will give an extremely positive grip.

to be checkered. Don't attempt to draw the hardness by heating, because this will also soften the surfaces that should remain hard. An example of this is Mauser safeties. They usually have a glass-hard surface and pretty well resist a file. However, the crust is easily ground off or can be "wiped" away with a bit of sandpaper wrapped around a file. If you attempted to soften the crust by heating you would also soften the wearing surface where the safety cams in front of the cocking piece. Once this hard surface is gone the safety starts to wear and is much harder to operate.

For our European sporter, three areas should have some checkering: the finger tab on the bolt release, the safety, and, or course, the bolt knob. Done in this order the projects range from quick and easy to relatively difficult. So

A very delicate checkering job on a Mauser bolt-release tab.

you'll be gaining experience as you work your way along toward the hardest part.

My personal choice for checkering size for these three areas is forty to fifty lines to the inch for the bolt-release tab and thirty lines to the inch for the safety and bolt knob. This is following the general rule of thumb of putting finer-line checkering on smaller parts. However, if you wish to invest in only one checkering file for the present, all of the parts can be checkered the same size, and they will look fine. As a matter of fact, all of the checkering shown in the illustrations is thirty lines per inch.

The bolt-release tab is a simple project and should present no problems whatever. The safety is slightly more difficult because it has a slightly curved surface. But once you get the lines in order it should go quite easily.

The bolt isn't all that much harder as far as the actual checkering goes, but it does present the problem of checkering within a bordered area. As with checkering on wood, the idea is to avoid runovers at the pattern's border. But in fact you have a bit of leeway because the runovers can be filed away.

The first step in checkering the knob is marking the outline of the pattern. The most common pattern, and one that always looks good, is the classic teardrop. This is a simple teardrop shape that covers about a third of the knob

Another beautifully done bolt-handle checkering job.

with the point of the tear running up toward the bolt shank. With teardrop panels on the top and underside of the knob, the coverage is two-thirds or so and thus very ample for a really nonslip surface. The outline can be marked with a needle-fine scribe or any other marking device you can think of that won't rub off. Begin the checkering in the center of the pattern and then work your way toward the sides. Don't worry if you nick the outline a little. Just try to get the grooves right up to the edge of the pattern and as deep as possible. In some cramped areas, such as near the root of the bolt shank, you may find it works better to cut the lines only lightly with the checkering file and then cut to full depth one by one with a sharp-edged needle file.

After the panel is completely checkered, deepen the border with a needle file. This will get rid of any runovers, provided they aren't too deep.

A handy hint, if you haven't already guessed, is to checker the underside of the bolt first. This part doesn't show, so any bobbles will be hidden most of the time. After you have done one panel the other should go much better. Of course, the really ideal situation is to have a spare bolt handle or two around to practice on before you attempt the real thing.

Newly cut checkering can be razor-sharp and have a few slivers hanging on just waiting to stick into your fingers. So give the pattern a thorough scrubbing with a wire bristle brush. This gets out the debris, dulls the diamonds somewhat, and polishes the work up a bit.

Aside from the purposes listed here, other likely places to apply your newly learned skill with the checkering file is on handgun backstraps, hammer spurs, triggers, all types of safeties, and the front of handgun trigger guards for two-handed holds. The surface doesn't have to be checkered with the usual diamonds. You may sometimes want to cut simple serrations with a one-way (not crossed) cut. These are especially nice on areas where you want a nonglare surface. Examples of this are the rear edge of front sights, front sight ribs, or pistol-barrel ribs. The possibilities go on and on and the only limiting factor is your imagination. Some gunsmiths, for example, get a nice effect by checkering the heads of active screws. Use your own ideas.

34

Lapping an Action for Better Smoothness and Accuracy

Some of the finest features of a really great custom rifle are details not readily apparent to the eye. But whether you see them or not, these details have a lot to do with how a rifle functions and performs.

If you look inside the action of a bolt rifle that has been customized by a really good professional gunsmith, you'll notice that the blue has been polished away on the rails and on the inside of the receiver walls. This is a final effort to make the bolt work as smoothly as possible. You can test your own bolt-action rifles by working the bolt in and out slowly and noting any tight spots. If the bolt doesn't feel as if it is sliding on greased ice, there are improvements to be made which you can do yourself.

One way to make a bolt run smoothly is simply to lay on the buffing wheel with a heavy hand and thus peel off a few thousandths. Actually, this may do more harm than good, because it makes the bolt loose and wobbly and just as likely to "grab" in the receiver. Bolts that slide in and out with silky smoothness are usually rather closely fitted to the receiver but have no "catch" or "grab" points. Examples of this are Krag and Mannlicher actions, which are extremely close-fitted yet are unmatched for smoothness.

After a bolt has been worked a bit, the points of maximum resistance will become apparent in the form of line-like worn spots. These lines may run the full length of the action but also can be found running radially or in an angled direction. The angled wear lines are caused by abrasive points on the downstroke.

First of all, match these lines up with the offending points in the receiver and see if there are any burrs resulting from the manufacturing process. If so, these should be polished out at once. Also, check for "puckers" where the receiver has been drilled and tapped for sights or scope mounts. It is even possible that sight-mount screws are extending through the receiver walls and scraping against the bolt.

Perhaps the most common offenders are the top, lower, and outside surfaces of external claw-type extractors on Mausers, Springfields, pre-'64 Winchester Model 70s, etc. A quick glance will show where they are rubbing. The situation can be corrected by stoning the scraped areas until contact is reduced or eliminated. Friction between the bolt lugs and bolt ways is reduced by stoning the lugs with a hard Arkansas stone and polishing the ways with fine (400-grit or finer) finishing paper. A good technique here is to cut a piece of hardwood so that it approximately matches the inside cut of the receiver. Attach the finishing paper to the stick with glue or staples and proceed to polish the inside of the receiver to a fine brightness. Not only does this make the action work smoother, it looks a lot better. Most custom gunsmiths prefer to polish the inside of the receiver in this manner after the gun has been blued. This takes out any final roughness, and the brightly polished inside looks mighty good against the blue exterior. Very professional.

A handy tool for "erasing" rough or high spots is the Dremel Moto-Tool with an abrasive-impregnated rubber wheel. These wheels come in assorted sizes to match different contours. My personal experience with the Dremel tool is that the variable-speed rheostat is very worthwhile, because the tool's normal top operating speed causes the polishing wheel to skip and bounce. Reducing the speed makes it much easier to handle and the results are as good as fine hand polishing. So I consider the Dremel variable-speed unit a good investment. You can use it on your other power tools, too.

When an action such as this is properly smoothed and lapped, it not only feels and looks better but may also perform better.

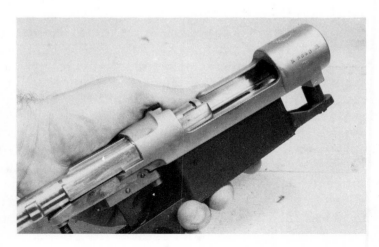

A head-on view of a Mauser action showing the bolt sliding up the bolt ways.

An Arkansas stone can also be used to polish the bolt at points of hard contact with the receiver. This sounds like work, but removing only a slight bit of roughness will sometimes work wonders. Remember, even if the inside of the receiver and the bolt's surface are both rough, you only have to polish one or the other to make the contact comparatively friction-free. A rough surface rubbing over another rough surface causes lots of friction. A slick surface against a rough surface is nearly as good as two slick surfaces. If you doubt this, try running a piece of sandpaper over a piece of glass. This is why an action can be made to work so much more smoothly by simply having a few key contact points on the bolt.

One final thing: Be sure to remove the trigger assembly, sear or cocking piece, and firing mechanism before attempting any lapping or polishing projects. Abrasives will play hell with a trigger mechanism and won't help the rest of the delicate parts either.

Polishing the action of a rifle improves the function in obvious ways. But did you know that lapping the locking lugs can improve accuracy? Though only a tiny percentage of modern actions fail under the pressure of test firing, the odds against a new two-lug bolt bearing evenly in the receiver are something like three to one. While one lug holds firmly, the other (or others) may be free of any contact by as much as .006 inch. This, of course, means that all is not well, because a single lug is holding the entire load.

This is more prevalent with new actions simply because in some older actions, especially if they are of rather soft steel, the condition will correct itself; the lug receiving the greater pressure sets back until the pressure is more or less equalized. This is not good either, because excessive headspace may

267

have been created. It may take surprisingly few shots, by the way, for the lugs to set back in the rear wall of the lug recess of some actions — helping to make it difficult to open. Some of the otherwise beautifully made '98 Mausers shipped to the South American republics are so soft that the lug will set back when the piece was test-fired and have excessive headspace thereafter.

I've personally inspected a number of what appeared to be new and unused arms that had a distinct depression in the lug recess where one of the lugs set back. I suspect that these rifles were fired no more than twice: once by the German manufacturer and once again by the purchasing government. The soft receivers notwithstanding, there would surely have been less setback, or none at all, if the two lugs had borne evenly.

In the case of harder receivers, especially those of more recent American manufacture, the lugs probably won't set back at all and a single lug continues to hold all the pressure. I recently removed the barrel from a Model 70 Winchester of about 1960 manufacture in .264 Winchester Magnum chambering and found no sign of setback despite the fact that the "lazy" lug had never contacted the receiver.

From this one might assume that only one lug is needed anyway, so there is no need to worry about it. An action with two primary lugs was designed with the intent of both lugs bearing evenly and fully. Likewise, modern high-intensity cartridges are loaded to pressure levels which assume maximum holding efficiency from the rifle's action. A bolt that is hanging on by only one lug certainly is not performing at the anticipated level.

Also, lugs which bear unevenly do not in any way contribute to top accuracy. This is why knowledgeable bench-rest shooters insist on lapped locking lugs and top gunsmiths consider lug lapping, or at least an inspection for proper bearing, an important part of fitting a barrel.

The importance of at least a lug inspection was made startlingly clear to me only recently when a routine lug check of a new action of excellent reputation disclosed that neither lug was in contact and the full load would be placed on the safety lug. If that action had fallen into the hands of a gunsmith who fitted barrels without checking the lugs, the results might have been unfortunate indeed. A check for relative contact is accomplished easily enough by simply coating the rear of the lugs with layout blue and then closing the bolt in the receiver. Some care, however, must be taken to make sure that the bolt is being pushed straight to the rear just as it would be by the rearward thrust of a cartridge at the instant of firing.

You cannot, for example, duplicate this rearward pressure simply by exerting rearward pressure on the bolt handle. Nor will the mainspring's rearward pressure on the bolt when the piece is cocked suffice. The natural looseness in the receiver (some have more than others) will allow the bolt to cock out of

Steps in Lapping an Action

1

This is what you need for a proper lug lapping operation. At upper left is a discarded barrel which fits the receiver you intend to lap. Below is a spud which, when pressed in, centers the bolt face and forces the locking lugs back against the receiver locking recesses.

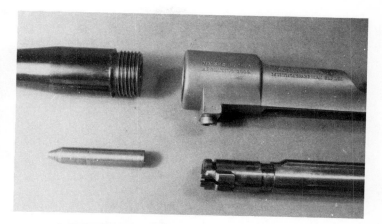

2

The locking lugs are coated with layout blue. When the layout blue dries the bolt is fitted into the action and worked a few times, and then the mating surfaces are examined for uneven lug contact. The blue will be wiped away where the surfaces mate.

3

This closeup shows where the layout blue was worn away where the lug contacted the receiver locking recess.

4

A small amount of lapping compound is applied to the contact surface of the bolt lugs.

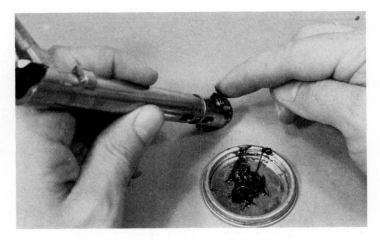

5

The lapping spud in the chamber of the discard barrel.

6

The receiver is screwed onto the discard barrel to the point where fairly firm bolt contact is made against the spud. As pressure is maintained the bolt is worked up and down, lapping the mating surfaces.

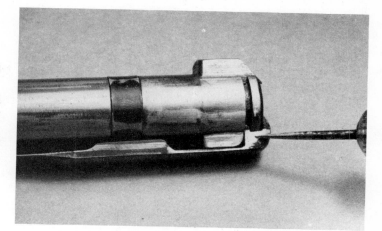

7

The pointer indicates a rubbed spot on the extractor caused by hard friction. This type of friction causes the bolt to operate harder than necessary.

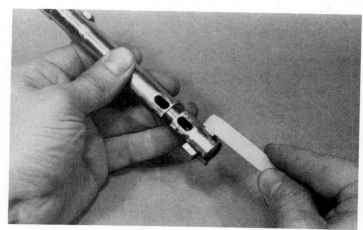

8

A hard Arkansas stone is used to hone the top and bottom surfaces of the locking lug. This ensures smoother operation as the bolt rides back and forward over the receiver ways.

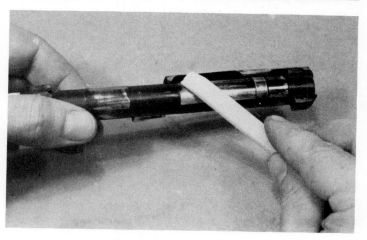

9

The hard Arkansas stone is also used to polish other contact points of the locking lug.

10

On this Springfield bolt you can see where a polishing stone has honed contact points.

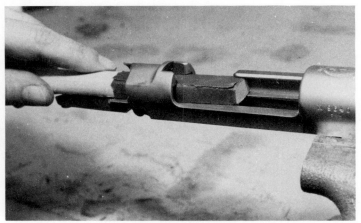

11

The receiver ways and inside walls are being polished with finishing paper. The polishing stick has been shaped so that it closely fits inside the receiver.

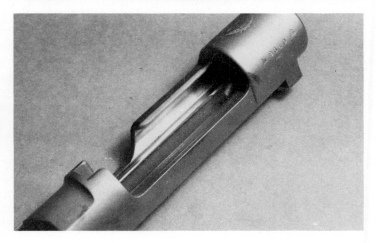

12

The receiver after interior polishing. Note the bright finish on the bolt ways and interior receiver walls. This is a very fine custom touch.

proper alignment and give a false reading. This false reading, by the way, will usually show that the lugs are bearing evenly.

The correct technique is to use a headspace gauge, dummy cartridge, or even a cartridge case with the necessary thickness of shim material between the face of the bolt and the head of the case—after removing the cocking piece and extractor. The idea is to get a firm in-line pressure parallel to the axis of the bore. With the pressure distributed over the face of the bolt and thus holding it at a right angle to the axis of the bore, "cocking" out of true alignment will be largely eliminated and the lugs will bear on the receiver as they do when the rifle is fired.

If the layout blue is scraped from the rear of both lugs smoothly and fully, it means that both lugs are bearing evenly, and all is well. On the other hand, if the blue is peeled from only one lug, it means that that lug is taking all the load. There are, of course, any number of conditions which will be indicated by the imprint on the blue. One lug, for example, may be found to bear fully while only a part of the other lug touches. Or only a small part of both lugs will touch. Any of these conditions is just cause for lapping. You may wonder at this and question the need for lapping when both lugs are contacting equally if not fully. If the lugs do not contact the receiver fully, it means that the full thrust, when transmitted to the receiver, is distributed over a relatively small area. This is more likely to result in setback and also tends to make the bolt harder to open.

The same principles which apply to checking the lug's contact also apply to the actual lapping operation—namely, that firm, direct pressure must be applied to the face of the bolt. Perhaps the best and simplest method is that shown in the accompanying illustrations.

An old barrel is used in conjunction with a steel dummy of approximate cartridge dimensions. The dummy, however, is longer than a normal cartridge. For actions with difficult-to-remove extractors, such as the Remington 700, the head of the dummy should be less than normal case-head size, so the extractor can be left in place without bearing. With the barrel held fast in a vise, the action is screwed on and the dummy inserted in the chamber. Since the dummy is longer than a cartridge, the bolt will not close; so, with closing pressure held on the bolt handle, the receiver is backed off the barrel shank until the bolt will just close. This gives a firm rearward force to the bolt lugs against the receiver. Lapping is accomplished by coating the lugs with a lapping compound and raising and lowering the bolt handle in rapid cycle. As the lapping advances there will be a corresponding lessening of pressure on the bolt handle. To increase the pressure, simply advance the receiver on the barrel shank.

I've heard it suggested that a spring-loaded dummy be fashioned which will

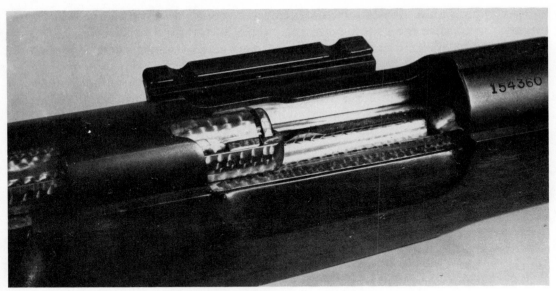

Another receiver which has had considerable polishing on the outside and inside of its action plus a bolt jeweling job.

keep a steady pressure on the face of the bolt during the lapping operation. This sort of a device, however, would not be good. It would aid in polishing the mating surfaces, to be sure, but the spring load would allow the lugs to ride over the high spots and at the same time apply pressure to the low spots. In other words, lap the "valleys" as well as the tops of the mountains. The advantage of the solid dummy is that pressure is applied only to the high spots.

It is possible to lap the lugs with the present barrel in place by using a carefully fitted dummy, a headspace gauge, or even a shimmed cartridge case. Of course, shims must be added as the lapping progresses. The wisdom of using a good headspace gauge for this work is questionable, simply because of its contact with an abrasive action. A maximum gauge may thus become a minimum gauge after a few jobs.

Another problem of lapping lugs with the fitted barrel in place is that you may create a condition of excessive headspace. On an average, a lapping operation will remove from .002 to .003 of metal, but in extreme cases as much as twice that may be removed. Thus, if you already have maximum headspace, the additional removal of metal could result in a critical situation. In this case the correct procedure would be to have a gunsmith turn the barrel in a thread and rechamber — or else use only neck-sized handloads that have been fire-formed in that chamber.

The lapping medium can be fine grinding compound or a fine abrasive flour (about 120 grit) mixed in light grease or petroleum jelly. Simply smear a bit of the lapping compound on the rear surfaces of the lugs and have at it. Be sure to keep the compound off the face of the bolt or you'll be lapping it too. In fact, it's a good idea to put a dab of lubricant on the bolt face to reduce friction against the dummy or whatever you're using.

There are some "self-destructing" lapping compounds available which break down with use and offer no further abrasive action. The one I tried, however, quit before the job was completed and required additional applications.

When the lugs are completely and properly lapped, the surfaces are well polished and it is easy enough to tell by looking that the bearing surfaces contact fully and evenly. Just out of curiosity, however, you may want to put on another coat of layout blue and check everything again. Now, wash the lapping compound off and the job is done.

V

Making Muzzleloaders

35 / Building a Harper's Ferry Pistol from a Kit

Making and shooting muzzleloading rifles, pistols, and shotguns is a popular activity. Much of the charm of black-powder burning is the do-it-yourself.

In these chapters we will discuss the construction of three kits: a pistol, a musket, and then a graceful "Kentucky" rifle. Each project is progressively more difficult, so that beginners can develop their skills at a logical pace without getting over their heads too soon. But at the same time, each project produces a highly authentic muzzleloading gun which not only shoots but makes a handsome decoration mounted on the den wall.

Both the Harper's Ferry pistol and the Brown Bess kits used here feature stocks which are pre-inletted for the barrel, lock, and other accessories, and are precarved to close to final dimensions. The Kentucky-rifle kit takes you a step further, because it is only rough-carved and gives you a chance to exercise your own ideas as to overall shape. The inletting of the long, octangular barrel comes completed, but it is necessary to inlet the lock mechanism. But by this time, with the experience gained with earlier projects, you will be able to handle this in a thoroughly professional style.

The Harper's Ferry and Kentucky-rifle kits described in the text are produced by Dixie Gun Works, and the Brown Bess kit by Navy Arms Company (see Appendix for addresses). Other kits of this general type are available from Connecticut Valley Arms, Classic Arms, Sharon Rifle Barrel Company, and Thompson Center Arms. Write for their catalogs to get an idea of what they have to offer.

The final project in this series offers some time-saving hints for home craftsmen who want to do their own thing and build muzzleloaders entirely from scratch. This is the next logical step after completing the Kentucky-rifle project. Though carving a graceful rifle stock from a plain slab of wood can be a fascinating creative exercise, there's no getting around the fact that inletting a long muzzleloading barrel can be a tedious, time-consuming task. The hints provided can change hours into minutes. But here we are getting ahead of ourselves.

Aside from the historical significance of the 1805 Harper's Ferry pistol, the first handgun produced in this country by a government-operated arsenal, much of the fascination of this famous gun lies in its graceful appearance. At a time when martial pistols tended to be plain, awkward, and clubbish, the Harper's Ferry with its trim lines and striking brass fixtures was a distinctively beautiful handgun.

This is the prime reason why the Harper's Ferry is a collector's favorite and will command a price eclipsing that of even rarer pistols. Though the price and scarcity of the Harper's Ferry makes it unlikely that many of us will ever own the genuine article, this project results in a close lookalike to the real thing with all the grace, balance, and bright brass trim of the original. It's a real eyecatcher hanging on the den wall and lots of fun to shoot—something owners of real Harper's Ferry pistols would never dream of doing.

As far as construction is concerned, few, if any, kits offer the degree of completeness and preshaping of this Dixie kit: The stock is preturned to near-final shape and all inletting for barrel, lock, sideplate, gripcap, trigger guard, ramrod, and ramrod pipe is so nearly complete that only a bit of cutting and scraping here and there is required.

This does not mean that all the work—and fun—has been removed, but quite the contrary. Actually the work which is finished or nearly so is that which requires tools and equipment, such as specially curved gauges and long-shanked drills (for drilling the ramrod hole), which the average home workman probably will not have available. The work that remains is a lot of fun and requires only a few simple hand tools. If you own a narrow chisel (or even a jackknife), a hand drill, a few drill bits, a file, a set of needle files, a half-round wood rasp, and two or three sheets of sandpaper, you're ready to build your Harper's Ferry.

Though I kept no accurate record of construction time, it is safe to say that the Dixie Harper's Ferry kit will pretty well fill the weekend for the inexperienced craftsman. My time, including picture taking, was about ten hours.

The Dixie Harper's Ferry kit is totally complete except for the stock finish and browning solution. No extra parts are required and nothing is left over—screws, pins, everything is there. The lock, which is a faithful reproduction of the original, comes fully assembled and strikes a good shower of sparks with no hardening of the frizzen or additional modification. The barrel, which is .56-caliber and rifled (a worthwhile departure from the original, which was smoothbore), comes with breech plug fitted, under rib attached, loop in place, and even the flashhole drilled. It has been proofed and bears Belgium proof marks. Buttcap, trigger guard, trigger plate, lock screws, barrel key, and pins are all there. The stock is of rather dense-grained European walnut and, as I say, is very nearly complete. The quality of the wood is good; it cuts cleanly and can be sanded to a high polish. The wood in my kit was rather light in color and required staining to match the rich brown of the original Harper's Ferry. The ramrod, which comes complete, features a flared brass button tip for seating the ball, and on the other end there is a worm for removing the ball if the need arises.

Begin work by fitting the barrel in the stock channel. You'll find that a small amount of wood must be removed before the breech-plug extension will seat fully. This is a minor job and is best done with a narrow chisel. You may find that the under rib prevents the barrel from fitting all the way back at the breech, so a bit of trimming may be required.

The lock on my kit fit into its precut recess with nothing more than a press and a slight tap. There are absolutely no gaps and the fit is perfect. If, however, your lock should require more than only moderate pressure to press in place, it is wise to scrape away the tight places. Fitting the lock too tightly may split the stock or splinter the edges of the recess when the lock is removed. The lock is fully seated only when the flash pan comes to rest against the barrel. Don't get alarmed if a bit of the lock plate extends above the surface of the surrounding wood. Look closely and you'll notice that the edge of the lock plate is cut to a slight bevel around the entire border. The lower edge of the border should be level with the wood. My kit came out perfect.

Once the barrel and lock are fitted, leave them in place throughout the assembly of the kit. Otherwise the sharp edges of the inletted recesses may become damaged. The hammer, frizzen, and frizzen spring will get in the way a lot, so it is a good idea to remove them at this point, but don't put them where they will be misplaced or accidentally discarded—it has happened!

The sideplate recess also has some sharp edges which should be protected, so put the sideplate in now. You'll be amazed at how closely it fits; Dixie Kits are precision-engineered.

Fitting the butt cap with its long side extensions may look a bit tricky, but with proper care you should have no difficulty. The surest way to get a good fit is to bend the extensions slightly outward until they do not touch the stock. Now the lower part of the grip cap can be fitted without interference. If there is too much wood at the bottom of the grip, simply rasp it away until the cap fits all the way flush to the inletting recesses. This may take a little time, but for a good fit you shouldn't rush things. The old cut-and-try method is the only way. Just be sure to cut a *little* at a time.

With the lower part of the butt cap in place you are ready to bend the extensions back in place and proceed with their inletting. Actually you want to bend the extensions in enough so there will be some spring pressure against the wood.

You'll note that there is an inward bevel at the upper points of the extensions. This bevel fits in *under* the wood and holds the extensions in place. Don't try to drive the beveled points of the extensions into the wood without first undercutting, as splitting will most likely occur. Undercut with a narrow chisel or, if you don't have a chisel of the required width, make one from a 1/8-inch screwdriver.

Inletting for the buttcap extensions on my pistol was slightly oversize, so I used walnut-tinted plastic wood to fill the gaps. When the filler is sanded flush it is hardly noticeable. Now secure the buttcap with the largest of the three brass screws which comes with the kit, and you're ready to move on to the trigger installation.

How to Build the Harper's Ferry Pistol

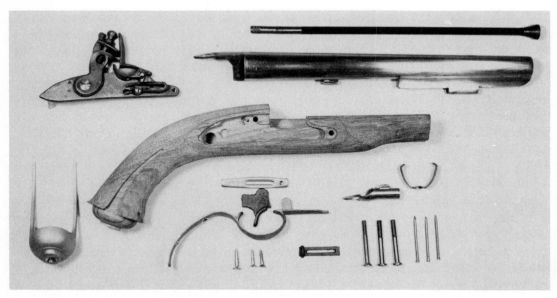

1 All the parts for a Harper's Ferry pistol. The kit includes twenty components. The lock is complete, assembled, and fully shaped. No other parts except stock finish and a piece of flint are needed.

The trigger comes "as cast" and will require a bit of smoothing up and polishing before installation. A piece of 280-grit or finer finishing paper wrapped around a small file is fine for polishing small parts. The trigger plate is a stamped item and thus is smooth enough as it comes. After fitting the trigger into the slot in the trigger plate, locate the proper position in the stock which allows the trigger lever to contact the sear arm, keeping in mind that the trigger will pivot from the front upper corner of the lever. Once the trigger is accurately located, mark the spot and inlet the trigger plate.

With the trigger held in the proper position, use a $1/16$-inch drill to drill through the stock and trigger at the pivot point. If properly located, this will be inside the lock recess. There is no need to drill all the way through the

2
The breech tang fits into the pre-inletted recess. The tang screw hole is already drilled and countersunk. During the final shaping operation the wood surrounding the tang will be filed to a flush surface.

3
The precut lock inletting is very nearly completed. As a matter of fact the lock can be forced into the stock the way it comes, but it is a good idea to loosen the fit somewhat so the stock will not split.

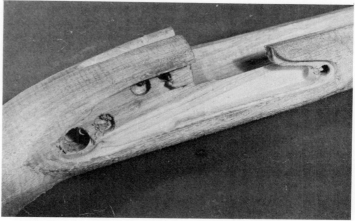

stock. About ¼ inch past the trigger is far enough. Thus when the lock is in place the trigger pin is completely hidden. When cutting the pin to length, do not cut it flush with the wood but allow it to extend as far as possible without interfering with the action of the lock. It may thus be extracted with pliers if ever necessary.

With the trigger plate in place the tong screw can be located. This screw does double service by holding the tong down and the plate up. Since the screw must pass completely through the stock and line up with an exact spot on the front of the trigger plate, some pretty tricky drilling is required unless you are using a drill press, in which case there is no problem. It is helpful to draw a line along the side of the stock at the angle the drill must take. This

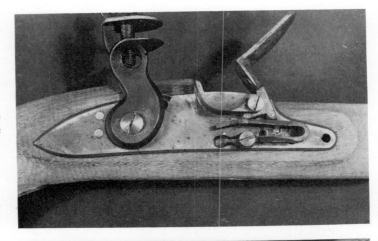

4
A detail of the lock fitted into the pre-inletted recess. Note the perfect wood-to-metal fit.

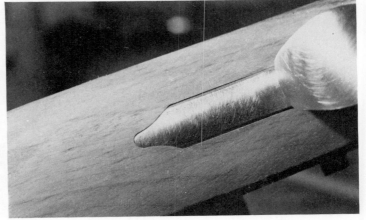

5
The forward extension of the brass trigger guard already fitted into the stock. The advantage of a well-finished kit on your first muzzleloader attempt is well evident here. The nearly finished precut inletting rules out any opportunity of serious mistakes or poor fitting.

6

The two nails protruding here are the hingepin and the trigger retaining pin. Do not trim these nails to length until the work is very nearly completed, because it will be necessary to remove them from time to time.

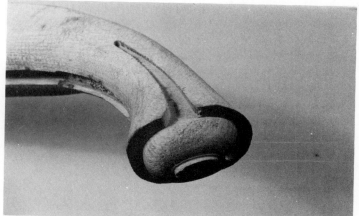

7

The machine-cut inletting for the buttcap. Though the machine inletting is very nearly complete, some handwork is still required for a perfect fit.

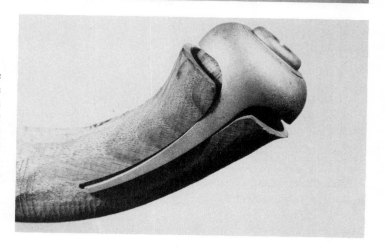

8

The side extensions should be bent slightly outward while the butt section is being fitted. The extensions are then bent in for final fitting. Note the bevel at the top of the extension. These fit into specially undercut recesses in the stock to hold the extensions in place.

way you can pretty accurately eyeball the correct route by lining up the drill bit with the line. If the drill comes out somewhat off center, simply enlarge the hole through the stock with a ¼-inch bit, and this should allow ample clearance for correct screw alignment. Now countersink the tong and tap the trigger plate. The tong screw is somewhat overlength, so trim it so a thread or two extends below the plate, as on the original Harper's Ferry.

The trigger guard goes in with practically no effort at all, but first give it a polishing with finishing paper and steel wool. Now place it in the pre-inletted recesses and locate the two remaining brass screws in the rear extension. The front extension is attached by the traditional pin-and-lug technique. Simply drill a ¹⁄₁₆-inch hole through wood and lug and insert the pin. As with the trigger pin it is a good idea to leave an extension so the pin can be withdrawn.

The ramrod pipe, as it comes with the kit, lacks the detailed molding of the original Harper's Ferry. However, the brass is amply thick for the correct shaping and the only tool you'll need is a fine-cut needle file. Shape to the detail shown in the photographs and polish with finishing paper and steel wool.

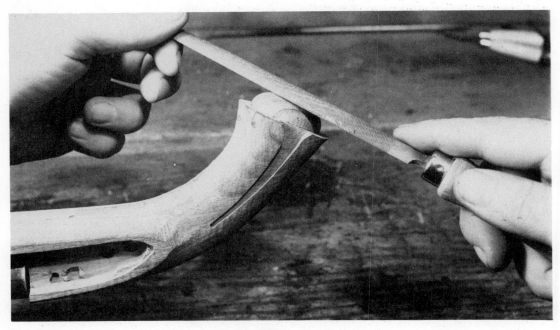

9 The excess stock wood at the butt of the grip is easily worked away with a stockmaker's rasp. File away a bit at a time until the fit is perfect. The best fitting procedure here is a cautious cut-and-try method.

10

As it comes with the kit the lower ramrod pipe lacks the detailed molding of the original. However, there is plenty of excess metal for correct forming. As seen here, the lower ramrod pipe fits into the stock easily.

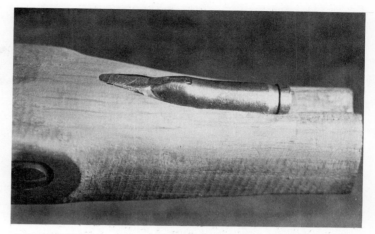

11

A bit of reshaping with a fine-cut needle file and the ramrod pipe is ready for finishing with polishing paper and steel wool. Note the detail of the molding, which is a close reproduction of original Harper's Ferry pistol.

12

The lower ramrod pipe is fitted into the stock after final finishing and polishing. Compare this picture with that of the unfinished pipe and you'll get an idea of the work that needs to be done for best appearance and authenticity. The ramrod pipes are held in position by a pin through the retaining tab, just as is the trigger guard.

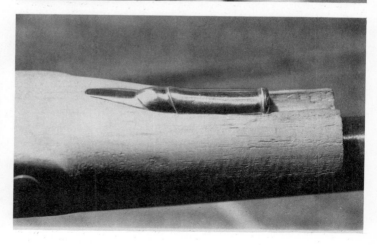

13

The forend band is installed by cutting with much care a shallow recess around and over the top of the forend with a narrow file. Note that the forend band begins just at the forward edge of the lower ramrod pipe. This makes proper positioning easy. The brass forend band extends around the stock and then tucks into the barrel channel, where it is clamped in place.

14

The final finished forend band after the stock has been rounded off and sanded smooth.

15

The brass buttcap and grip are finished together. This makes a smooth, flush union of wood and metal. Note that the stock is being sanded by a brisk shoe-shine motion with cloth-backed sandpaper. This is a good sanding technique for all types of rounded surfaces.

The ramrod pipe, like the trigger guard, is held in place by the pin and lug method. Before drilling, however, be sure that the pipe is in the proper position to allow the ramrod to pass freely. Now drill *all* the way through the stock, insert the pin, and trim flush.

The forend band is installed by simply filing or cutting a shallow recess around and over the top of the forend. Bend the band so that it lies flush in the ramrod groove, then bring it up the sides and clamp down into the barrel channel, about ¼ inch or so. The barrel will then hold the ends firmly in place.

The only piece left to be assembled is the barrel wedge, which holds the barrel in place by passing through the stock and the loop under the barrel. This is another "blind" drilling operation requiring accurate measurements and careful drilling. Locate the proper position for the wedge by measuring the depth of the barrel channel where the loop is located and mark this depth on the outside of the forend opposite the loop. Now, drilling very slowly so the drill won't tend to lead off, drill halfway through the stock. If the drill bit passes cleanly through the loop without any sign of being off course, continue on through the stock. Now drill a series of holes the width of the wedge. Wobbling the drill bit back and forth will usually break the wood between the holes and leave a neat slot through which the wedge may be inserted. Or you can use the old-timer's method of heating the wedge red-hot and letting it scorch its way through the holes. Whichever way you use, be sure the slot is cut cleanly and close with only enough space for a snug, pressure-tight fit.

With all the parts now assembled, all that remmains is shaping, sanding, and finishing.

The stock is so nearly shaped that all you need to do is shape up the moldings around the lock and off-lock sides and trim down the grip as shown in the photos. The quickest way to sand rounded surfaces such as the grip is a shoeshine motion with cloth-backed sandpaper. The same technique is good for polishing the barrel. Use finishing paper wrapped around a file to polish the lock plate, hammer, and frizzen, then give everything—wood, brass, and steel—a brisk rubbing with steel wool. You are now ready for finishing.

As mentioned earlier, my stock was of rather light-colored wood. A home-brew stain of brown liquid shoe die darkened with a bit of black die gave just the right shade of chestnut brown. However, any number of commercial stains will do perfectly if your stock needs a bit of darkening. If the color comes out too dark, just rub with steel wool until you get a lighter shade.

Finish with any good grade of stock finish or varnish, or, if you prefer, do as I did and rub in several coats of boiled linseed oil for a rich "antique" glow.

The barrel, lock, and other iron fixtures can be left bright, or again, as I did, you can brown them for that authentic antique look. Two browning solutions

The finished Harper's Ferry kit really shoots. Here the priming charge in the pan goes off with a satisfying puff of smoke. Keep in mind that the Harper's Ferry pistol is a powerful, big-bore handgun, and treat it as carefully as a modern cartridge-firing pistol.

which work well are Birchwood-Casey's Plum Brown, a chemical preparation which works instantly but requires that the metal be preheated, and Dixie browning solution, a slower-acting preparation which works on cold metal. After browning the metal, rub in a coat of oil and you'll be amazed at the beauty and "class" of the color.

Now reassemble the pistol and take a long admiring look at what your efforts have produced. Take care when showing it to the wife, however, for the Harper's Ferry is such a handsome decorator that right away she'll want to hang it in the den.

Bore size of the Dixie Harper's Ferry is .562 inch, so a .550-inch ball works best. As a matter of fact, it is a good idea to order a Dixie mold and a few flints when you order the kit. Of course, you'll also need some black powder, but as this cannot be shipped it must be purchased locally. *It is absolutely essential that you use black powder only!* Try using smokeless powder and you'll blow your fine Harper's Ferry all to hell and probably your hand along with it.

A good powder charge for the 245-grain .55-caliber bullet is 40 grains of FFG powder. Search around until you find a thickness of cloth that gives a medium snug patching. Also you'll need some finely granulated black powder for the priming. FFG is best but is usually hard to find. FFG works about as well and is the most common granulation.

When firing your pistol keep in mind that it is by no means a toy. The big ball packs a big punch and it can cover a lot of territory, so be sure of what is behind what you are shooting at!

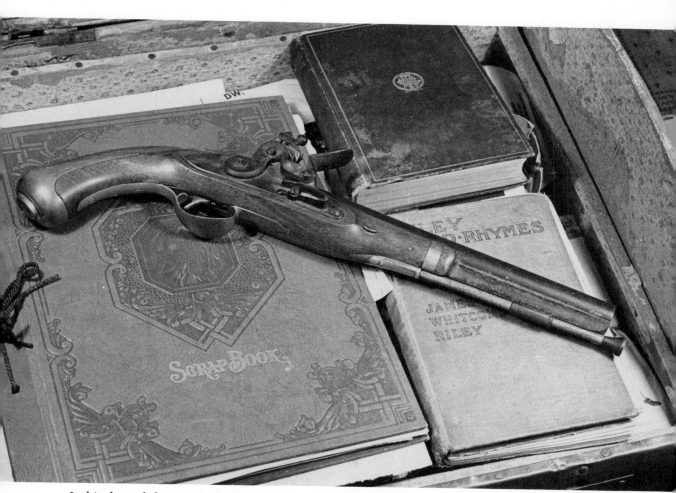

Is this the real thing tucked away in a Grandmother's chest or only a replica made from a kit? It's hard to tell the difference. This is the Harper's Ferry replica made from the kit described in this section.

36 / Building a Brown Bess Musket from a Kit

With the twenty-twenty vision of hindsight it is always easy to peer back a couple of decades and see where we really missed the boat. I can remember when original Brown Bess muskets were so common (or at least so it seemed) that they didn't even qualify as collector's items.

Then they started getting more and more scarce as foresighted collectors and dealers began gathering them up and hoarding them in the back room. Well, you know the rest; today a good Brown Bess will fetch several hundred dollars. At the same time it appears that everyone is getting the Brown Bess bug. And no wonder. This kingsize musket, which was the standard British infantry weapon for well over a century, is a strikingly handsome piece which adds distinction to any collection. The long barrel, giant lock, and broad expanses of gleaming brass make it one of the most desirable of decorator pieces. A big Brown Bess over the fireplace creates a magnificent focal point in early American decorator schemes. I suspect interior decorators who don't know or don't care about the fascinating history of this legendary piece have had a good bit to do with driving the price up on Brown Bess muskets simply because of their demands for it as a decoration.

Whatever the reasons may be, the simple fact of the matter is that relatively few of us who would like to own a Brown Bess are able to afford one. And even if we could there simply aren't enough to go around.

In terms of both quality and completeness the Navy Arms Brown Bess kit is one of the better kits offered the home craftsman. The buttplate, nose cap, trigger guard, ramrod pipes, sideplate, and grip escutcheon are high-quality brass castings. The steel barrel is nicely polished and comes complete with fitted barrel loops, bayonet stud, fitted breech plug and tang, and a decorative molding at the breech just like the originals.

292

The lock, frequently a stumbling block in such do-it-yourself projects, is not only completely finished and polished but is even hand-engraved, marked "GRICE 1962," and bears the distinctive GR and crown stamp of "Georgius Rex," King George II.

The trigger, sling loops, and matching screws are nicely polished and blued steel, and all necessary threading and tapping has already been done. Likewise all the pins, miscellaneous screws, and odd parts are right there with the kit. You even get a musket-size piece of flint.

The stock is a cleanly carved and precision-inletted piece of what appears to be a medium-hard grade of straight-grain maple. The reason I say it "appears" to be maple is that the kit is of European origin and the stock may be of some sort of wood that only looks like maple. But what the hell, let's call it maple and be done with it. At any rate it cuts cleanly, is easy to sand, and accepts stain readily. The preshaping is so complete that the distinctive "nose" on the comb, the molding around the tang, and even the traditional beavertail carvings at the rear of the lock moldings are already carved to final shape, and the characteristic hand-filling swell of the forend just below the lower ramrod pipe is preshaped in authentic detail. In other words, if you're concerned about getting a good authentic shape, there's no cause for worry. Just sand this stock smooth and it looks right—how can you go wrong?

This isn't one of those long-drawn-out projects designed for Eskimos who are snowed in for nine months. Timewise, you can figure it for about one weekend or a full week of evenings. As to tools, all you'll need are an electric drill and two or three bits, a couple of curved and straight chisels, a sanding block, a couple of rasps, two or three files, and various screwdrivers. You'll also need some sandpaper, walnut-toned woodstain, and stock finish.

The first step in building the Brown Bess is fitting and attaching the buttplate. The reason for doing this first is that the sharp edges and inletting at the butt will then be protected from any accidental battering, denting, or chipping which might happen during construction. The only chore here is inletting the buttplate's upper extension. The inletting here is so nearly completed that there may be a strong temptation to try to force the metal into the wood. This, however, is an open invitation to disaster in the form of an ugly split or crack. So slice and scrape the inletting until the buttplate slips easily in place. Next step is to drill the butt for the two buttplate screws. You may be shocked to discover that these screws are steel rather than brass and thus don't match the buttplate. But this is the way they're *supposed* to be. After pulling the screws up tight, file the heads to match the contour of the plate and the buttplate chapter is closed. Except for final polishing of the brass, that is—but we'll come back to that later.

So now we move to the barrel. In my kit the barrel channel was so nearly completed that only a bit of light slicing with a curved chisel was required before the barrel fell snugly in place. Likewise for the barrel tang; here the outline was traced with a sharp scribe, then the recess was cut to full size and depth with a flat chisel. Also the tang was a bit too straight to fit the curve of the stock. This was easily remedied by bending it downward with pliers bit by bit until it was right.

A bit of work is required to inlet the recesses for the barrel loops. These so-called "loops" (also known as "tenons") are the small, squarish lugs attached along the bottom of the barrel. (An additional lug on top, near the muzzle, serves to hold the bayonet in place and also serves as a front sight of sorts.)

The recesses for these lugs can be easily cut with a narrow $1/8$-inch or so chisel. Don't worry about getting a perfect inletting job on these little cavities as they are hidden when the barrel is in place anyway. By the same token, however, don't go too deep lest you cut through into the ramrod channel on the underside of the forend. Don't worry too much if you do, but be advised that it was considered poor form to do so two hundred years ago if you happened to work at His Majesty's Brown Bess factory.

The purpose of these loops or tenons, as you are about to learn, is to hold the barrel in place by means of a simple but secure pinning arrangement. After calculating the proper location a $1/16$-inch hole is drilled completely through the stock and lug. Next one of the pins supplied with the kit is tapped into the hole. When all of the lugs have been drilled and pinned, the barrel is held securely in place. Eventually the pins will be trimmed flush with the wood, but for the time being leave them long. They're easier to remove this way and you'll be removing the barrel a few times before the job is done.

Now is as good a time as any to fit the lock. Actually the job is all but done for you. The only additional lock inletting required for my kit was to enlarge a portion of the inletting to make room for the mainspring and to cut a small recess of the "rat tail" at the extreme rear of the lock plate.

After that everything worked perfectly. The holes for the two sideplate screws are already drilled, so that all you have to do is pull the screws up tight and the lock is secured in place.

The inletting for the brass sideplate is absolutely perfect. Just press it in and the job is done! Simple enough. Now all it takes is a dressing down with the file and final polishing with the fine sandpaper.

Now we can move on to the trigger and trigger plate. The trigger plate, you will note, has a threaded shank at the forward end. This is a clever attaching arrangement for the tang screw. Simply locate and drill a $3/16$-inch or so hole down through the tang and stock so that it is in alignment with the threaded hole in the trigger plate. After countersinking the tang, insert a screw to hold both the tang and trigger plate securely in place.

With the trigger plate in position you can now mark the location where the trigger slot is to be cut. This slot is only about $1/16$ inch wide and nearly $1/2$ inch deep. Cutting a deep, narrow slot such as this could be a problem. But not if you do it this way. Simply drill a row of narrow holes as close together as you can manage. Next gently rock the turning drill back and forth, causing it to act like a rotor and open up the slot. It couldn't be easier.

Next step is to insert the trigger blade (the narrow upper area which contacts the lock's sear arm) into the slot. The trigger is held in place by a pin which also acts as the trigger pivot. So with the trigger held in proper position, drill a "blind" hole into the lock recess, through the trigger blade, and into the wood beyond. Be careful not to drill so deep that the bit will exit on the other side of the stock. Since this pin is inserted into the lock cavity it will be invisible when the lock is in place. Be sure to leave enough of a stub sticking up ($1/8$ inch or thereabouts) so that it can be grasped with pliers and withdrawn.

The stock which came with my kit had a rib of wood running up the underside from about midway up the butt section all the way to the lower ramrod pipe. Why this was left on I can't guess, but if your stock has one too now is as good a time as any to cut it off. I simply planed it away with a Stanley Surform shaper, then dressed up the area with a cabinet rasp. Takes about ten minutes all told.

Now you can go ahead and fit the trigger guard. First, however, it's a good idea to dress up the guard a bit and square the edges with a file. The edges of these castings are slightly rounded, and this makes for sloppy-looking inletting.

Next it is necessary to cut the mortises for the attaching lugs—just as you did for the barrel loops. Don't drill for the pins this time, however, as the guard is to be inletted into the wood somewhat yet. With the lug mortises cut to full depth, position the guard on the stock and trace the outline with a small, narrow-bladed knife. Next, remove the guard and retrace the outline to a depth of about $1/16$ inch or so. With this border cut, your next act is to recess the wood within the outline. This is easily done with a flat-bladed chisel. As long as your tool is sharp and you pay attention to the direction of the grain, you'll have no trouble here. Just take it slow and easy when you get close to the edge.

After two or three fittings the trigger guard will fit flush. When it does, go ahead and fit the anchoring pins.

Now that you've got the hang of inletting the brass parts, go ahead and fit the ramrod pipes. These are inletted to half-depth and held in place by the now familiar pin-and-loop method. My technique for this was to dress off the rough surface with a fine-cut file, then polish with emery cloth. The brass was then brought to a nice polish by scrubbing with fine steel wool.

The only trouble you're liable to have here is with the lower thimble. This is due to the rather long rearward extension. This extension is inletted just as you did the trigger guard, so take it easy and you should have no trouble. Once it is in place, file the surface so metal and wood are perfectly flush. Also, before the final finishing be sure to insert the ramrod to see if it passes down the channel and through all the pipes without binding or sticking. If it does stick, a few adjustments may be necessary.

While you're up on this end of the rifle, why not go ahead and attach the nose cap? This is as easily done as said. The cap is slipped in place, a screw is inserted from the inside of the channel, and the job is finished. Phew!

By now you're just about going to run out of parts to fit. All except for that odd-looking shield-shaped brass casting. This, dear reader, is a wrist escutcheon or thumb plate.

How to Make the Brown Bess Musket

1 The Navy Arms Brown Bess musket kit is one of the most complete kits I've ever seen. Everything you need, including screws, pins, and even a piece of flint, is included. Other than a few simple tools and a few hours' time the only other thing the maker needs to supply is finishing material such as sandpaper, stain, stock finish, and barrel browner.

2

A curved chisel is used to slightly open up the barrel channel. The barrel channel as well as other inletting is so nearly completed that only a few minutes' work is required to bring it to final dimension.

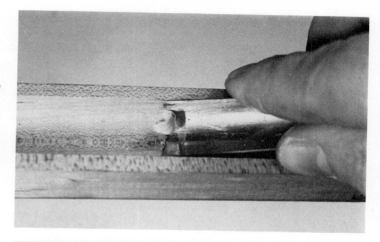

3

Detail of breech tang.

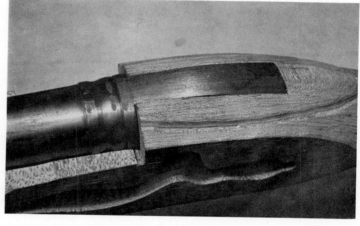

4

With the barrel fully in place a hole that will take the barrel pin is bored through the stock and the barrel lug.

5

A pin fits through the stock and lug, thus holding the barrel securely in place. This is the traditional method of holding the barrel and other metal parts in the stock.

6

Inletting of wood in this kit is so precise and nearly finished that only a small amount of additional handwork is required.

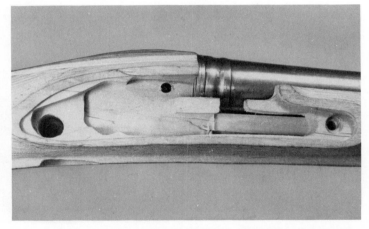

7

Absolutely no additional hand inletting was required to fit this heavy brass sideplate.

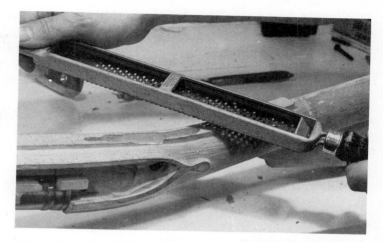

8

The Stanley Surform shaper is a good tool to work the stock down to final shape.

9

The technique used to cut small, deep slots. Narrow holes are drilled side by side, then the drill is rocked back and forth to open up the slot. This particular slot is to be used for the trigger assembly.

10

A narrow chisel is used to open up the recess for the trigger-guard tab.

It is inletted in the top of the grip and is held in place by a screw running up from the underside of the grip under the rear trigger-guard extension. Square up the edges with a file and inlet it the same way you did everything else. As this has more curves it may require a bit more care for a perfect hairline fit. Just take your time. When it is fully inletted, smooth it down to the wood and admire your fine inletting.

Now you can drill the hole for the front sling swivel. This is located about 1/2 inch forward to the second ramrod pipe.

Now that everything is together you can reverse the process and take everything apart! It's time to sand the stock.

Tell you what—let's make a deal. If you're tired and not much in the mood

11
A fine-cut file is used to square up the edges of the forward trigger-guard extension. The edges of brass castings tend to be somewhat rounded with imperfect edges, thus it is a good idea to square up the edges before beginning the inletting process. This makes the inletting look better and also makes it easier for you to do.

12
With the trigger guard in correct position, a narrow-bladed knife is used to trace the outline. Needless to say, much care must be exercised here if a perfect inletting job is expected.

for sanding, let's just put it off until another time. Lots of otherwise fine stocks have been ruined simply because they were given a lick and a promise by someone too eager to get the job finished. So if you don't want to do it correctly now, do yourself a favor and wait until you do. Likewise with polishing the brass. Save these jobs for an evening when you're in the mood for an easy but slow session of sanding and finishing.

The first step in the final finishing process is to rasp away the rows of shallow grooves on the stock's surface left by the carving machine. This can be done with a fine-cut wood rasp or even a metal file. Just take long, lengthwise strokes with the rasp and they fade away. The only actual stock shaping you'll have to do is slightly taper the forward end of the forend so that it flows

13

With the edges of the inletting cut to full depth, a sharp chisel is applied carefully to remove the excess wood.

14

The same inletting process is used to inlet the shield at the top of the grip, or "wrist." Here the outline of the inlay is being traced with a sharp narrow-bladed knife.

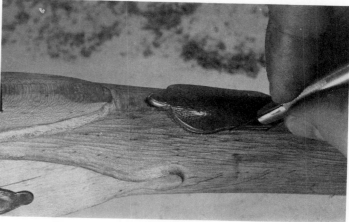

inward to the nose cap. The swelling at the forend just at the lower ramrod pipe (where it looks like a snake that swallowed a rat) is supposed to be that way, so don't cut it off.

Also a bit of wood trimming might be necessary around the buttplate, but only a little. Begin sanding with fairly coarse paper of about 120 grit to take out whatever tool marks might have been left by the rasp. Follow this up with 180-grit or 220-grit paper. Always sand with the grain, and by all means use a sanding block on these long, straight surfaces. These rather stark lines, by the way, make the Brown Bess stock quite easy to sand, and the job goes along rather speedily despite its size.

15
A ramrod pipe being polished by a back-and-forth shoeshine motion with flexible sandpaper. Both cloth-backed and plastic-backed sandpaper are appropriate for this job.

16
Cast-brass ramrod pipes before and after polishing. Extra time spent in the polishing operation makes a better-looking gun.

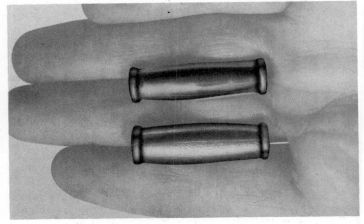

17

A detail of the lower ramrod pipe after final polishing and fitting in the stock. Note the close inletting. The rear extension of the ramrod pipe, like all castings used in this kit, is extremely heavy. The inlay, for example, goes into the wood for nearly ⅛ inch. This makes for a high-quality reproduction.

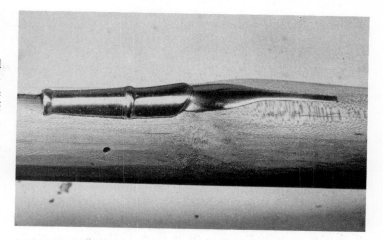

18

The lock is here fitted into the stock but before any other finishing of the wood. Note the very close inletting.

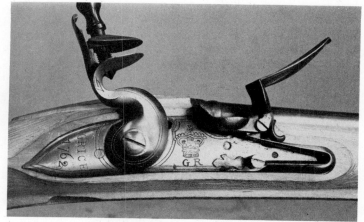

19

A detail of the barrel tang, showing the rough-filed finish after final shaping of the wood.

20

Preliminary finishing of the tang and other metal parts needing finishing is best accomplished by using a small piece of 120-grit sandpaper wrapped around a file.

21

A strip of abrasive finishing material is used to polish the barrel. Again, a simple shoeshine motion is best.

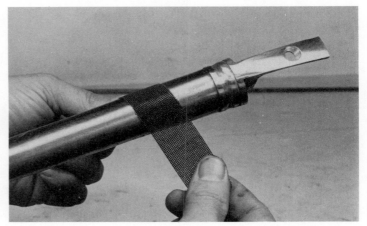

22

The final polish is applied to metal parts with steel wool.

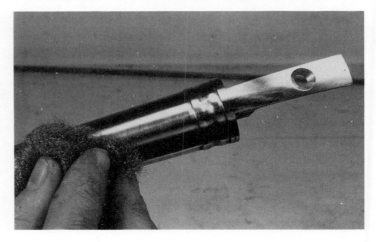

Finally, give the wood a final slicking-up with 280-grit or 320-grit paper and set the stock aside for the time being. Now turn your attention to the brass castings. Despite all this expanse of metal, the job of polishing the brass fixtures can be accomplished pretty quickly. My technique is to wrap 220-grit paper around a file and have at it. When the grainy surface left by the mold has been rough-polished away, switch to 400-grit paper and go over everything again. Finally a hard scrubbing with fine steel wool will bring the brass to a nice shine.

For final finishing I used the new Muzzle Loader's Barrel & Stock Finishing Kit sold by Birchwood-Casey. This kit includes everything you'll need—stock stain, stock finish, metal browner, swabs, finishing paper, steel wool, etc.

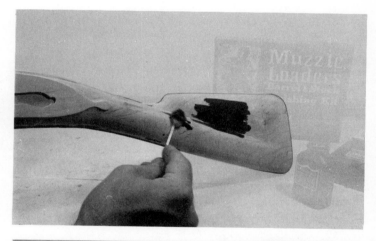

23
Stain is applied to the final sanded stock. Original stocks were made of walnut, so a walnut-type stain is used here.

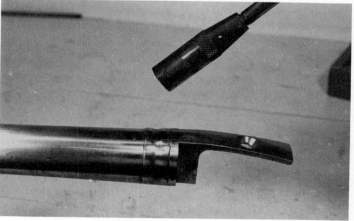

24
Heat is being applied to the barrel with a butane torch.

Two applications of the Colonial Red Stain which comes with the kit brought the maple stock to a deep reddish-brown hue that looks just like old walnut. I gave the wood a final rubdown with steel wool and rubbed on three coats of Tru-Oil with my fingers.

Brown Bess muskets were originally issued with the steel lock and barrel left bright. So if you want your Brown Bess to look new, just leave the metal the way it is. However, most of the surviving specimens are aged and browned to a rich brown patina. So, since I wanted my Brown Bess to look *old*, I used the Plum Brown metal-browning solution that comes with the kit. The results could not have been more satisfying.

25

This simple barrel-holding cradle was made by bending a wire coat hanger. The purpose of holding the barrel in a cradle such as this while being heated is so the barrel will heat uniformly without any "cold" spots. If the barrel is held in a vise or other heavy-metal heat-robbing fixture, the barrel will not heat uniformly and the brown color will not be uniform as it should be.

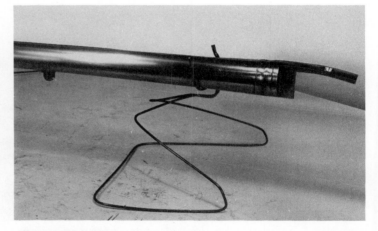

26

When the barrel metal reaches a sufficient temperature, the Birchwood-Casey Plum Brown browning solution is swabbed on it. The browning effect is immediate and uniform.

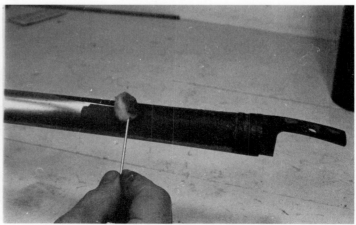

27

After the browning solution is swabbed over the barrel and allowed to cool somewhat, the metal part is rubbed down with an oily cloth.

28

Before you attempt to brown the lock it is necessary to disassemble it completely.

29

For browning or bluing to look best the metals parts must be absolutely clean and free of greasy fingerprints. Here Birchwood-Casey cleaner and degreaser is used to clean the surface of the lock plate. Note the rubber gloves to help prevent contaminating the surface with fingerprints or other marks.

30

After the lock plate is cleaned, it is heated. Note that the lock plate is being held simply by use of a pair of pliers.

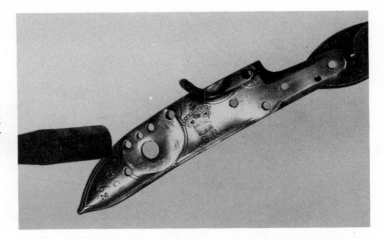

31

A butane torch is used to heat the hammer.

32

Some browning solution is swabbed on the hammer. Note the immediate browning effect.

As mentioned earlier, the Navy Arms Brown Bess Musket is definitely a shooter. The frizzen is well hardened so that a nice shower of sparks fall when the hammer falls. Balls are cast of soft scrap lead in molds that are available from Navy Arms and Dixie Gun Works. Since the Navy Arms Brown Bess is .750 caliber, you can use any size ball from about .69 to .72 inch in diameter with complete success. For plinking try 50 grains of FFG black powder. For splitting logs increase the charge to about 80 grains.

33
After browning, the lockplate is rubbed down with an oily cloth.

34
The reassembled lock after browning. Note the even texture of the coloring.

35   A detail of the lock area after final finishing.

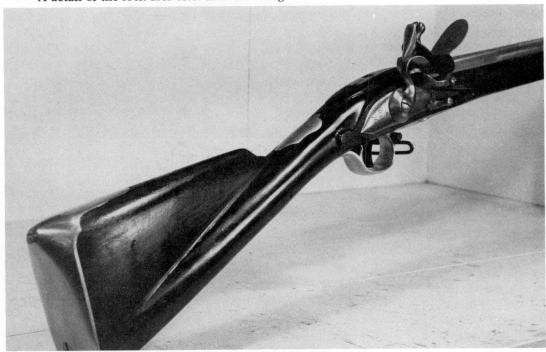

36   A detail of the butt section after completion.

I try a shot with the newly crafted Brown Bess musket. Note the typical cloud of smoke that swirls up from the pan.

The finished musket and the finishing materials used. The Birchwood-Casey muzzle-loading finishing kit includes stain, stock finish, cleaner and degreaser, And Plum Brown metal finish in addition to sandpaper and other finishing materials.

37

Building a Kentucky Rifle from a Kit

This final do-it-yourself muzzleloading project is somewhat more difficult than the earlier two projects, because the stock has not been preshaped to near final dimensions. But by the same token, it is far more exciting because it gives you a chance to express your individual ideas as to final shape. In fact, the finished rifle will so clearly bear the stamp of your individual taste that it will be all but impossible for anyone to know for sure that you worked from a kit. About the only stockwork that has been done for you is to rough-shape the wood and cut the barrel channel. This pre-inletted barrel channel will save you several hours of tedious labor, which will be better spent on shaping the outside of the stock.

The kit described here is Dixie's Number 101 Standard Precision Rifle Kit, which, in 1977, sells for a bit under a $120 and comes with a choice of .32, .36, .40, .45, and .50 caliber. This kit includes the same parts which make up Dixie's Squirrel Rifle, which in finished form sells for more than twice the price of the kit. If you prefer a flintlock rifle to percussion, order kit Number 102. Or after looking at the Dixie catalog you may decide to try one of their other kits. (See the Appendix for Dixie's address.)

The barrel, which can be ordered in $^{13}/_{16}$ or $^{15}/_{16}$ inch, fits into the precut channel with no cutting, no scraping, and no gaps. About two inches of channel at the breech end must be finished by hand, but this represents no problem at all. One needs only to continue the straight lines of the barrel channel back through the unfinished portion and remove the wood with the straight-edged chisel.

The breech tang can be precisely inletted by simply placing the barrel in the channel with the tang in position over the grip or "wrist" of the stock. Enough of the barrel will remain in the channel to ensure perfect alignment so all you need to do is scribe the outline of the tang and cut to depth, and the job is done.

Now you are ready to move on to the only part of the entire operation which may be considered somewhat tricky: inletting the lock. Actually it isn't tricky at all. Just take enough time to get the preliminary layout correctly aligned and you'll save yourself considerable aggravation later.

The vertical placement of the lock represents no problem whatsoever, because the top edge of the lock follows the top line of the forend. The lateral positioning, however, must be exact, because the hammer must hit the nipple squarely.

For layout purposes, use a centerpunch to mark a spot midway across the right outer barrel flat at a point ¾ inch forward of the rear of the barrel. Later you will use this punchmark to drill the hole for the drum, but for the present it will do service for positioning the lock. Simply hold the drum and nipple assembly in relative position by hand and eyeball the lock into proper position by arranging it so that the arc of the hammer nose coincides with the axis of the nipple. You'll find this easier if you remove all lock parts from the lock plate except the hammer and the tumbler. The lock will thus lay nearly flat and quite close to the stock so that accurate eyeball alignment of hammer and nipple will present no problem, provided you are reasonably sober. Now remove hammer and tumbler and you are ready to continue.

The lock plate, as it comes with the kit, is of a pleasing traditional shape, but you may wish to reshape it to a more distinctive outline. There is sufficient metal for fairly extensive reshaping, but don't get carried away and file away so much metal that parts of the mechanism will extend beyond the plate profile when you reassemble the lock. This will cause embarrassment and no end of difficulty. Also be sure to file a slight inward bevel on the edges. This will facilitate inletting as well as making the lock easier to remove once it is tightly inletted.

Begin lock inletting by holding the lock plate in the exact position and tracing the outline with a scribe or sharp pencil. Deepen the outline by tapping straight and appropriately curved chisels into the line to a depth of about ⅛ inch. For the sake of a hairline fit it is a good idea to keep the outline cuts slightly inside the scribed outline. This will allow you to remove the wood speedily from the lock area without fear of gouging where you shouldn't. As you are inletting the lockplate you will have cause to appreciate the fact that the Dixie stock is so precisely preshaped that the lock contacts the side flat of the barrel exactly when the plate is flush with the surface of the wood! Before this happens, however, you will find it necessary to do a bit of careful cutting and scraping along the edges of the lock-plate recess. You'd better be careful if you want a close, tight fit.

When the plate is inletted flush, reassemble the complete mechanism and begin cutting the various recesses for the various parts. One school of thought on this is simply to dig out one big space into which the mechanism or "guts" will fit. This is quick and easy, but it is nearly as easy to inlet specific areas to receive the variously shaped parts of the lock. This method is preferred because it doesn't weaken the stock as much as does the dig-out technique and is a hell of a lot more satisfactory to the craftsman who takes pride in his work. Also, it doesn't take a lot of fancy tools; a single ⅜-inch gouge will do the whole job.

With the barrel and lock in place you'll want to start a bit of stock shaping. Proper shaping is the key to an attractive, graceful Kentucky rifle, and it is just here that many otherwise well-made rifles come up lacking. While it is certainly not impossible to louse up a shaping job on the Dixie kit, it is highly unlikely, for the simple reason that much of the bulk has already been removed, thus allowing you to concentrate on the final form. Too, the forearm of the Dixie Kentucky Rifle Kit is completely finished to shape, thus freeing you from that arduous task.

The first step in shaping the butt portion of the stock is fitting the buttplate. This must be done first, because the buttplate establishes the cross-section dimension from which further shaping proceeds. If you own or have access to a bandsaw, the sharply curving buttplate can be fitted with little effort. Otherwise you'll just have to rasp it out the old-fashioned way. A good amount of time and effort can be saved by using a fairly wide (¾-inch or so) Forstner or paddle bit in an electric drill. Just drill overlapping holes along the buttplate line and you'll get rid of a lot of surplus wood. Smooth with a rasp and you are ready for a final close fit. The cast-brass buttplates are fairly rough at best, with rather rounded edges and corners that should be sharp. Square up the edges and corners and the buttplate will be easier to fit and look a lot better when the job is done.

The brass buttplate is held in place by two 1-inch brass or steel flathead wood screws, one down through the top tang of the buttplate and the other about three-quarters of the way down the rear curve. Countersink the holes so the screw heads will pull up flush.

With the buttplate in place the terminal points of the comb and "shin" (the underside of the butt) are established. The top line should curve gracefully forward to the nose of the comb, and the shin line curves gently upward until it flows into the straight line of the forend. The graceful top and bottom butt lines of the semi-shaped Dixie stock are hard to improve on, and actually one needs only to alter them enough to meet the top and bottom edges of the buttplate. This requires very little cutting, but it is important that these top and bottom surfaces be cut *flat*. Later the comb will be rounded, but at this point it is important to keep them flat for the sake of drawing various reference lines.

The lower edge of a Kentucky rifle's buttstock, unlike that of a modern rifle, is cut flat and level, with the flat surface continuing undiminished from the buttplate to the trigger guard. This unique feature is one of the most characteristic elements of the Kentucky rifle, and therefore considerable care must be taken to ensure that it is properly formed. This flat "shin" was as much as an inch wide on early-eighteenth-century flintlock rifles, but by the percussion era it had been reduced to as little as ½ inch. The bottom edge of the buttplate furnished with the Dixie Kentucky Rifle Kit measures about ⅝ inch and is highly authentic for the percussion period. This, of course, means that a ⅝-inch flat surface has to extend from the "toe" (the bottom of the buttplate) through the trigger-guard area. Since the shin is already flat, all you need to do is draw a pair of straight lines ⅝ inch apart from the corners of the buttplate up through the underside of the grip and lock area. These lines will be a reference for further shaping. Another line, drawn from the top center of the buttplate to the breech tang, establishes the centerline of the comb.

With the buttplate and guidelines to serve as references, even the beginner should have little difficulty in achieving a fine graceful shape. The preshaped cheekpiece has an excellent shape and it comes so that all you need to do is blend the front and rear ends into the grip and rear of the butt with a shallow concave slope. The rounded side of a half-round rasp is the tool for this.

Another highly characteristic feature of the Kentucky rifle is the stock shaping or "molding" around the lock. If properly shaped this molding adds considerable style and grace to the long rifle. The outline of the molding generally follows the profile of the lock, so a simple way to get the molding started right is to draw a border around the lock plate as shown in the illustration. You then need only to reduce the wood around this line so that the molding shapes into the grip to the rear and the forearm to the front. Those two guidelines you drew on the underside come in handy here, for the bottom side of the lock molding slopes directly to this line. The top side of the molding curves around to the top of the tang. Trace a template of the molding, transfer it to the left side, and duplicate the shaping.

With the completion of the lock moldings you will probably need to take a few swipes with the rasp to blend all the stock lines together, and as you do so this mess of wood and metal will begin to materialize into a long graceful Kentucky rifle. At this point you will no doubt lay down your tools, lift the rifle to your shoulder, and squint down the slender barrel. . . . If this is your first effort at building a long rifle, now is when you join the elite group who have performed the same joyous ritual for hundreds of years.

The trigger assembly which comes in the Dixie rifle kit features a trigger with a broad flat face and a traditional "pigtail" curl on the tip. Locate the proper position for the trigger plate by positioning it so that the trigger is pulled. Center the trigger plate between those two handy lines on the under-side of the stock. The trigger assembly can be held in place by the traditional method of running a long machine screw down through the breech tang and into the trigger plate. An unthreaded screw is provided for this purpose, but you must drill a perfectly centered line from the tang to the trigger plate, thread the screw shank, then tap the hole in the plate. I fudged a bit by using wood screws to hold both the tang and the plate.

The trigger guard comes next, but, like the buttplate, it must first be dressed up a bit. The guard, when installed, is partially inletted with a molded portion rising above the wood. Prepare the guard by shaping up the exposed portions with a fine-cut file and polishing with fine (400-grit) finishing paper and super-fine steel wool. The insides of the various curves can be efficiently polished by wrapping the finishing paper around a dowel or round file.

Building a Kentucky Rifle from a Kit

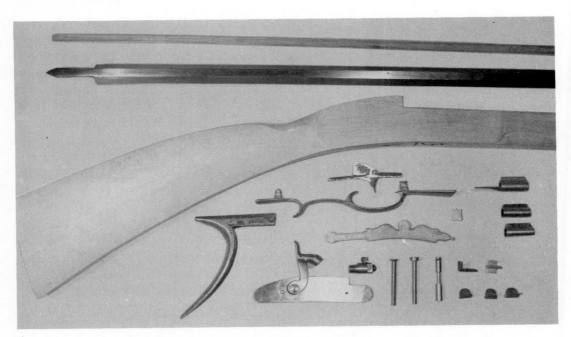

1   The Dixie Kentucky rifle kit. These kits are available in both caplock and flintlock form. This is the caplock version. Note that the stock is roughly cut to shape but leaves enough room to express your own ideas as to styling and design.

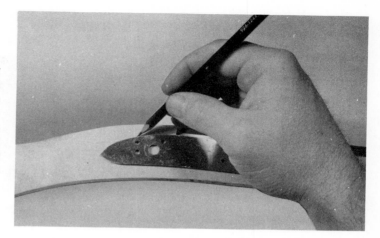

2

After determining the proper position of the lock, remove the working parts and place the lock plate flat on the stock. Next trace the outline with a sharp pencil. Note that the lock plate shown here has been somewhat reshaped from the original form.

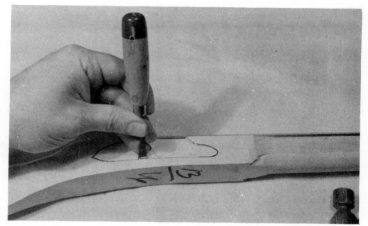

3

After the lock-plate outline has been traced, the next step is to cut the outline to full depth with sharp-edged carving tools. After this the wood is cut away so that the lock plate fits flush in the recess.

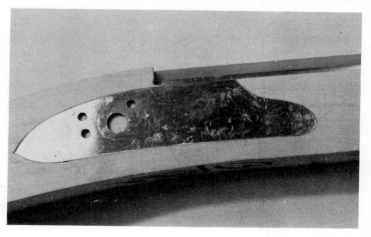

4

The lock plate in place in the inletted recess. Note the close wood-to-metal fit, the sign of careful craftsmanship.

5

The next part of the inletting process is to cut the inletting deeper to accommodate the lock mechanism. For inletting with router, see next chapter.

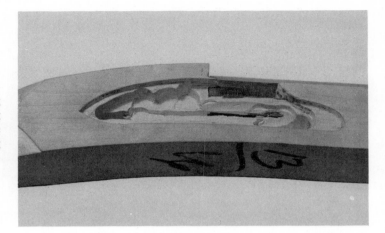

6

The assembled lock in place after the stock has been sculpted to near final shape. Pay particular attention to the molding around the lock plate. Note that the outline of the molding was first sketched on the wood; also note how the final shaping was worked around the outline.

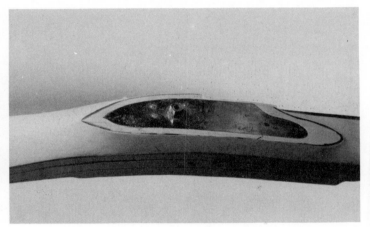

7

The brass buttplate is fitted to the stock before working the wood down flush with the buttplate. At this stage the buttplate still has the rough-cast finish, which will be polished off after final stock shaping.

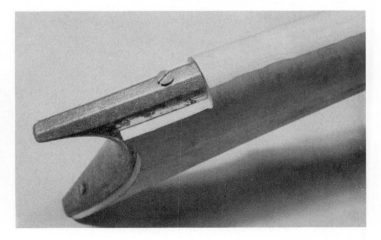

8

Another view of the buttplate fitted to the stock. With the buttplate in place as shown here it forms a template which determines the final stock dimension. This is why it is necessary to fit the buttplate before it is given its final shape.

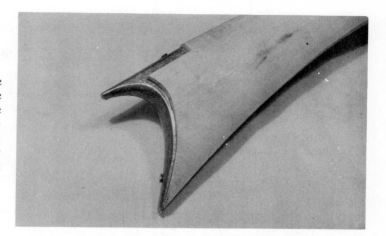

9

The barrel-tang inletting. This chore is accomplished in a matter similar to the lock-plate inletting; the outline of the tang is traced on the wood and then cut to full depth.

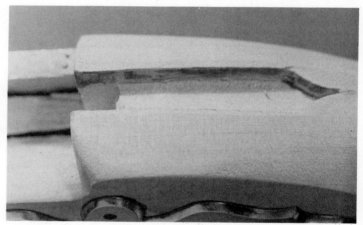

10

The tang in position but before final polishing and shaping. Note the close wood-to-metal fit, which is always important.

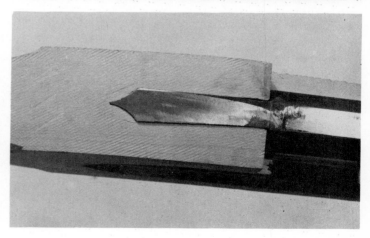

The trigger guard is held in place by inletting the "ears" and inserting cross pins through the stock. This method has been used for hundreds of years and is a tradition well worth continuing. The inletting for the ears is rather deep and narrow but can be quickly accomplished by drilling a row of ⅛-inch holes where the ears are to be inserted, then routing out the slots by wobbling the drill back and forth. After the fore and aft tangs of the guard are inletted, run a ¹⁄₁₆-inch drill through the stock and ears, insert two penny finishing nails, and the job is complete. Don't trim the nails flush at this point, however, as you will need to remove the guard soon.

Next chore is inletting the ramrod pipes. Locate the upper pipe about 3 inches from the muzzle and place the center pipes halfway between the upper and lower pipes. Inletting the pipes presents no special problem, though the tang on the lower pipe may require a little bending to match the curve of the stock. They are secured in place by the traditional pin method.

By now you're about ready to install the side plate, but it suddenly occurs that it can't be positioned properly until the lock screw hole is drilled. Trying to figure out where the lock screw will go may cause you a few anxious moments. To be sure there isn't much room, but there is enough—just barely. Locate the center of the lock screw about ¼ inch forward of the upper bridle screw (the dohickey that holds the tumbler in place) and about ¼ inch from the top of the lock plate. This should clear the rear of the barrel by ⅛ inch or so. Now you'll discover that the lock screw will pass through the wrench web below the tang. This problem can be cleared up by simply cutting a notch in the web.

11
The sideplate is inletted in the same manner as the lock plate. However, here it is inletted to only half of its actual depth. The other half-thickness of the sideplate extends above the surface of the wood.

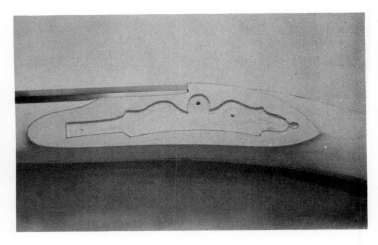

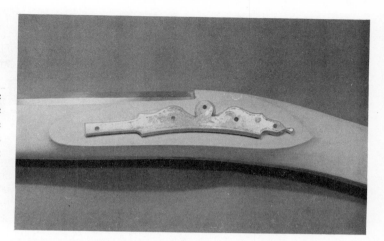

12
The lock plate in position. Note that the surface of the lock plate is still rather rough as it came with the kit. After the plate is securely fastened in the wood it is easier to file flat and polish.

13
A half-round cabinet rasp is used to put the final shape on the cheekpiece. Note that the cheekpiece slopes away both on the front and rear edges.

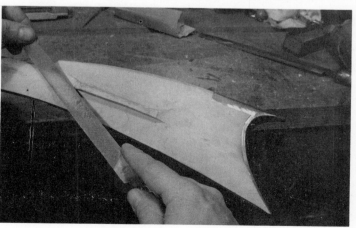

14

The trigger-plate assembly has been inletted into the stock. Before inletting the plate, however, it is necessary to make sure that the trigger is properly lined up with the sear arm of the lock.

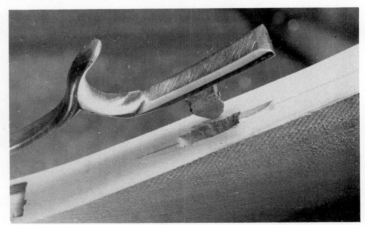

15

A closeup of the first step in fitting the trigger guard. Note that the trigger-guard tab, which will eventually hold the guard in place by use of pins, has been inletted into the bottom of the stock. Since this cut will not show, it is not necessary, or even desirable, to make an extremely close fit.

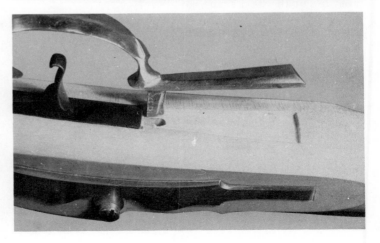

16

The inletted recess for the forward extension of the trigger guard, and also the deep-cut hole for the trigger-guard attachment tab. Also note that the lock plate has been filed flat and polished with the lock screw in place.

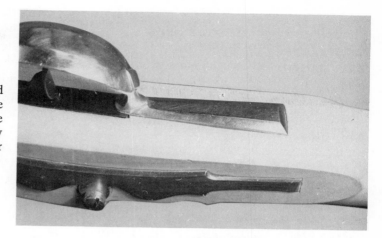

17

The trigger-guard unit is fitted into the inletting. Note how the trigger guard overlaps the trigger plate and holds it tightly in position with no need for screws or pins.

18

A bit of finishing paper wrapped around a small file is used to put a final polish on the trigger guard. Final polishing is done with fine steel wool.

19

With the trigger guard held in position, the retaining-pin hole is drilled through the stock and retaining tab. This way perfect alignment is assured, but it is very necessary that the trigger guard be properly aligned and held flush with the stock.

Now you can drill the lock screw hole and, with the lock in place, continue the hole through the stock. Now you know exactly where to put the sideplate! In addition to making a firm backing for the lock screw (or screws) the sideplate decorates the otherwise plain offside of the lock molding. The sideplate furnished with the Dixie kit is of a beautiful old original design, but, like the guard and buttplate, it is of cast brass and requires a bit of dressing up for best effect. Traditionally the sideplate is installed half in and half out of the wood with the exposed edges beveled. The Dixie sideplate is amply thick for this application, but it takes a bit of work with a file to get the bevel right. After inletting, secure the plate with three or four ¼-inch brass wood screws. Do not countersink the heads full depth but just enough so that the slotted portion of the screw head will protrude above the plate surface. File the heads flush and you have a neat installation with all but invisible screws.

This pretty well wraps up the stockwork except for final sanding and finishing. A nice touch is a brass muzzlecap. Though the muzzlecap comes with the more expensive Dixie kits, it is not part of the $79.90 (current price) New Dixie kit which I built. Muzzlecaps can be purchased separately from Dixie for about two dollars and are well worth the extra expense and time required to install. (Be sure to specify the barrel size when you order.)

To fit the drum of the barrel, remove the breech plug (hold the barrel in a vise and use an adjustable wrench on the plug), then drill and tap for the 5/16-inch 24-thread drum shank. If you don't have tapping tools, you can have this work done at a machine shop. You spotted the location for the drum when you were working on positioning the lock—remember? File a bevel on the right side of the breech-plug face so there will be plenty of space for proper ignition. With the drum in place you'll now discover that the lock plate will have to be notched before the barrel will return to position. Small problem—just mark the position on the lock plate and use a rat-tail file to make a semicircular cut to receive the drum. Check for fit and proper location as you proceed so the fit will be close and the position correct.

When the barrel comes to proper position, check to see how the hammer lines up on the nipple. Adjust to a proper striking angle by tilting the angle of the nipple as needed. Also you may find it necessary to screw the drum in or out until the nipple is properly aligned with the hammer.

The next job will require a lot of cutting and filing, but it can't be put off any longer. Five dovetail slots—two for the sights and three for the barrel loops—must be cut. A good bit of metal can be removed pretty quickly by sawing a close row of slots with a hacksaw. The remaining metal can be removed with a file. A simple triangular file is all that's needed for undercutting the edges of the dovetail slots.

20

The dovetail cut which is filed on the bottom surface of the barrel, shown here with the barrel loop in place.

21

Two finishing nails are used as retaining pins. The pin to the left passes through the stock and barrel loop. The other pin is through the ramrod thimble retaining tab. Note that the pins are left overlength. This is a good idea until the rifle is completely finished, because there will be several occasions to disassemble the rifle and it is easier to extract the pins when they are extra long. Later they will be cut to proper length.

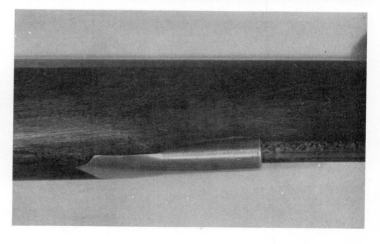

22

A closeup of the lower ramrod thimble, or pipe. Note that it is neatly inletted and blends with the natural lines of the stock. The holding pin has been cut flush with the stock surface.

The front barrel loop should be about 5 inches from the muzzle and the rear loop about 9 inches from the breech. Position the center loop halfway between the other two loops. Before you start cutting, please make sure that you are on the proper flat of the barrel. Occasionally an overeager craftsman will discover that he has located the loops or sights on the *side* of the barrel. No insult to your intelligence intended.

With the loops attached you go through the through-pin drilling routine again, polish and install the sights, and suddenly your rifle is all but finished!

At this point remove the barrel, lock, and trigger guard and give the barrel and lock a good scrubbing with steel wool, apply a coating of Dixie browning solution, and set it aside for the rust coating to form. The amount of time spent on final sanding pays dividends, and since so much good work has been invested in the rifle it's not very smart to fudge on the sanding. Using progressively finer-grit paper, work until the stock is as slick as a buckeye, and then give it a final rubdown with superfine steel wool.

For a dark, rich color which brings out the character of the wood, use Dixie's stain for antique guns or a similar stain such as the Birchwood-Casey Colonial Red stain. Some builders prefer to leave the wood its natural blond color, and the effect is indeed striking. My own choice of finish was Casey's polyurethane spray-on stock finish. This easy-to-apply finish is tough and will remain bright and beautiful through a lot of hard use.

So now the long rifle is finished. Oil the lock, reassemble the parts, insert the pins, and clip the pins flush. You are now the proud owner of a beautiful, highly shootable, custom *handmade* Kentucky rifle. Hang it on the wall and it will draw lots of admiring comments, or take it to the range and draw a crowd. It's the only one like it in the world.

The underside of the stock, showing the finished trigger guard, trigger assembly, etc., in place. The stock has been final-sanded, stained, and finished. Particularly note that the work is clean and neat with everything properly fitted. This is a sure sign of careful workmanship.

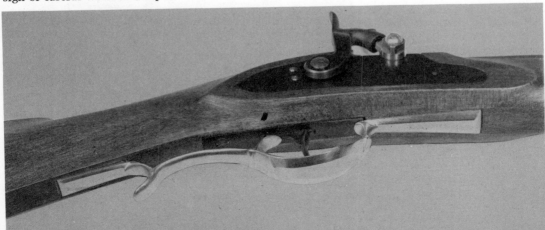

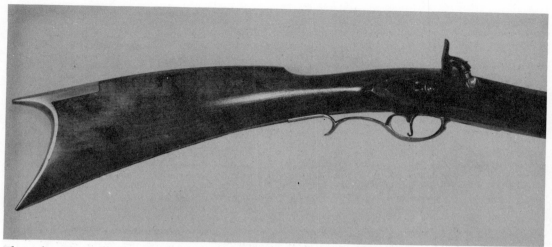

The right side of the butt section. Compare this final shape with the shape of the original, semi-finished stock. This will give you a good idea of the individual styling possible with the Dixie kit. The secret to making attractive Kentucky-style rifles is using simple but graceful curves such as I did here.

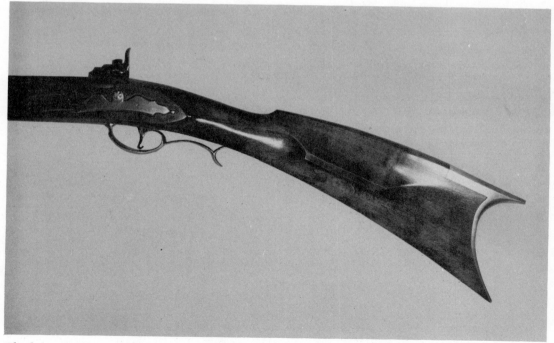

The left side of the butt section of the Kentucky rifle stock, showing the simply but gracefully styled cheekpiece.

The final test: I fire at a target with my just-completed Kentucky-style rifle. The cloud of smoke can be seen just ahead of the muzzle. I'm wearing shooting glasses, always a necessity when firing muzzleloading firearms.

38 / A Fast and Accurate Way to Inlet Barrels and Stocks

This final section is not a complete project but just some mighty helpful hints. After building the muzzleloading rifle and pistol kits described in the preceding chapters, there's not much more to be gained by working with kits. Now you're ready to step out on your own and build and entirely original piece. Finished locks and barrels are available from several sources, and nearly all professional muzzleloading gunsmiths buy these parts readymade. The big chore is making a stock from a plain block of wood. Awesome as working on that much wood may appear, you'll find that it isn't all that much more difficult than building the Dixie "Kentucky" rifle kit. Probably the biggest difference is inletting that long barrel into the stock.

When I was in college I picked up tuition money by making reproductions of Kentucky-style rifles. The memory of those days is well impressed on my person in the form of a scar where a barrel inletting chisel got out of control and field-dressed my left thumb. Since this barrel-inletting procedure was proving painful as well as time consuming—I usually spent a whole day inletting a 40-inch barrel into rock-hard curly maple—I began casting about for a better way to get the job done.

The only advice I could get from local woodworkers was to grind a special cutter for a power shaper. This, however, would involve a different cutter for every barrel size. Also, this technique didn't offer the degree of flexibility I wanted; I was planning ahead for the application of power equipment in other areas of rifle building.

It had been pointed out that a router offered the flexibility I needed, but that the available router bits would not give the cut we needed for barrel inletting. Thinking this over, I came up with the idea that perhaps a combination of router bits would do the job. After all, a barrel channel was only a series of vertical, horizontal, and 45° cuts. So why not use a plain ¼-inch bit for the sides and bottom, then use a bit with a 45° cut for the two corner flats? Also, as I was delighted to discover, there were bits available which would be perfect for cutting the ramrod groove (another job I hated with a passion).

The only tools needed are a router, an edge guide, and two bits, one ¼-inch straight edge and a ⅜-inch V-groove bit. To be sure, routers are fairly expensive, especially if you intend to make only one rifle. The ideal arrangement in such cases would be multiple ownership. A muzzleloading club, for example, could share a commonly owned router. Or perhaps your neighborhood has a rental shop where you can rent a router for an hour or two.

The first step is to bandsaw your stock blank to profile. Be sure the top and bottom edges of the forend are straight and parallel. It is a good idea to have the top and the sides planed smooth. The router and the edge guide will move more easily if they are smooth.

There is some dilemma in sawing the top edge of the forend, because you have to choose between sawing to the finished stock line or cutting only on a false line where the top of the barrel will be. The dilemma is created by the "hump" or rise in the stock just aft of the breech. If the top of the forend is cut to finished dimensions, the channel cannot be routed to full depth because the router's base plate will stop against this hump at the rear of the channel. Thus the last 4 inches must be inletted by hand. This, of course, is not much of a job.

If the stock blank is profiled so that the top line is straight all the way back, the barrel channel can be cut to absolute length. But then you have to go back and saw, or cut by some means, the forend down so that the barrel will lay half-depth in the stock. This latter method is a bit speedier if you have a bandsaw or table saw close at hand, but you can run the risk of splintering the edges of the inletting somewhat. The decision is yours.

Quite frequently, drying stock blanks will take on considerable amount of warpage, with the full length of the blank being out of line an inch or more. Obviously, since the router guide follows the edge of the wood, the routed channel will be ahead and will cut the channel to the correct barrel size. When the forend is worked down to the final shape it will be flexible enough to be held straight by the barrel.

Also there is the matter of where to locate the channel in respect to the center of the blank. The answer to this is simply to allow the thickness of the lock plate along the right side of the stock between the edge of wood and the barrel channel. The top edge of the lockplate is usually something like ¼ inch or so. The beauty of this technique is that since the lock is to be inletted flush against the barrel, the surface of the lockplate and the side of the stock will already be level and will require no additional work. Too, and of even more importance, offsetting the barrel this way allows additional wood on the left side for the cheekpiece! Now how about that? Of course if you're left-handed and using a left-handed lock, just reverse the process.

Begin in the routing by cutting the vertical sides of the channel. Cut only to the depth of the corners of the side flats. Don't try to cut it all at once, just take a cut the router can handle easily. Too—and this is important—when you cut the left side of the channel set the router up so that the edge is on the

Using Routers for Inletting Work

1 Two types of routers that are mighty handy for inletting muzzleloading rifles. At left, the Dremel Moto-Tool with routing attachment. At right, a Black & Decker router with straightedge attachment. The other tools needed are a precise measuring rule, as in foreground, and the three router bits as shown (see next photo). The wrenches are used for changing router bits in the Black & Decker tool. In the background is an inletted muzzleloading barrel and stock resting on a Black & Decker tool kit.

right side! Then reverse the position when cutting the other side of the channel. There is a very good reason for this: If the router "jumps" it can only jump into the channel area where the miscut can do no harm. I learned this trick when I ruined the first stock I routed.

Also, to play it extra safe, you might cut the sides of the channel 1/64 inch or so undersize. Later you can use the router to shave this open bit by bit until the barrel fit is absolutely perfect.

With the sides cut to full depth, the next step is to cut the 45° flats running inward to the bottom of the channel. The bit I use cuts this strip about 3/8 inch wide. If the flats on the barrel require a wider surface, set the router in and down a little until the bit lines up with the surface and make another pass. Getting this overlap to line up perfectly is best done by stopping the router—and unplugging it—and eyeballing the bit just where you want it.

Now with the two sides and the inside flaps cut to shape, all that's left is a ridge running up the center. This is quickly sliced away with the straight-sided bit. So there you have it—the job is finished and the job is perfect.

2
These three basic router shapes are all you need to completely inlet a muzzleloading barrel and ramrod. The half-round router shape at left is used to cut a perfect ramrod groove. These bits come in several sizes to correspond with whatever ramrod size may be needed. The 45° cutter in the center is used to cut the inside corners of the barrel channel. At right is the straight cut, or bit box, which is used to cut the vertical and flat surfaces in the barrel channel. A 1/4-inch bit such as this can be used for all barrel sizes simply by moving back and forth and overlapping width of the cut.

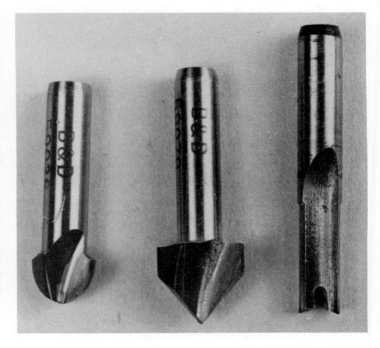

3

The two sides of the barrel channel are being inletted with the simple box bit. Note the use of the straightedge guide. It is important that only one side of the stock be used as a guide reference. This is necessary because stock blanks may vary in width and if the guide is used on either side the barrel channel may not be uniform.

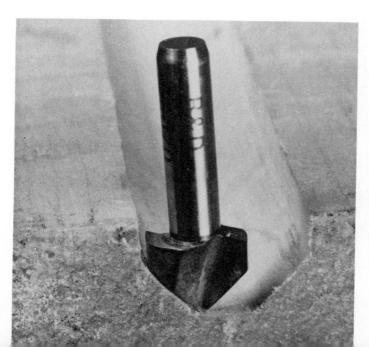

4

This setup shows how the 45° angle cutter is positioned and moved when it cuts away the inside corners of the channel.

5
A cross section of a typical muzzleloading barrel channel for octangular barrels. Despite the seemingly complex shape of the cut, actually only three angles are cut.

6
An octangular muzzleloading barrel fitted into a router-cut barrel channel. The fit is very precise.

Always—and I mean *always*—play it safe when using a router or any other piece of power equipment. Always be sure that the tool is *unplugged* when changing bits or making adjustments.

Now, moving on to the ramrod groove, fit a ¼-inch or ⅜-inch half-round bit in the cutter and set the guide so the groove will be directly under the bottom flat. The thickness of the web between the channel and the groove is a matter of personal taste, but for those really slim, graceful forend lines this web has to be pretty thin. About ¼ inch is the most you'll want. Actually all you need is enough room for the barrel loops.

There are other applications for the router, such as cutting the recess for the patch box and even inletting the lock. The torque of a big router makes it pretty tricky for freehand work when you get close to the line, but they are fine for hogging out most of the inletting. For really fine, detailed inletting, the little Dremel Moto-Tool with routing kit is about perfect. The light weight and low torque of this tool plus the excellent visibility makes it possible to make right-up-to-the-line cuts for a perfect metal-to-wood fit.

If you really want to do yourself proud, try this technique. Completely disassemble the lock and position the lockplate exactly where it is to be inletted. Now mark the outline of the plate with a sharp scribe—a pencil mark is too wide. Now rout the plate to its final depth. Cut the inside area out first, then work cautiously up to the scribed line.

7
The first step in inletting a lock with a router is determining the proper position of the lock plate on the stock and then scribing the outline.

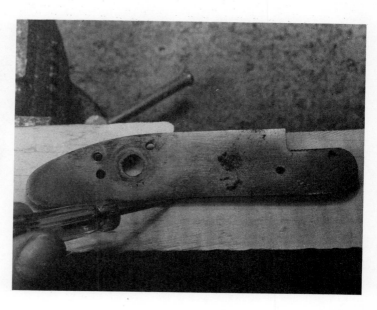

When the lockplate is fitted, begin adding the "guts"—bridle, sear, springs, tumbler, etc.—one by one and inletting them to their various and individual shapes and depths. The effect of this technique is to give the inletting a very professional look, and even though it can't be seen there is a great personal satisfaction in knowing it is done right. "Gravedigging," the technique of hogging out a big cavity for the lock, isn't all that much quicker and weakens the stock in a critical area.

After the lock and action parts are fully inletted, check all the moving parts to make sure that there is room for free operation. The sear arm and tumbler require special attention in this respect.

With the barrel and lock inletted and ramrod groove cut, you are ready to move on to the more creative and pleasant tasks of shaping the stock. So from here on out you're on your own. . . .

8
The Dremel router attachment with a router bit in use.

9

Here the lock-plate inletting has been very nearly completed with the router. Note that the router cut came quite close, but not quite entirely up to the scribed outline. It is possible to route all the way to the outline if you have a sure hand with the router. Otherwise it may be a good idea to do the finishing touches with hand tools.

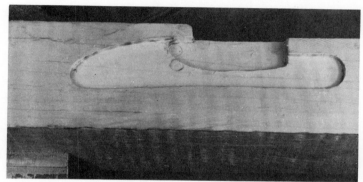

10

The completely finished lock-plate inletting.

11

The lockplate in position. Note the very close wood-to-metal fit with no gaps.

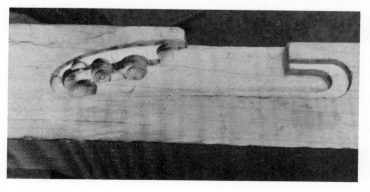

12

The inletting of the "guts" or mechanism of the lock has been completed with a router. Remove only enough wood to allow the lock to fit close but work freely. Additional removal of wood has a weakening effect.

VI

Making Semi-portable Shooting Benches

39 / Making a Wood Shooting Bench

A semi-portable bench rest is a happy medium between the light folding types and the rigid, nonmovable bench. For rifle clubs and individuals who must share their shooting space between bench-rest shooters, position shooters, and pistol buffs, the advantages of a movable bench are obvious.

These features make these benches especially attractive for clubs and private ranges which must make sure that *all* rifle bullets hit in a rather restricted impact zone. With a fixed bench it is frequently necessary that all shooting be done at a specified distance so that all shots will strike a given impact area. With a semiportable bench, however, the target can be properly positioned in front of the embankment, or whatever the impact area happens to be, and the bench located at whatever range one desires. Thus all shots strike in the specified area and maximum safety is assured.

A bonus to this arrangement is that you can zero your rifle at a given range — say 100 yards — then conveniently move the bench, rifle, shooting kit, and all back to 200, then 300 yards, or wherever you want, observing all the while the shift of impact on the target.

Sound interesting and useful? It is!

Of course just how quickly and easily the bench can be moved from one place to another depends on your source of power. Many rifle clubs have invested in small tractor-type riding lawnmowers. This is a most ideal means of pulling the bench about. Also a jeep-type vehicle or even your automobile. If nothing else is at hand, two men can move the bench along without too much sweat, but as I say, it's *semi-portable.*

Built entirely of 2 × 6-inch lumber, the bolted-together frame is designed so that each structural member contributes to the overall stiffness of the unit. Even the built-in seat lends additional strength. The design is so efficient, in fact, that the bench will withstand constant movement and use without getting loose and shaky.

For maximum ease and speed of construction, all structural members of the bench, such as legs and braces, can be precut to proper length before beginning assembly. This is especially time-saving if you're building more than one bench. A pre-sawing guide is included with the bill of materials.

Begin work by cutting the two runners. (You'll note that the runners are beveled on each end so the bench can be pulled in either direction without having to turn it around.) The two 64-inch runners can be cut from a single 10-foot length of lumber if you make a diagonal cut in the exact middle of the piece. This saves a few inches and forms the bevel too.

Now position the upright members, drill, and bolt together. These upright members are located so that there is a 1-inch clearance above the lower edge of the runner. This in no way reduces the strength but makes the bench considerably easier to pull about. It is also important that the uprights be perfectly positioned and absolutely square with the runners. If you get them right to start with, the rest of the bench can be assembled without need for further measuring or squaring—provided your sawing is accurate.

With the uprights secured in position, add the top supports and the two halves are completed. Now all you need to do is put the cross members in place, bolt them to the sides, and the frame is pretty well finished. In fact, as soon as you nail the diagonal top brace in place the frame *will* be finished!

As soon as you've taken a breather, the top and the seat can be nailed in place. Since most of the big 12-penny nails will be driven pretty close to the end of the board, there is some danger of splitting. This can be avoided by predrilling with a $3/32$-inch, or thereabouts, bit.

Starting at the right side of the bench, position the first top board so there is a $1\frac{1}{2}$-inch overhang to the side and an equal overhang fore and aft. Now nail it in place and work your way across. The curved body recess can be accomplished as shown in the photographs by cutting the rear ends of the top pieces at increasing angles. Of course, if you have a bandsaw available you'll probably want to cut a fancy curve.

The seat is simple enough to nail in place, but don't forget to alternate the plank after each angle cut. This way the angle keeps matching up so as to save you a lot of sawing. Now position the foot rest to suit yourself.

Now all you need to do is drill a couple of holes for the tow rope in the front and rear runner crosspieces and the job is done and you're ready to shoot.

If the bench is to be exposed to the elements, a coat or two of paint won't hurt a thing. Also, if you really want to get fancy, drill a few holes along the side of the bench for mounting your reloading press, powder measure, etc. The bench top is amply wide for your shooting gear plus your reloading stuff, and loading at the bench can save a lot of legwork. Too, you might attach a mounting bracket for a beach umbrella. . . .

How to Make the Wood Shooting Bench

1 All the precut parts, ready for assembly. Though the parts can be easily cut by hand, a radial-arm saw or similar power equipment speeds up the process considerably. The list of materials and precut lengths given in the text makes it possible to precut all parts to finished length.

2

The basic skids and uprights laid out together. Note that the uprights do not go all the way to the bottom of the skids. This makes the bench easier to move than if the uprights went all the way to the ground and snagged on grass, rocks, etc.

3
The author's son drills holes in one of the sides for bolts. This is a job the whole family can participate in.

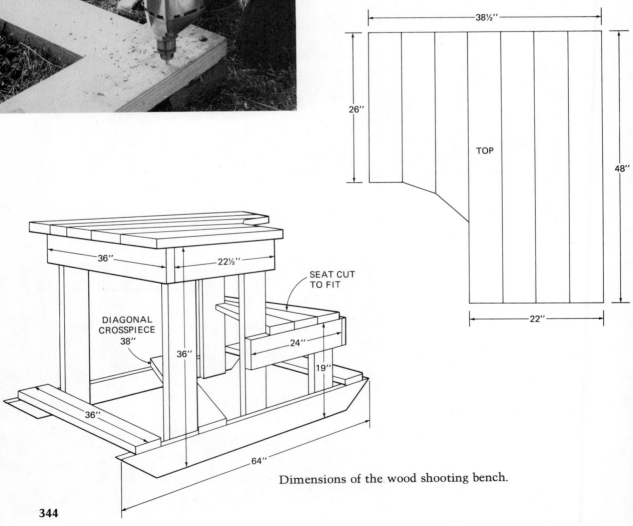

Dimensions of the wood shooting bench.

4

The left side of the bench is assembled and ready to be attached to the right side with the cross members. Note how the bolts are staggered to avoid splintering. This looks like sloppy work but actually it is good procedure.

5

A detail of how the uprights attach to the runners, showing the 1-inch clearance to help prevent snagging.

6

The two sides have been joined with the ends of the four basic cross members.

7   Pre-drilling the top pieces keeps them from splitting when they are nailed down. This drilling can be done quite easily with only a nail chucked into the drill.

8   The top pieces are nailed to the cross members.

9
This closeup shows how the top pieces are cut to achieve a reasonably well-curved recess for the shooter's body. This can be rounded even further with a saber saw or with a rasp.

If the bench is to be stored or moved to a new location, all you need to do is pull off the top and seat, take out the crossmember bolts, and the bench collapses into a neat little pile which takes very little room.

BILL OF MATERIALS

2	12′	2″ × 6″
3	10′	″
4	8′	″
16	8″	⁵/₁₆″ carriage bolts with washers
44	3½″	⁵/₁₆″ ″ ″ ″ ″

2 lb. 12-penny common nails

(Total cost runs from $15 to $20 depending on local prices.)

Sawing Guide:
1. Cut the two 12-foot boards into eight 36-inch pieces. These are the four uprights and four crossmembers.
2. Cut the two runners from one 10-foot piece.
3. Cut four 48-inch pieces from two 8-foot pieces.
4. Cut the 38-inch diagonal top crosspiece, and the 42-inch and 22½-inch top supports from one 10-foot piece.
5. Cut the 43-inch foot rest, 19-inch seat upright, and 24-inch seat support from one 8-foot piece.
6. The seat (cut-and-try) and remaining top pieces are cut from remaining lumber.

347

The portable wood shooting bench can be dragged along by hand, but for really stylish transport a garden tractor, such as shown here, tops the bill. As a matter of fact, I mowed my shooting range as I moved the tractor to the various ranges.

I give the bench a workout. The footrest can be positioned according to your leg length.

40

Making a Concrete Shooting Bench

For individuals or clubs wanting something less portable but more substantial than an all-wood bench, the best choice is a portable (barely) concrete model. The bench described here was designed and built by the Prescott Sportsmen's Club of Prescott, Arizona.

Their problem was pretty much the same as that experienced by shooting clubs all over the country—too many groups of different shooting interests and not enough room for all their different kinds of shooting on the club range. To be sure, there was a nice pistol setup, a covered concrete-floored smallbore firing line, and a half-dozen or so plywood bench rests for plinking, black-powder shooting, and rifle testing. Normally, the benches were positioned on the concrete firing line and simply carried out of the way whenever smallbore or pistol tournaments were held.

The arrangement proved pretty much satisfactory until the increasing benchrest-shooting segment of the club began thinking about holding formal benchrest competitions. Two things were clearly evident: The flimsy plywood benches, serviceable as they were for most types of shooting, were not rigid enough for competitive shoots, and there wasn't enough room to install permanent benches.

Obviously, the only solution was benches that could be positioned on the concrete firing line for bench-rest competitions and then moved out of the way for other types of shooting. But this meant portable benches and the inherent lack of rigidness of nonfixed benches—or did it?

First, the question of "portability" was analyzed in terms of how far and how often the benches had to be moved. In this case it means moving the benches only two or three times a year for the major smallbore tournaments, and even then they needed to be moved only to the rear of the firing line, some 10 feet or so. During the rest of the year the benches could be left in position and still leave plenty of room for the practicing position shooters.

Since the benches could not be made rigid by permanently attaching them in the ground or cementing them to the concrete slab, sheer mass would be required to make them sturdy. This, of course, meant using concrete and lots of it, but it also meant the problems always encountered when trying to move a concrete object.

Being a nonflexing material, concrete is notoriously bad about cracking and breaking when subjected to uneven pressures or uneven supporting surfaces. Some permanently fixed concrete benches, for example, have been known to crack simply because the legs settled into the ground at an uneven rate.

Now perhaps you understand the problem of building a massive concrete bench than can withstand the rigors of being moved—without cracking or breaking.

In engineering terms it was a problem of weights, stresses, counterstresses, and reinforcements. Also, the time and expense involved in building forms ruled out any try-and-see techniques. Instead, the project was approached as an engineering problem, pure and simple. Plans were drawn, weights calculated, stresses estimated, and a reinforcing structure designed. Also, since several benches were to be made, the forms had to be designed so that they could be rapidly dismantled and reassembled.

The results are actually better than we had dared hope. This is no doubt due to the engineering talents of Paul Marquart, Doye Phillips and Paul Hosman, who did most of the design and actual work. To date the benches, which weigh approximately 800 pounds each, have demonstrated their ruggedness. They have been hoisted into the back of a pickup truck by means of winch lift, survived a trip over rugged, unpaved roads, and endured being slid out of the truck via an improvised ramp and pipe rollers, moved along the firing line on rollers, and, finally, being dragged off the firing line and then back on again. All this without so much as a crack!

From a standpoint of sturdiness they compare very well with permanently mounted concrete benches. In fact, they are more rigid than benches I've tried with concrete tops and metal legs set in concrete footings. Naturally they are far more solid than any wooden benches. The only thing we've found that is more sturdy is concrete mounts set on a concrete slab. But an arrangement like that is far from portable.

The most striking feature of the portable concrete bench is that the two top extensions (making the bench equally suitable for right or left-handed shooters) and the legs are all of a single unit of concrete. The bench top and legs are all poured at one time! Thus, when the bottom skids are bolted in place and the cross bracing added, each part reinforces another part. This way uneven pressures on the unit, such as being set on an uneven surface or even being dragged over rough terrain, are distributed over the entire structure rather than finding their way to the weakest part and causing a fracture.

Begin work on the form by cutting the sixteen side pieces for the four leg forms from ¾-inch plywood. The legs measure 26 inches from the tops of the skids to the underside of the top, 8 inches wide at the tops, and 4 inches wide at the bottom. In order to make the forms come out right, cut eight of the sides so they will be 26 inches high, 8 inches wide at one end, tapering to 4 inches at the other. Then cut the other eight sides 26 inches high, 9½ inches at the top, tapering to 5½ inches at the bottom. This additional width allows for the overlapping at the corners so there will be a perfectly square cavity.

Assemble the leg forms by nailing together lightly and adding some scrap-wood crossmembers across the outside for additional support. Finally, bind the leg forms with wire bands in a couple of places to prevent the forms from gaping open at the seams under the weight of all that concrete.

The form for the bench top is made of a single piece of plywood measuring 45×45 inches. The body recess, 21×21 inches, is cut into one side of this piece of plywood, thus forming the right- and left-hand extensions. This makes the extensions 12 inches wide and 21 inches deep, ample for comfortable shooting.

The next step is cutting the four 8×8×8 inch holes where the leg forms join. These holes are easy to cut with a saber saw but must be carefully positioned so that everything will line up properly when the form is assembled, so follow the scale drawing carefully.

In order to keep the top form from sagging under the weight of the concrete, it must be reinforced with 2×4 strips along the outer edges around the leg openings and across the center area. The 2×4 reinforcing strips around the leg openings should be set back exactly ¾ inch from the edge of the hole to hold the leg forms in good alignment with the hole and at the same time keep the tops of the leg forms from spreading out under the pressure of the concrete.

The final step in building the form is attaching the edging around the top form. The width of the material doesn't much matter, just as long as it extends up a uniform 4 inches all around the sides. Now, with the form completed, you are ready to pour a bench.

The first step is to cut and drill the two bottom runners from 4×4 hardwood. Cut these 42 inches long and bevel each end about 45° or so, to make the bench skid more easily. Drill a ½-inch hole through the center of each runner 8 inches from the front edge, and the second hole 25 inches to the rear of the front hole. Now, countersink the *underside* of the holes with a 1-inch bit to a depth of an inch or so. This will allow room for a washer and nut to be added later.

With the runners in proper position on a hard, level surface, insert the leg-reinforcing irons. The reinforcing irons were made of foot-long, ½-inch diameter bolts with the top 2 inches or so bent at right angles. This gives a better hold in the concrete. Welded to the bolts is a 27-inch length of ⅜-inch reinforcing rod. The top 3 inches of the rods are bent at a 90° angle and the bottom end overlaps the bolt 2 inches. This gives the leg reinforcing rod a length of 32 inches overall, from the threaded end of the bolt to the top bend of the rod.

With the leg rods in position, drop the leg forms on top of the runners and then set the top form on top of the legs. Adjust the runners until the legs align perfectly with the openings in the top form.

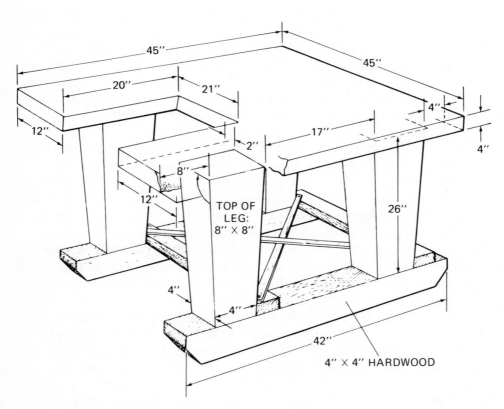

The concrete bench rests on a pair of hardwood 4-by-4s.

At this stage you're almost ready to start pouring concrete, but first wax the inside of the form. This helps waterproof the plywood, gives a smoother surface to the concrete, and makes the forms easier to remove. Simply melt two or three cakes of paraffin in a pan and brush or swab it on the inner surfaces of the form and you're ready to go.

Reinforcing material for the top is 6-inch-mesh welded wire and $3/8$-inch reinforcement iron. The wire mesh must be bent slightly so that it does not lie flat on the bottom of the form but rather extends up about 2 inches or so. This will put it near the center of the 4-inch-thick top where it will do the most good. *(Text continues on page 359)*

Making the Concrete Shooting Bench

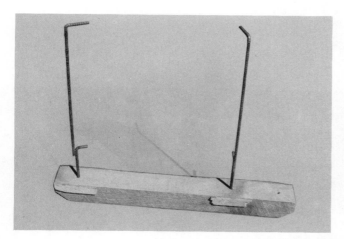

1

The first step in assembling the form is inserting reinforcing rods in the hardwood skids. Eventually the rods will be bolted to the skids, but not until after the concrete has set and the form removed. The undersides of the skids are countersunk deep enough to allow for a washer and nut. Note that the reinforcing rods are simply welded to bolts.

A shooting-club member attaches leg forms over the skids. Note the wire bands which hold the sides together and help prevent bulging when the leg forms are filled with concrete. The leg forms are supported by blocks temporarily nailed to the skids. These are knocked off and the wire is removed when the form is disassembled from around the hardened concrete.

3
A closeup of the assembled leg mold. The wooden blocks, which help hold the form together, are lightly nailed so that they can be easily removed.

4
The underside view of the form shows the 2×4s used for bracing. Note bracing around the leg holes. This bracing both aligns and supports the leg forms.

5

A detail of the bracing around the leg holes which aligns and supports the leg forms.

6

The completed form ready for the concrete. Note how reinforcing rods in legs extend up into the top slab.

A detail showing the inside of the leg form with reinforcing rod in place.

355

7

One of the designers of the bench applies a coat of melted paraffin to the inside surface of the form. This helps waterproof the plywood and prevents it from sticking to the concrete.

8

Concrete for the benches can be conveniently mixed in a wheelbarrow. If you don't have a wheelbarrow, borrow or rent one.

9

When the leg forms are filled with concrete to within about 2 inches of the top, a tarpaper seal is inserted around the leg joint and folded over the top. This keeps concrete from seeping into the joint, making the form difficult to disassemble.

10

As the concrete is poured into the leg forms it should be constantly tamped in order to eliminate bubbles and voids which might weaken the structure.

11

After about 2 inches of concrete have been poured into the top form, reinforcing wire and bracing are added as shown here. Note how the rod is bent so that it extends from the main body of the slab to the right and left.

12

After the form is filled the slab is smoothed by simply brushing a straightedge board across the top molding. Final smoothing is done with a trowel.

13 After the concrete has set for several hours a final once-over will give an extra-smooth surface.

14
Extra bracing of 2×6 hardwood cross members bolted to the skids plus X-bracing of steel straps makes the concrete bench a virtually indestructible unit, capable of withstanding a considerable amount of dragging about.

15 Club members setting the top form over the leg forms. After the concrete hardens the top form is removed by simply dropping it down over the legs after the leg forms have been removed. It is also necessary to detach the skids at this point. After the form is removed the skids are permanently attached by tightening the four nuts at the undersides of the skids.

The iron rod is bent in a U shape with either end reaching well into the right and left "arms" or rear extensions. These extensions are the most vulnerable part of the bench and must be reinforced accordingly.

Mixing concrete is an art unto itself and well beyond the scope of these pages. My mix, however, was seven parts fine gravel, five parts sand, and three parts cement, tastefully blended with appropriate amounts of water.

Actual pouring begins with filling the leg forms up to within 3 inches of their tops. It is important that the concrete be tamped well as it is poured, to avoid any air pockets which might weaken the structure.

To keep the liquid concrete from seeping between the leg forms and top forms, and thus blocking the easy removal of the top form, strips of tarpaper can be fitted around the union and folded over at the top. This forms an effective seal. The pressure of the concrete holds the tarpaper seal firmly in place

A finished bench. The advantage of the prefabricated form is that any number of benches can be made from one form.

and presses tightly against the inside walls. From here on out it is simply a matter of filling the form up to the top.

Smoothing and leveling the top of the slab is accomplished by sliding a 2×4 leveling bar across the top edges of the form. Be sure to agitate the concrete sufficiently to remove any voids. A final troweling before the concrete sets hard puts a dead-smooth surface on the top of the bench.

When the concrete has cured for a day the forms can be removed. This is surprisingly easy provided everything was assembled right to start with. The sides of the top form are simply knocked off. The leg forms come off next, but they cannot be simply pulled off because they are interlocked with the top form. Using jacks, or a hoist or lever arrangement, the bench must be raised about 6 inches. The runners, which will probably stick to the legs, are removed by tapping lightly until they fall off. This in turn allows the leg forms to be slipped free, the wire bindings cut, and the sides dismantled.

With the leg forms out of the way, the bottom of the top form will drop straight down and can then be removed intact. Now the runners are once more fitted in place; washers and nuts are put in place at the underside of the runners, drawn up tight, and the bench can be lowered.

Final bracing is accomplished with 2×4 hardwood strips connecting the runners fore and aft and held in place by heavy nails or lag bolts. A final X-bracing between the legs, of 1-inch strap steel or iron rods, completes the bracing. These can be anchored by the same nails or lag bolt that attaches the cross-members to the runners.

Notice that no provision has been made for a built-in seat, though this would have made the bench easier to build. Seats built integral with a shooting bench tend to transmit body movement and tremor to the bench, and hence to the point of aim. It is better to have the stool, chair, or whatever separate and detached. So the matter of what to sit on is entirely up to the club or individual.

A wooden bench top is desirable, particularly for precision rest rifles, so rests may be "nailed" to the bench. A thick plywood top can be attached to this bench with lag bolts, or by other means.

Five of these benches received their "trial by fire" at a nonregistered bench-rest match. The shooters who were there have competed at almost all, if not all, of the major bench-rest clubs in the country, and they gave these barely portable benches high marks for both shooting comfort and rigidity.

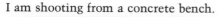

I am shooting from a concrete bench.

Appendix

Sources of Tools, Supplies, and Equipment

Many ordinary tools such as drills, files, rasps, etc. that are used for gunsmithing can be bought at your local hardware store. But other tools are of such a specialized nature—stock, checkering and carving tools—that they usually must be ordered either from the manufacturer or a distributor such as Brownell's.

The following is a listing of the major suppliers of tools and gunsmithing supplies. Many of these cater specifically to the amateur craftsman and offer instructive as well as interesting catalogs. Many of the suppliers listed here make an initial charge for their catalog. This price is listed where known. The catalog price is refunded on the first order. Some manufacturers and distributors send a free brochure, and request only a stamped self-addressed envelope (as noted here, SSAE).

Alley Supply Co., Corson Valley Industrial Park, Gardnerville, Nev. 89410: tools and specialty items.

Atkinson Barrel Co., P.O. Box 512, Prescott, Ariz. 86302: rifle barrels made and fitted.

B-Square Co., P.O. Box 11281, Fort Worth, Tex. 76109: tools and specialized equipment; free catalog.

Al Biesen, 2039 Sinto Ave., Spokane, Wash. 99201: semi-finished stocks, steel buttplates and gripcaps; SSAE for catalog.

Birchwood-Casey Co., Eden Prairie, Minn. 55343: stock finishes, stains, cold blues, and other gunsmithing chemicals.

E. C. Bishop & Co., Warsaw, Mo. 65355: semi-finished stocks; catalog $1.

Bonanza Sports Co., Box 278, Faribault, Minn. 55021: gunsmith's screwdrivers.

Brookstone Co., 16 Brookstone Bldg., Vose Farm Rd., Peterborough, N.H. 03458: tools and specialty items.

Brown Precision Co., 5869 Indian Ave., San Jose, Calif. 95123: fiberglass stocks.

Leonard Brownell, Box 25, Wyarno, Wyo. 82845: classic-style gripcaps, bolt handles, and scope mounts; SSAE for catalog.

Brownell's Checkering, 1852 Alessandro Trail, Vita, Calif. 92083: checkering tools; SSAE for catalog.

Brownell's, Inc., Montezuma, Iowa 50171: best single source of gunsmithing tools and related equipment; catalog $2.

Chicago Wheel and Mfg. Co., 1101 W. Monroe Street, Chicago, Ill. 60607: hand grinders and accessories.

Classic Arms Intl., Ltd., 547 Merrick Rd., Lynbrook, N.Y. 11563: muzzleloading kits; catalog $1.

Jim Cloward, 4023 Aurora Ave. N., Seattle, Wash. 98102: semi-finished target stocks.

Connecticut Valley Arms, Saybrook Rd., Haddam, Conn. 06438: muzzleloading kits and accessories.

Albert Constantine & Son, Inc., 2050 Eastchester Rd., Bronx, N.Y. 10461: tools, woods, and finishing supplies.

Craftsman Wood Service Co., 2727 S. Mary St., Chicago, Ill. 60608: tools, finishing supplies, wood.

Dem-Bart Electric Checkering Tools, 117-5th St., Edmonds, Wash. 98020: electric checkering tools and hand checkering tools; SSAE for catalog.

Dixie Gun Works, Union City, Tenn. 38261: tools, supplies, and muzzleloading specialty items; catalog $2.

Douglas Barrels, Inc., 5504 Big Tyler Rd., Charleston, W.V. 25312: rifle barrels, modern and muzzleloading.

Dremel Mfg. Co., 4915-21st St., Racine, Wisc. 53406: miniature power tools.

Reinhart Fajen, Warsaw, Mo. 65355: semi-finished stocks; catalog $3.

Jerry Fisher, Box 66, Kalispell, Mont. 59901: semi-finished stocks and inletting tools; SSAE for catalog.

Flaigs, Millvale, Pa. 15209: semi-finished stocks.

Foredom Electric Co., Bethel, Conn. 06801: flexible-shaft grinders and accessories.

Forster Products, 82 E. Lanard Ave., Lanark, Ill. 61046: tools; catalog 25 cents.

Gunline Tools, 719 North East St., Anaheim, Calif. 92805: checkering tools.

Herter's Inc., Waseca, Minn. 56093: semi-finished stocks and specialty items; catalog $1.

Jet-Aer Corp., Paterson, N.J. 07524: finishing chemicals.

Marquart Precision Co., P.O. Box 1740, Prescott, Ariz. 86302: rifle barrels made and fitted.

Bill McGuire Inc., 541 S. Kentucky St., E. Wenatchee, Wash. 98801: checkering tools and finishing supplies.

Michael's of Oregon, P.O. Box 13010, Portland, Ore. 97213: tools, sling swivels, and specialty items.

Earl Milliron, 1249 N.E. 166th Ave., Portland, Ore. 97230: semi-finished stocks; SSAE for catalog.

Frank Mittermeirer, Inc., P.O. Box 2, New York, N.Y. 10465: gunsmithing tools and equipment; catalog $1.50.

Navy Arms Company, 689 Bergen Blvd., Ridgefield, N.J. 07657: Brown Bess musket kits.

Norton Abrasives Co., 50 New Bond St., Worcester, Mass. 01606: abrasives, stones, wheels.

Numrich Arms Co., West Hurley, N.Y. 12491: gun parts; catalog $2.

Oakley & Merkley, Box 2446, Sacramento, Calif. 95811: stock wood.

Pachmayr Gun Works, 1220 S. Grand Ave., Los Angeles, Calif. 90015: semi-finished stocks, stock blanks, and recoil pads.

Richards Micro-Fit Stocks, P.O. Box 1066F, Sun Valley, Calif. 91352: semi-finished stocks

Richland Arms Co., 321 W. Adrian St., Blissfield, Mich. 49228: tools and specialty items.

Roberts Gunstocks, 1400 Melody Rd., Marysville, Calif. 95901: semi-finished stocks.

Royal Stock Co, 10064 Bert Acosto St., Santee, Calif. 92071: semi-finished stocks; catalog 50 cents.

A. G. Russell, 1705 Highway 71N, Springdale, Ark., 72764: sharpening stones.

Sears, Roebuck & Co. (catalog and retails stores): hand grinders and accessories.

Sharon Rifle Barrel Co., P.O. Box 1197, Kalispell, Mont. 59901: muzzleloading barrels and kits.

Shilen Rifles, Inc., 205 Metro Park Blvd., Ennis, Tex. 75119: rifle barrels; catalog $1.

Simmons Gun Specialties, Olaf, Kansas: ventilated ribs, shotgun barrels.

Southwest Smelting & Refining Co., Box 2010, Dallas, Tex. 75221: jewelry supplies.

Stoeger Arms Corporation, 55 Rutta Court, South Hackensack, N.J.: variety of gunsmithing supplies and tools.

Thompson Center Arms, Farmington Road, Rochester, N.H. 03867: muzzleloading kits.

Weller (Cooper Industries), Box 728, Apex, N.C. 27502: mini-shop hand grinders and accessories.

Williams Gun Sight Co., 7389 Lopeer Rd., Davison, Mich. 48423: finishing supplies and specialty items.

Woodcraft Supply Co., 313 Montvale Ave., Woburn, Mass. 01801: woodworking tools and equipment; catalog 50 cents.

Index